P9-CJF-154

# Southern Living®
# BIG BOOK OF
# CHRISTMAS

# Southern Living

# BIG BOOK OF
# CHRISTMAS

Edited by Rebecca Brennan

©2010 by Time Home Entertainment Inc.
135 West 50th Street, New York NY 10020

All rights reserved. No part of this book may be reproduced in any
form or by any means without the prior written permission of the
publisher, excepting brief quotations in connection with reviews
written specifically for inclusion in magazines or newspapers, or
limited excerpts strictly for personal use.

ISBN-13: 978-0-8487-3333-9
ISBN-10: 0-8487-3333-9
Library of Congress Control Number: 2009937180

Printed in the United States of America
First Printing 2010
Abridged version of previous hardcover edition

Oxmoor House
VP, Publishing Director: Jim Childs
Editorial Director: Susan Payne Dobbs
Brand Manager: Daniel Fagan
Managing Editor: Laurie S. Herr

*Southern Living₀ Big Book of Christmas*
Senior Editor: Rebecca Brennan
Project Editors: Diane Rose, Vanessa Lynn Rusch
Senior Designer: Melissa Jones Clark
Director, Test Kitchens: Elizabeth Tyler Austin
Assistant Director, Test Kitchens: Julie Christopher
Test Kitchens Professionals: Jane Chambliss, Kathleen Royal Phillips,
   Catherine Crowell Steele, Ashley T. Strickland, Deborah Wise
Photography Director: Jim Bathie
Senior Photo Stylist: Kay E. Clarke
Associate Photo Stylist: Katherine Eckert Coyne
Production Manager: Tamara Nall

*Contributors*
Foods Editor: Julie Gunter
Designer: Carol Damsky
Compositor: Rick Soldin
Copy Editor: Julie Gillis
Proofreader: Lauren Brooks
Indexer: Mary Ann Laurens
Interns: Emily Chappell, Georgia Dodge, Allison Sperando,
   Angela Valente
Food Stylist: Kelley Self Wilton
Photographers: Beau Gustafson, Lee Harrelson, Becky Luigart-Stayner
Photo Stylists: Melanie J. Clarke, Kappi Hamilton

To order additional publications, call 1-800-765-6400.

For more books to enrich your life, visit **oxmoorhouse.com**

To search, savor, and share thousands of recipes, visit **myrecipes.com**

**Cover:** (left to right) Baked Ham with Mustard-Peach Glaze, page 133;
Carnation Ring, page 15; Banana Cream Cake, page 320

# Contents

# DECORATING ALL THROUGH THE HOUSE

Show your holiday spirit with festive décor
in every room. These delightful accents and
arrangements will trim your home with cheer.

# Ways to Say *Welcome*

*Give holiday guests a cheerful greeting with festive outdoor designs.*

## Extend a Warm Reception

Use lively colors, such as the red and chartreuse ribbons on these "presents" (actually empty boxes), to add surefire impact to your front porch decorations. The door is accented with a wreath and metal bucket attached with florist wire. Flowers and greenery tucked in the bucket stay fresh for several days in moistened florist foam. Adding the bucket is a clever way to update the traditional wreath.

### ◄ Add Accents in Unexpected Places

Try a shutter instead of a window as the backdrop for natural decorations. Fill a wire wall basket with greenery and berries, and wire it in place. This is one of the easiest decorations to make: The clippings practically arrange themselves, and they'll stay fresh for several days even without florist foam. Pinecones hide the stems and help hold them in place.

### ▼ Go Natural

Simple touches often convey the warmest greetings. For this quaint embellishment, wire together oversize pinecones and loop them over a lantern. Tuck greenery boughs behind the pinecones for a rich contrast. If you don't have large pinecones, wire together several small ones to achieve a similar effect.

### tools for natural decorations

*Gather key items before you start decorating so that you can concentrate your creative energy and make the whole process more fun. Here are some suggestions:*

- Pair of sharp clippers
- Bucket of water to hold greenery clippings
- Assorted vases and containers
- Florist foam, florist wire, and florist picks
- Wired ribbon

## Spell Out a Sentiment

Send a seasonal greeting by shaping letters from plastic craft foam and covering them with sprigs of boxwood or mixed greenery. In cool weather the greenery looks fresh up to two weeks. For a permanent version, use faux greenery. These evergreen letters work well indoors hanging in a window or propped on a mantel.

## Make Your Own Reindeer Family

Cut wood sections from a small tree trunk or branch for the bodies, heads, necks, and legs; use twiggy branches for the antlers and magnolia leaves for the ears and tails. Drill holes to assemble the pieces; if desired, glue to secure. Add bows to dress them for the holidays.

# 25 Classic *Wreaths*

*From a simple evergreen to a circle of chocolates, the wreath is the quintessential holiday trim. On these pages we share a variety of festive designs.*

◀ Holly and Pine

Express the essence of the season with a red-and-green
wreath—perhaps the most traditional composition of all.

▲ Merry Bells

Hang small wreaths from ribbons accented with bells.
Every time the door is opened, you'll enjoy a cheery hello.

## tried & true tips for making wreaths

*Hanging a wreath on the front door signals the start of the Christmas season and extends a warm welcome. Here are some tools that make wreath making easy.*

### base basics

**Florist foam.** Soak this wreath form in water, and let it drain before adding decorations. It's the best choice for keeping such materials as greenery and flowers fresh. Mist with water every few days for maximum freshness.

**Plastic craft foam and straw.** Perhaps the easiest forms to embellish, use these for wreath decorations that don't need to be kept moist, such as magnolia leaves, moss, ornaments, and pinecones.

**Grapevine.** This base doesn't have to be covered entirely, so you may need fewer materials to finish the wreath. Grapevine wreaths are especially good for wiring on decorations, such as ornaments and holiday trinkets. For greenery and berries, just tuck the stems between the branches of the wreath.

### strong attachments

**Florist wire.** Whether on a spool or in single pieces, florist wire is an essential tool for decorating a wreath. Use it to attach ornaments, greenery sprigs, berries, pinecones, and ribbons. It's very flexible and easy to use.

**Florist picks.** Use picks to attach fruits to wreaths. Picks are available either plain or with wire attached to one end. If decorating a grapevine wreath, for example, use picks with wire so that you can stick the sharp end of a pick into each fruit and use the wire end to attach it to the wreath.

**Florist pins.** U-shaped florist pins hold leaves, greenery and berry stems, and moss securely in place on straw and plastic craft-foam wreaths. These pins can be removed easily and used again.

**Hot-glue gun.** Use a hot-glue gun to permanently attach such items as ornaments, pinecones, moss, and ribbons to a wreath you plan to use again next year.

### where to find it

Look for all the materials mentioned at crafts and discount centers.

### Fraser Fir and Flowers
Update a standard greenery wreath with chartreuse 'Kermit' mums and bronze ribbon.

## ▲ Feathers and Magnolia

Fashion a splendid circle of pine, magnolia, and cypress. Crown it with feathers and faux apples.

## ▲ Ornaments Abound

Hot-glue bright ornaments in varying sizes to a straw wreath for a fun decoration that will last for years.

## ▲ Aucuba and Nandina

Add pizzazz to an evergreen wreath by wiring on aucuba leaves, nandina berries, and lotus pods.

## ▼ Carnation Ring

Snuggle together bright red carnations on a florist-foam wreath for a fresh twist on tradition.

## ▼ Garden Inspired

Adorn a wreath with wild abandon. Give plum branches, cedar, dried hydrangea, and beautyberries a try.

## ▼ Winter White

Think of red birds in the snow when you pair red ribbon and berries with baby's breath and paperwhites.

## ◢ Williamsburg Classic

Evoke Colonial times with an evergreen wreath adorned with fresh fruits, including that Southern symbol of hospitality: the pineapple.

### ◢ Stocking Stuffer

Start with a twiggy wreath. Then lavish it with magnolia leaves, holly, seeded eucalyptus, and red and white gerbera daisies. Complete the look with a jaunty bow and a velvet stocking for a touch of whimsy.

### Southwestern Flavor ▼

For regional flair, include dried peppers along with traditional adornments on a grapevine wreath. Enhance the theme with a burlap bow, dried grasses, and feathers.

## Vine-Wreath Snowman

Build the perfect Southern snowman with three grapevine wreaths, a stovepipe hat, a scarf, and boots. To make the hat, shape sheet metal and spray-paint it black; or affix a large coffee can to a semicircle of wood, and paint it black.

17

## Herbs and Toile

Wrap a straw or plastic craft-foam wreath form with strips of toile fabric. Wire on clay pots filled with herbs and berries. Accent with gingham fabric.

## ▲ Sand Dollar Adornments

Garnish an evergreen wreath with creamy white sand dollars for a seaside theme.

## ▲ New Heights

Suspend a double-sided wreath (greenery on both sides) with ribbons above a table for a fresh approach.

## ▲ Market Fresh

Check out the produce aisle to trim a festive kitchen wreath with vegetables and gerbera daisies. Finish the look with a gingham bow.

## ▼ Family Treasures

Fill a wreath with favorite collectibles, and bring back fond memories season after season.

## ▼ Chocolate Treat

For a sweet decoration, use a low-temp glue gun to secure candies and a bow to a grapevine wreath.

## ▼ Simple Statement

Use a ribbon hanger as the only embellishment for a wreath made by pinning leaves to a plastic form.

## ▲ Apples and Holly

Tuck small lady apples, sprigs of holly, and greenery clippings among the branches of a grapevine wreath for a casual look with lots of charm.

## ▲ Berry Blend

Cover a small grapevine wreath with pepperberries and holly berries. Stick the sturdy holly stems between the vines; wire the pepperberries in place with florist wire.

## ▲ Golden Fruits and Berries

Use permanent materials for a wreath that makes return showings for years to come. Wire together pears, apples, pomegranates, and berries; then shape the garland into a rectangle.

## ▼ Urn of Plenty

For a tabletop showpiece, stand a vine wreath laced with holly-berry stems in an urn mounded with flowers and fruits. Secure pieces in florist foam with florist picks.

## ▲ Natural Selection

Hot-glue nuts, pinecones, and star anise to a grapevine wreath. Sprigs of pine provide a woodsy accent and fresh Christmassy scent.

# Christmas Cottage
## *Charm*

*Feel the magic of the season in a cozy home that overflows with holiday delights.*

### Conjure a Holiday Fairyland

The enchantment begins at the front door of this charming abode (above) that opens onto a roomy screened porch that's decked from floor to ceiling with Christmas cheer (right). The traditional red-and-white theme is updated with generous doses of natural colors and materials, as seen in the linen pillows, pinecone garlands, ornaments, gift wrappings, and chocolate brown dinner plates.

# get the cottage look

*Gather your favorite decorations and then add some new ones for a beautifully coordinated Christmas setting.*

## start with a plan

• Decide on the main colors you want to use. You may want to stay with red and green but accent with another color, as with the brown accessories used for this home.
• Think about all the areas and ways you want to decorate, including centerpieces and other table decorations that you want.
• Make a list of the decorations you need to replace and the new things you want to add.

## consider flowers and greenery

• Outdoor garlands and wreaths stay fresh longer than the same greenery indoors due to cooler outdoor temperatures. Misting the greenery helps keep it fresh. Plan on greenery staying fresh for a week to 10 days indoors and up to a couple of weeks outdoors.
• Arrange flowers just before a special party for maximum freshness. Or use such flowering plants as paperwhites, poinsettias, cyclamen, and amaryllis that last throughout the season and beyond.

## accessorize

• Browse cabinets and cupboards for everyday items that carry out your decorating scheme.
• Incorporate natural materials for a cozy ambience.

## *all in the details*

▲ Tie felt ornaments to the tree to add a handcrafted touch.
◄ Incorporate angels or other symbols of the season in outdoor containers for quick holiday embellishments.

Wrap gift packages with papers and ribbons that blend with other decorations. Tie ribbons in fluffy bows for a homey touch. ▼

▲ Adorn year-round items for the holidays, such as adding this evergreen collar to a wooden pony.

## ◀ Plan a Centerpiece with Staying Power

Topiaries—found easily during the Christmas season at grocery stores and home-improvement centers—can be the basis for a tabletop decoration that lasts for weeks. This topiary is encircled with pears and accented with berries. Use florist picks to hold the fruit in place.

## ▲ Keep It Simple

A pot of paperwhites, ruffly white anemones, and a scattering of fruits and greenery twigs are easy to assemble for a mantel decoration with loads of charm. Solid white pitchers and a red flowerpot allow the smaller elements to stand out.

## ▲ Do the Unexpected

Use Christmas stockings to add a holiday note all through the house. Even on a dining room hutch, a soft velvet stocking seems right at home and is a fitting complement to the seasonal display.

## ◄ Form a Group

Arrange several small items together for a big decorative impact. Here, the wreath and the pine sprigs that are sprinkled among the pieces provide a pleasing framework for the trees, reindeer, candles, and pitcher.

## Autumn Color

Begin this double-duty design by gathering items that work for both autumn and Christmas (see photo at right). Try containers, candleholders, and a scarf or length of fabric to add softness. Then decide on a focal point, such as a wreath, that can be switched easily to change the seasonal look of the mantel (see pages 32 and 33).

Tuck richly colored leaves and berries into the arrangement along the mantel, allowing naturals to softly drape over the mantel's edge.

Fill containers with branches of persimmon and bittersweet to add height to the arrangement and to balance the design.

For a cheerful glow, punctuate the mantel with candles. Be sure to keep greenery and dried plants away from candle flames, and never leave candles burning unattended.

# Two Seasons

season; then make a few quick
ready for Christmas.

## Christmas Greenery

After celebrating Thanksgiving, replace the focal point
with a Christmas wreath. We used a magnolia wreath
with twigs and berries (see pages 34 and 35). As an alternative to two different wreaths, for autumn, stick
fall-colored leaves and dried seedpods into an unadorned
grapevine wreath; for Christmas, replace the leaves and
dried materials with evergreen clippings and berries.

Replace the autumn leaves, and fill
in around the candles with small
bouquets of natural materials, such as
magnolia leaves, berries, eucalyptus,
and mossy twigs.

Use tall stems with red berries and moss-
covered branches in a glass container to
reflect the wreath's embellishments and to
add a dramatic extra punch of color and
texture.

For Christmas, replace the harvest
candles with holiday candles, varying
heights for interest. Form collars of
pepperberries, seeded eucalyptus, or
moss around the base of the candles
for a fancy finish.

Harvest Mantel

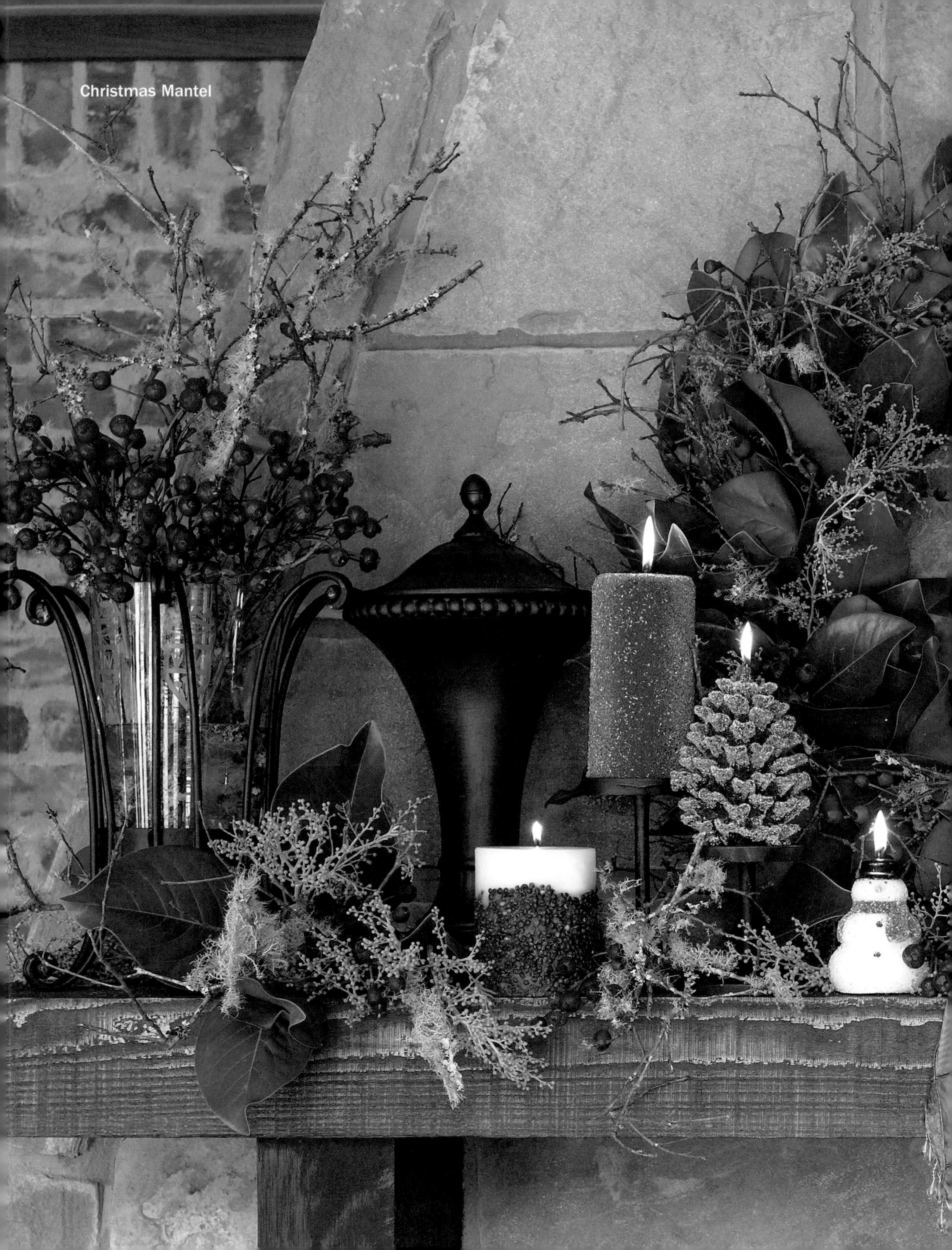

# Mantels
## for Many
## Moods

Plan your holiday mantel to complement the colors and ambience of your room. The decorations on these pages show a range of styles suitable for a variety of settings—all are equally festive.

## Serene Scene

A neutral-toned backdrop gets a warm holiday glow from a simple arrangement of
pillar candles and bud vases filled with bittersweet branches. For visual interest,
mix pillars of varying heights and hues and set them on small boxes or books to
add height where needed. Arrange the candles and vases of bittersweet before
Thanksgiving for an autumn decoration, and then all that's needed is an evergreen
garland to take the decoration through the Christmas season.

## Red-hot Style

Make a bold statement with vivid red. Fill containers with bright amaryllis blooms, pepper plants, and bunches of berries. Use red containers to give an additional pop of color. Then tuck pine clippings and pinecones around the bases of the containers. For guaranteed holiday sparkle, punctuate the look with votive candles.

## Grand Scale

An ornate fireplace needs only a few embellishments to set the holiday mood. For a room with high ceilings and a large mantel, opt for tall decorations, such as these silver twig trees that grace each end of the ledge. A glittery star garland and silver ornaments echo the metallic theme. Fill in with smaller items, such as these clear vases holding tiny nosegays of freesia and berries. Add a fun detail to the arrangements by knotting a narrow leaf around each bunch of flower stems (see detail at right). Then place pillar candles along the mantel for a cheery glow, and soften the arrangement with clippings of evergreen.

## Refined Approach

To create a floral extravaganza, start by protecting the mantel ledge with plastic (use a large trash bag or other waterproof covering). Arrange water-soaked blocks of florist foam on top of the plastic. (For best results, use florist-foam blocks in cages or on trays to help prevent water damage.) Now, for the fun part! Assemble your choice of flowers, dried materials, and fruits. Insert the stems into the florist foam; use florist picks to add fruits to the arrangement.

For a design that transcends the seasons, gather an assortment of dried materials, seedpods, and pinecones (no need to soak the florist foam for dried materials). At Christmastime, swap out the dried materials or just fill in around them with fresh flowers and fruits. For a special party, layer on lushness with grapefruit and pomegranate halves secured with florist picks. To balance the arrangement, place clear urns filled with pinecones, nuts, fruits, ornaments, and feathers at the ends of the mantel.

## ▲ Staying Power

Go easy on your holiday flower budget by glorifying inexpensive blooms, such as carnations. To achieve the look pictured here, place a water-soaked florist-foam sphere in a decorative container, and insert carnation stems to completely cover all visible areas of the foam. The moistened foam will keep the blooms fresh for several days.

## Cheerful Expression ▶

Red and green set an instant holiday scene. Hang richly colored stockings for the ultimate declaration of traditional style; then add a snow, white stocking to the mix to make the colors really pop. For the mantel, create a display from favorite accessories. Here, metal letters on stands take center stage, with flower-filled pots, crimson candles, and a fragrant wreath playing supporting roles. Use books and boxes to vary the heights of the individual elements.

# DO-IT-YOURSELF HOLIDAY STYLE

Get crafty with decorative touches
you can create yourself. The photos and directions on
these pages show you how.

# Decorating Classics in 3 Easy Steps

Whether looking for an exquisite bow to trim a gift or the best way to embellish a plain wreath, you'll discover step-by-step photos that reveal how to decorate like a pro.

## Decorate a Wreath

*Transform a wreath from blah to breathtaking with the simple addition of wired-on bows and bouquets.*

**You will need:** wire-edge ribbon • evergreen wreath • thumbtack • dried flowers • berries • wooden florist picks with wires • florist tape and wire • ornaments

1 Use a length of ribbon to hang the wreath, tacking the ribbon in place at the top of the door.

2 To make each bouquet, attach dried flowers and berries to a wooden florist pick with wires. (We used dried hydrangea blooms and pepperberries.) Wrap the stems with florist tape to secure each bouquet. Wire several small bouquets to the wreath.

3 To make each bow for the wreath, form 2 loops from a length of ribbon. Cinch the center of the bow with a wooden florist pick with wires. Stick several bows in the wreath, filling in among the flowers. Wire ornaments to the wreath for pops of color.

## Tie a Package Bow

*A well-tied bow is the secret to a beautiful package.*

**You will need:** wire-edge ribbon • wrapped package

1 Center the middle of a length of ribbon on top of the package. Wrap the ribbon down 2 sides of the box, cross it underneath the box, and bring it back up the other 2 sides. Tie the ribbon in a knot on top of the package, leaving several inches for the tails.

2 Starting about 4 inches from the end of a length of ribbon, make a loop. Pinching the ribbon between your thumb and index finger, make a loop on the opposite side; repeat to make 2 loops on each side.

3 Center the bow on top of the package, and secure it in place by tying the ribbon tails around it. Fluff the loops to shape the bow.

# Make a Big Bow

*This is the classic bow for decorating. Use it on garlands, on wreaths, and even as a tree topper.*

**You will need:** 5 to 6 yards wire-edge ribbon • florist wire

1 Starting about 8 to 10 inches from the end of a length of ribbon, make a loop. Pinching the ribbon between your thumb and index finger, make a loop on the opposite side.

2 Continue making loops in this back-and-forth manner until you are happy with the fullness of the bow.

3 Tie a length of ribbon around the center of the bow, making the knot on the back of the bow. Let the ribbon tails fall from the bow, and fluff the loops to shape the bow. Use florist wire to attach the bow where desired.

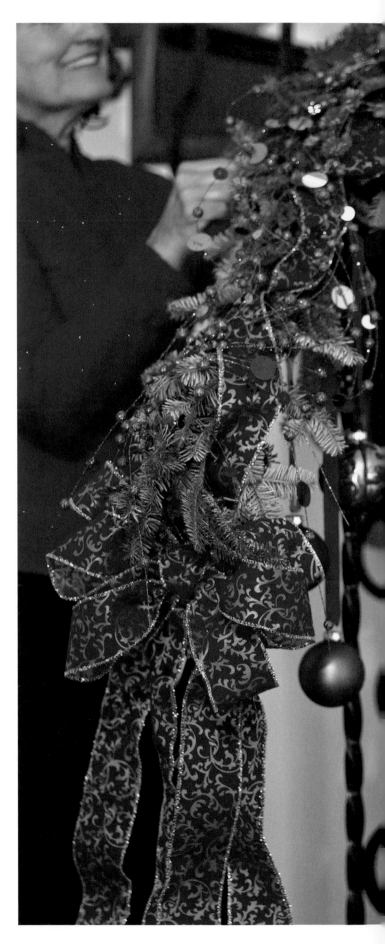

# Create a Floral Centerpiece

*Styling a professional-looking centerpiece is as easy as 1–2–3.*

**You will need:** florist foam • container • flowers • pillar candle • berries • greenery sprigs • wire-edge ribbon

1 Place moistened florist foam in the container. Stick the stems of the flowers into the foam, forming a collar around the top of the container.

2 Center a pillar candle on the florist foam. Stick the stems of the berries around the candle. (We used pepper-berries.) Fill in any gaps with sprigs of greenery.

3 Tie a bow around the candle, securing small blooms in the knot.

# Quick-as-a-Wink *Centerpieces*

These tabletop accents can be arranged in minutes, thanks to
the handy materials lists and easy directions.

## Stacked Packages

**You will need:** 2 cake stands (one larger than the other) •
small, wrapped boxes • berries •
greenery sprigs

1 Place the smaller cake stand atop the larger stand.

2 Arrange the wrapped boxes on the cake stands;
place a tallish box in the center of the small cake
stand to give the centerpiece a pleasing shape.

3 Tuck the berries and wispy sprigs of greenery, such as
cedar or cypress, among the boxes.

## Tiers of Fruit ▶

**You will need:** assorted fruits • tiered compote •
holly berries or herb sprigs

1 Arrange the fruits on each tier of the compote. (If you
are using grapes, allow them to drape over the edges.)

2 Add a few stems of the holly berries to the arrangement for decoration only (the berries are non-edible);
or tuck sprigs of fragrant herbs, such as rosemary or lavender, among the pieces of fruit.

## ◀ Ornament Collection

**You will need:** container • tissue paper (optional) •
assorted ornaments • hypericum berries •
greenery clippings

1 For a large container, fill the bottom of the container
with crumpled tissue paper. Arrange a variety of ornaments in the container, using different shapes and styles
to add interest.

2 Fill in around the edges of the arrangement and
among the ornaments with the berries and greenery.
(A box similar in size to the one pictured is best suited
for a sideboard decoration; for a dining table, choose a
bowl or basket that's low enough for guests to see across.)

## Flowers and Ornaments

**You will need:** vases in various heights • assorted flowers, berries, and greenery clippings (we used amaryllis, seeded eucalyptus, tulips, anemones, ranunculus, fir clippings, and holly berries) • ornaments • (the gift boxes are ornaments)

1 Arrange the vases, and fill with the flowers, berries, and greenery clippings. Group similar colors for maximum impact.

2 Scatter the ornaments around the vases to tie the arrangement together.

## More Ideas for Centerpieces

- Fill silver serving pieces with red carnations. Using one color makes an impressive presentation. ▶
- For a twinkling design, place tea lights on a tiered compote.
- To save money on flowers, use large blooms. For example, place a few calla lilies in a glass vase; add a couple of votive candles on each side of the vase for an elegant yet inexpensive table decoration.
- Instead of decorating with a large centerpiece, mark each place setting with a small vase filled with a few flowers, a sprig of greenery, and a snip of berries. Be sure to cut the stems short so that the materials hug the tops of the vases.

## Party-Ready Centerpiece

**You will need:** punch bowl, cups, and tray • holiday garland • small evergreen wreaths • tall cake stands with domes • small cakes or cookies • ribbons • flowers and berries • wrapped boxes

1 Set the punch bowl and cups on a large tray at the center of the table. Weave a holiday garland around the cups (see pages 132 and 133).

2 Place the small wreaths on each side of the punch bowl. Set a cake stand in the center of each wreath. Place decorated cakes or stacks of cookies on the cake stands.

3 Tie together small bouquets of flowers and berries with the ribbon. Lay the bouquets on the wreaths for colorful accents. Fill in along the back of the arrangement with the wrapped boxes.

# Pillows with Pizzazz

Give plain pillows extreme makeovers that are specially suited to the season.

## ◄ Stocking Pillow

**You will need:** fabric for stocking • hot-glue gun and glue sticks • plain pillow • yarn trim for stocking • trim for cuff • fake fur for cuff • tassels

1 Draw a stocking shape on the reverse side of the fabric, and cut it out. Hot-glue the stocking to the pillow.

2 Hot-glue the yarn trim along the edges of the stocking. Hot-glue the cuff trim to the top of the stocking. Hot-glue the cuff to the pillow, covering the top edge of the trim.

3 Stitch the tassels to the stocking toe and to each pillow corner.

## Wreath Pillow ►

**You will need:** hot-glue gun and glue sticks • looped chenille trim • plain pillow • small pompoms • ribbon

1 Hot-glue 2 rows of the chenille trim (to double the width) in a circle on the pillow.

2 Hot-glue the pompoms randomly on the wreath.

3 Tie the ribbon in a bow. Hot-glue the bow to the top of the wreath.

## Snowflake Pillow ►

**You will need:** hot-glue gun and glue sticks • narrow white trim • plain pillow • buttons • white pompom trim

1 Hot-glue the narrow trim to the pillow, using the photo at right as inspiration.

2 Hot-glue a large button to the center of the pillow where the trim intersects. Hot-glue a small button to the end of each point of the snowflake.

3 Hot-glue the pompom trim around the edges of the pillow.

# Spotlight on *Shades*

**Turn on a holiday look when you switch plain lampshades with these dressed-up versions.**

## Hand-Lettered Shade

**You will need:** pencil • ivory lampshade •
fine-tip permanent black fabric pen •
hot-glue gun and glue sticks • beaded trim

1 With a pencil, lightly mark a rule for the line spacing
at the overlap area on the shade. Use the fabric pen
to write seasonal sentiments on the shade. If you prefer
not to write the words freehand, use adhesive letters,
quotes, or stencils (found in the scrapbooking section of
crafts and discount stores) for a similar effect.

2 Hot-glue the trim to the top and bottom of the
shade.

## Drummer-Boy Shade ▶

**You will need:** pencil • red drum-shaped lampshade •
ribbons • small paintbrush • thick craft and fabric glue

1 Use a pencil to lightly mark the placement of the
ribbons on the lampshade. Cut the ribbons to
desired lengths.

2 Use the paintbrush to spread glue on the back of the
ribbons. Glue the zigzag design first; then glue the
ribbons to the top and bottom of the shade.

## Holly and Berries Shade ▶

**You will need:** heavy paper, such as thick
wrapping paper, handmade paper, or wallpaper •
thick craft and fabric glue • ivory drum-shaped
lampshade • black sequins

1 Using the photo at right as inspiration, cut out the
designs from the heavy paper.

2 Glue the cutouts to the lampshade. Glue the black
sequins in place to accent the holly-berry designs.

# SETTING THE SCENE

Prepare a feast for the senses and impress family and friends with table settings and centerpieces that are causes for celebration.

# Harvest *Celebration*

Thanksgiving heralds the start of the holiday season. Set the tone with a festive alfresco fete.

## Golden Opportunity

Savor the season by setting your Thanksgiving feast outdoors. Colored leaves of rich golds and rusts provide autumnal ambience. Enhancing the scene is a plethora of pumpkins and table decorations in shades of mulberry and mauve.

## Ornamental Orb

As the signature fruit of the season, pumpkins make a showstopping centerpiece. Fill a large container with moistened florist foam. Stack a large and a small pumpkin atop the foam. To secure the arrangement, insert a long florist pick into the top of the large pumpkin; then insert the pick into the bottom of the small pumpkin. Fill in around the pumpkins with a colorful mix of berries and leaves; insert stems lush with persimmons into the florist foam. Fit small pots of pansies between the florist foam and the sides of the container.

## Lay on the Charm

Embellish place settings to heighten the holiday attitude. Pair delicate dinnerware, such as this mulberry transferware, with woven chargers to harmonize with the casual outdoor surroundings. Add visual interest to the table by mixing and matching glasses, as evidenced here with a plum-colored goblet and a bronze tumbler. In lieu of traditional tapers, place pumpkin candles in saucers on the table to contribute a friendly glow. To fashion a place card, fold a rectangle of colored paper in half, and glue on a square of paper in a contrasting color. Then write a guest's name on another paper square, and glue it to the card at an angle.

## Clever Presentation

Instead of using a conventional tray, pull out a pretty platter to hold such items as cups and saucers for after-dinner coffee or dessert plates and forks.

## Gather Together

Pumpkin candles in various sizes grace this mantel, echoing autumn's splendor. If you don't have an outdoor mantel, use this setup on a side table or in a more diminutive form on the dining table. For the center of the arrangement, fill a container, such as a tureen, with small pots of pansies and leaves. Place pumpkin candles or small pumpkins on each side of the container, and link the individual elements by punctuating them with leaves, small berries, or rose hips.

# Holiday Bowl

**With this clever decoration, a colorful transition from Thanksgiving to Christmas can be just as natural inside as it is out.**

## Basic Construction

Choose a wide, sturdy decorative bowl. Gather candles of varying widths, heights, and shades. For an autumn look, select candles in rust, orange, and golden hues; or consider using white or cream ones that transcend the seasons. If necessary, securely elevate the candles on a base in the bowl to add height and to raise the flames above nearby foliage. Once you're happy with the candle arrangement, fill the bowl with dried leaves and berries, tucking in stems randomly around the candles. Scatter small gourds and pumpkins around the bowl.

## Christmastime Is Here

After Thanksgiving, substitute materials in the bowl to create a Yuletide array.
Replace autumn-colored candles with pillars in shades of green. Remove the dried
leaves, and tuck in an assortment of evergreen sprigs and berries. Complete the
look by surrounding the bowl with tiny wrapped boxes and bright green apples.

# From Everyday
## *to Holiday*

**Get your everyday table setting holiday
ready with just a few quick adjustments. These
photos show you how it's done.**

## Quick Change

Candleholders sporting pears and a wooden compote filled with fresh fruits form
an easy centerpiece that's both beautiful and functional for everyday. Two table
runners—placed across the table rather than lengthwise—stand in for separate
place mats. White plates, clear glassware, and wooden-handle utensils are basic
tableware (above). With these essentials in place, your table is set for a speedy
makeover that will make it ready for a holiday party in no time flat (right). See
*Stylish Substitutions* on page 150 for all the details.

## Stylish Substitutions

It's easy to make the switch from everyday to holiday with just a few key substitutions. Here's how:

| Everyday Table | Holiday Table |
| --- | --- |
| • White dinner plates | • Add cream-colored chargers. |
| | • Add mocha-colored salad plates. |
| | • Add pinecone candles, greenery, and berry clippings in small bowls at each place setting. Let each guest take home a candle as a memento. |
| • White napkins | • Substitute with red napkins. |
| • Clear glassware | • Substitute with red goblets. |
| • Fruit on compote | • Substitute with miniature Christmassy chapel surrounded with pine and berry clippings. |
| • Pears on candleholders | • Substitute with twig trees topped with bows. |

**Holiday extras:**

Add fresh clippings, tiny pinecones, and ornaments around the base of the compote and candleholders. Finish the look with additional twig trees and red pillar candles.

## Cup of Cheer

At each place setting, fill a small cup or bowl with a decorative candle (left), which doubles as a mood-setting detail and take-home party favor. Tuck in short stems of pine and berries to keep the candle company. Then knot brown satin ribbon around a fanned-out napkin for a rich contrast of colors and textures (above).

## Final Detail▶

Complete the seasonal transition with a charming chair decoration. Tie a twig star to the chair back with brown ribbon layered atop a wider red ribbon to repeat colors from the table setting.

# Tradition
## *with a Twist*

**Introduce unexpected accessories to the holiday table for a fresh look that's definitely not the standard bill of fare.**

## Showcase the Centerpiece

Consider using a glass terrarium as a centerpiece that's beautifully fresh all season long. Not only will this display last longer than a floral arrangement, but it will also bestow elegant sophistication to the entire room. Plant lacy ferns in the bottom of the terrarium; or tuck in small containers of ferns, and hide the pots with moss. Place a tall Christmassy accent piece, such as a mercury glass tree, in the center of the terrarium. Add similar accents or tall pillar candles on each side of the piece. Soften the edges of the arrangement with bits of evergreen.

## A Sparkling Setting

Select table decorations with reflective surfaces to set a refined table that is richly understated yet no less festive. Here, mercury glass trees and votive holders amidst circles of beaded garlands catch the twinkle of lights from the tree.

Add small details to the luxury of the setting. Layer a crochet-edged table runner atop a linen tablecloth, and use trimmed napkins in a soft shade of mauve as delicate complements. Choose mauve-colored glasses to enhance the color scheme.

## ▲Warm Glow

Place a candle at each seat for a welcome that shines with the warmth of the holiday spirit. Encircle the votive holder with a wintry glass garland to reflect the candle's light. When dinner is served, guests can set their candles aside to be carried home later as glowing reminders of a lovely evening shared with friends.

## Fast Fix ▶

Filling a decorative container with beautiful ornaments is one of the quickest ways to impart a seasonal accent to a room. Search out unusual pieces, such as this small terrarium, to boost the appeal of the arrangement.

## A Sterling Idea

Present flatware in stocking-shaped ornaments for a darling detail that will have everyone abuzz. This presentation works especially well at a buffet, since guests can easily collect their flatware while also holding their plates. Write the year and event on the back of each stocking for personalized favors.

# *Lighten* Up

**Send dark Christmas crimsons and greens on holiday, and rely instead on bright red accents paired with chartreuse for a simplified setting.**

## Ever Green

From lemon-leaf wreaths basking in the sunlight to wide ribbon simply tied to each chair, chartreuse exudes chic style in this modern holiday setting. Against a neutral background, this cool shade makes reds appear even more vivid.

Gather pale green and red amaryllis blooms to create an aromatic place card. The wide array of colors offered by this flower can pull together any nontraditional Christmas color scheme. For a favor each guest can enjoy at home, arrange the trumpet-shaped blooms in a bouquet tied with matching ribbon before placing them in a mug.

## Instant Success

Far from austere, these spiky holly boughs need no embellishment to achieve maximum results. Fill clear glass vases with a couple of inches of water, and then add holly stems—it's that simple. Placing the stems at angles in the vases fashions a bold, three-dimensional focal point that spreads its charm beyond the table to the entire room.

# Dressed
## for Dinner

A few snips of ribbon transform plain napkins into
showy table accessories that are striking yet simple.

## Terrific Tie-Ups

For a winning combination, pair two trims, such as the rick-rack and curly ribbon shown on the opposite page. (Clockwise from top, left) Add sparkle to a neutral place setting with shimmery ribbon; for a sweet finish, tie chocolates to the ribbon tails. Give red plates a sophisticated complement with decorative brown ribbon; here, a traditional bow ties a napkin into a neat package. Crisscross grosgrain ribbon around a napkin, and finish with a tiny treasure for a casual look that blends perfectly with a pottery plate. For a fancy touch, knot dramatic ribbon around each napkin.

# CELEBRATION MENUS

Treat your guests to memorable meals with
planned-to-perfection menus. We offer a selection
of festive updates to traditional favorites.

# 12 Menus of Christmas

With this grand array of menus, you'll entertain with ease.
Time-saving game plans, make-ahead options, and over 80 recipes
give you everything you need to host the most memorable
gatherings of the season.

Chocolate-Espresso Pots de Créme
(page 192)

# Beef Tenderloin Repast

Smoked Trout and Pecan Crostini

Baby Romaine and Blood Orange Salad

Bacon-Wrapped Beef Tenderloin with Madeira

Butternut Squash Mash     Balsamic Beans

Grilled Red Cabbage with Garlic Cream

Dark Chocolate Chunk Cherry Cake

**serves 10**

## menu prep plan

**3 days ahead:**

- Cook butternut squash and garlic; prepare Butternut Squash Mash. Chill.
- Prepare smoked trout spread; chill. Toast baguette slices; store at room temperature in an airtight container.

**2 days ahead:**

- Section oranges and prepare vinaigrette for Baby Romaine and Blood Orange Salad; chill.
- Microwave cabbage wedges, and prepare Garlic Cream for Grilled Red Cabbage; chill.

**1 day ahead:**

- Prepare Dark Chocolate Chunk Cherry Cake.
- Prepare Bacon-Wrapped Tenderloin, but do not cook; cover and chill.
- Trim beans; chill.

**2 hours ahead:**

- Cook beef tenderloin, and prepare Madeira sauce; keep warm.

**1 hour ahead:**

- Grill cabbage wedges; arrange on a serving platter and keep warm.
- Arrange smoked trout and baguette slices on a serving plate.

**30 minutes ahead:**

- Reheat Butternut Squash Mash in microwave.
- Prepare and bake Balsamic Beans.
- Reheat Garlic Cream to serve with Grilled Red Cabbage.
- Slice tenderloin; arrange on a serving platter.
- Toss lettuce with remaining salad ingredients.

*make ahead*

## Smoked Trout and Pecan Crostini

**Prep: 18 min.   Cook: 8 min.   Other: 1 hr.**

| | |
|---|---|
| 1 | (8-ounce) package smoked trout fillets, skinned and boned (about 2 fillets) |
| 1 | (8-ounce) package cream cheese, softened |
| ½ | cup chopped pecans, toasted |
| ½ | cup sour cream |
| 1 | shallot, quartered |
| 2 | teaspoons prepared horseradish |
| 2 | tablespoons fresh lemon juice |
| ½ | teaspoon freshly ground black pepper |
| ¼ | cup olive oil |
| 2 | teaspoons minced garlic |
| 1 | French baguette, sliced into ⅓" slices |

Combine first 8 ingredients in a food processor; process until smooth. Chill 1 hour or up to 1 week. Serve at room temperature.

Combine olive oil and garlic; brush both sides of bread slices with garlic oil; arrange slices on baking sheets.

Bake at 400° for 8 minutes or until crisp and golden. Cool completely. Serve with spread. Yield: 2¾ cups.

## Baby Romaine and Blood Orange Salad

**Prep: 15 min.**

| | |
|---|---|
| 5 | blood oranges or red navel oranges |
| ¼ | cup sherry vinegar |
| 2 | tablespoons honey |
| 2 | tablespoons minced shallot (about 2 shallots) |
| 1 | tablespoon minced fresh thyme |
| ½ | teaspoon salt |
| ½ | teaspoon pepper |
| ⅓ | cup extra-virgin olive oil |
| 10 | cups baby Romaine lettuce (9 ounces) |
| ½ | cup pine nuts, toasted |

Section oranges by cutting away the rind and white pith; carefully cut alongside each membrane to remove fruit, using a paring knife. Squeeze remaining membranes to extract juice. Combine juice, vinegar, and next 5 ingredients in a large bowl; slowly drizzle in oil while whisking constantly. Cover and chill up to 2 days (return to room temperature before serving).

Toss lettuce with orange segments, pine nuts, and desired amount of dressing. Serve immediately. Yield: 10 servings.

Bacon-Wrapped Beef Tenderloin with Madeira,
Balsamic Beans, Butternut Squash Mash,
Grilled Red Cabbage with Garlic Cream

*editor's favorite • make ahead*

# Bacon-Wrapped Beef Tenderloin with Madeira

*Beef broth and consommé appear in tandem to give the
Madeira reduction a richer flavor.*

Prep: 31 min.   Cook: 1 hr.   Other: 10 min.

1    (6- to 6½-pound) beef tenderloin, trimmed
1    tablespoon freshly ground pepper, divided
1½   teaspoons salt
½    cup chopped fresh flat-leaf parsley, divided
¼    cup chopped fresh rosemary
¼    cup fresh thyme leaves, divided

1    pound bacon slices (about 20 slices) (we tested with
     Boar's Head)
⅓    cup minced shallots
2    (3.5-ounce) packages shiitake mushrooms, stems
     removed and sliced
2    (3.5-ounce) packages oyster mushrooms, stems
     removed and sliced
1    cup Madeira
1    (14-ounce) can beef broth or fat-free, less-sodium
     beef broth
1    (10½-ounce) can beef consommé, undiluted
3    tablespoons unsalted butter
Garnish: fresh herb sprigs

Cut tenderloin in half crosswise; sprinkle both pieces evenly with 2½ teaspoons pepper and 1½ teaspoons salt. Combine ¼ cup parsley, rosemary, and 3 tablespoons thyme; rub over beef. Fold narrow end of tenderloin under to achieve a uniform thickness.

Wrap bacon around tenderloin pieces, and secure at 1" intervals with heavy string. Heat a 12" nonstick skillet over medium-high heat; add beef in 2 batches. Cook 8 to 10 minutes, turning often to brown all sides. Remove beef from pan, reserving 2 tablespoons drippings in skillet.

Place beef on a rack in a large roasting pan. Bake at 400° for 40 to 50 minutes or until a meat thermometer inserted into thickest part of tenderloin registers 140° (rare) to 160° (medium) or to desired degree of doneness. Remove tenderloin to a serving platter, and cover with aluminum foil; let stand 10 minutes before slicing. Remove string.

Meanwhile, heat reserved pan drippings in same skillet over medium-high heat; add shallots, mushrooms, and remaining 1 tablespoon thyme. Cook 3 minutes; add Madeira, stirring to loosen particles from bottom of pan. Add beef broth and consommé; bring to a boil. Boil 10 to 12 minutes or until reduced to about 3 cups. Remove from heat; add remaining ½ teaspoon pepper, remaining ¼ cup parsley, and butter, whisking until butter melts.

Slice tenderloin into ½"-thick slices; arrange on a serving platter. Garnish, if desired. Serve with Madeira sauce. Yield: 10 servings.

**Make Ahead:** Cover and refrigerate uncooked bacon-wrapped tenderloins up to 24 hours. Let stand at room temperature 30 minutes before proceeding with the recipe.

Wrap and tie tenderloin pieces to ready them for cooking.

*editor's favorite • make ahead*

## Butternut Squash Mash

*The subtle blend of sage and garlic enhances this yummy alternative to mashed potatoes.*

**Prep: 31 min.   Cook: 1 hr., 24 min.   Other: 10 min.**

| | |
|---|---|
| 3 | large butternut squash (about 3½ to 5¼ pounds each) |
| 2 | small garlic bulbs |
| 1 | tablespoon olive oil |
| 2 | tablespoons butter |
| ½ | cup half-and-half |
| 1 | tablespoon minced fresh sage |
| 2 | teaspoons salt |
| 1 | teaspoon freshly ground pepper |

To make squash easier to cut, prick squash with a paring knife; microwave each squash on HIGH 4 to 5 minutes. Carefully cut squash in half lengthwise using a sharp chef's knife, discarding seeds and membranes. Line 2 large baking sheets with aluminum foil; lightly grease foil. Arrange squash halves, cut side down, on baking sheets.

Cut off pointed ends of garlic bulbs. Place garlic on a piece of aluminum foil, and drizzle with oil. Fold foil to seal; place on 1 baking sheet with squash.

Place 1 baking sheet on upper oven rack; and 1 on lower oven rack. Bake at 350° for 1 hour, switching baking sheet positions after 35 minutes. Let cool 10 minutes.

Scoop out squash from shell, and place in a large bowl. Squeeze garlic cloves from bulbs; mash with a fork.

Melt butter in a small saucepan over medium heat. Stir in half-and-half and next 3 ingredients; bring to a simmer. Remove from heat.

Add herbed butter and mashed garlic to squash. Beat at medium speed with an electric mixer until smooth. Serve hot. Yield: 10 servings.

**Make Ahead:** Prepare Butternut Squash Mash. Cool, cover, and chill up to 3 days. Reheat squash mash loosely covered with heavy-duty plastic wrap, in the microwave on HIGH 6 to 8 minutes or until heated thoroughly, stirring after 4 minutes, or bake it in a covered casserole dish at 350° until hot.

# Balsamic Beans

*A quick-to-make balsamic syrup enhances these roasted green beans. The syrup is also good drizzled over pork roast or even sliced fresh strawberries.*

Prep: 6 min.   Cook: 27 min.

½    cup balsamic vinegar
2½   pounds green beans, trimmed
2    tablespoons olive oil
1    teaspoon salt
½    teaspoon freshly ground pepper

Cook vinegar in a small saucepan over medium heat 9 minutes or until syrupy and reduced to 3 tablespoons; set aside.

Toss beans with oil in a large bowl. Spread beans on a large rimmed baking sheet; sprinkle with salt and pepper.

Bake at 475° for 15 to 18 minutes or until charred in appearance (do not stir). Toss hot beans with balsamic syrup. Serve immediately. Yield: 10 servings.

**Fix it Faster**: Purchase prewashed, trimmed green beans available in the produce department.

**Make Ahead**: The balsamic syrup can be made a day ahead and stored at room temperature. Make a few extra batches of the syrup for gift giving.

*editor's favorite • make ahead*

# Grilled Red Cabbage with Garlic Cream

*Give yourself some extra time by following the make-ahead tips in the recipe. We also give an indoor cooking option that produces similar results.*

Prep: 10 min.   Cook: 24 min.

2    small heads red cabbage (about 3 pounds)
2    tablespoons water
2    tablespoons butter or margarine
1    tablespoon minced garlic, divided (about 3 cloves)
1    cup heavy whipping cream
¾    teaspoon salt, divided
¾    teaspoon freshly ground pepper, divided
¼    cup olive oil

Remove outer leaves from each cabbage head, and cut each head into 6 wedges, leaving core portion attached to hold the wedges together. Place wedges in a large glass bowl; add 2 tablespoons water, and cover loosely with heavy-duty plastic wrap. Microwave at HIGH for 9 minutes or until tender.

(**For make ahead**: Arrange cabbage wedges on a jelly-roll pan, and refrigerate to cool quickly and stop the cooking process. Cover and chill up to 2 days.)

Meanwhile, melt butter in a small saucepan over medium heat; add 1 teaspoon garlic, and sauté 1 minute or until garlic is golden. Add cream, and bring to a boil. Reduce heat, and simmer over medium-low heat 10 minutes or until slightly thickened. Add ¼ teaspoon each of salt and pepper. (**For make ahead**: Cover garlic cream, and chill up to 2 days; reheat in microwave or saucepan.)

Combine olive oil and remaining 2 teaspoons minced garlic in a small bowl; brush oil over cabbage wedges. Sprinkle cabbage with remaining ½ teaspoon each of salt and pepper. Grill, covered with grill lid, over medium-high heat (350° to 400°) 12 minutes or until browned and slightly charred, turning once. Arrange cabbage on a serving platter; drizzle each wedge with about 1 tablespoon garlic cream. Yield: 12 servings.

**Indoor Cooking Option**: Broil steamed cabbage on ungreased baking sheets 5½ inches from heat 24 minutes or until browned and slightly charred, turning once.

*editor's favorite*

# Dark Chocolate Chunk Cherry Cake

Prep: 20 min.   Cook: 1 hr., 4 min.   Other: 18 min.

Unsweetened cocoa
1    (18.25-ounce) package yellow cake mix with pudding
½    cup sugar
1    (3.8-ounce) package devil's food instant pudding mix
4    large eggs
¾    cup vegetable oil
½    cup water
1    (8-ounce) container sour cream
1    tablespoon vanilla extract
5    (3-ounce) dark chocolate bars, divided (we tested with Ghirardelli)
½    cup coarsely chopped dried cherries
1    tablespoon butter
⅓    cup heavy whipping cream

Grease a 12-cup Bundt pan, and dust with cocoa; set aside.

Combine cake mix, sugar, and pudding mix in a large mixing bowl.

Beat eggs and next 4 ingredients at medium speed with an electric mixer until blended. Gradually add oil mixture to dry ingredients; beat 2 minutes. Coarsely chop 3 chocolate bars; fold cherries and chopped chocolate into batter. Pour batter into prepared pan.

**Dark Chocolate Chunk Cherry Cake**

# Dried cherries and dark chocolate transform cake mix into this ultra-decadent dessert.

Bake at 350° for 1 hour or until a wooden pick inserted in center comes out clean. Cool cake in pan on a wire rack 15 minutes. Remove from pan; cool completely on wire rack.

Coarsely chop 1 chocolate bar. Place chopped chocolate and butter in a small bowl; set aside.

Bring whipping cream to a simmer in a small saucepan over medium-high heat. Remove from heat, and immediately pour over chocolate and butter. Whisk gently until smooth. Cool glaze 3 minutes or until slightly thickened. Drizzle glaze over cake. Coarsely chop remaining chocolate bar; sprinkle chopped chocolate over cake. Yield: 12 servings.

# Turkey and All the Trimmings

Cauliflower Bisque

Green Salad with Cranberry-Champagne Vinaigrette

Roast Turkey with Cider-Rosemary Gravy

Roasted Garlic and Herb Potatoes

Green Beans with Roasted Shallots

Ginger-Rum Carrots

Caramel Chess Tart

**serves 10**

## menu prep plan

**4 days ahead:**
- Place turkey in refrigerator to thaw, if frozen.
- Toast seasoned pecans for salad; place in airtight container.
- Roast garlic for potatoes; chill.

**1 day ahead:**
- Prepare Cranberry-Champagne Vinaigrette; chill.
- Trim green beans, and cook; chill.
- Slice carrots; chill.
- Prepare Caramel Chess Tart; cover and store at room temperature.
- Prepare Cauliflower Bisque; chill.

**4 to 5 hours ahead:**
- Whip cream for Caramel Chess Tart; chill.
- Combine ingredients for salad except oranges, vinaigrette, and pecans; chill.
- Bake turkey; keep warm.
- Prepare Roasted Garlic and Herb Potatoes; keep warm.

**1 hour ahead:**
- Prepare Ginger-Rum Carrots; keep warm.
- Complete preparation of Green Beans with Roasted Shallots; keep warm.
- Prepare Cider-Rosemary Gravy; keep warm.

**last minute:**
- Reheat Cauliflower Bisque.
- Carve turkey.
- Add oranges, pecans, and vinaigrette to green salad.

## Cauliflower Bisque

*To preserve the creamy white color of this soup, sauté the veggies just until soft, but not browned.*

**Prep: 32 min.  Cook: 45 min.**

| | |
|---|---|
| 3 | tablespoons butter or margarine |
| 2 | cups chopped leeks |
| 1 | cup chopped celery |
| 3 | garlic cloves, chopped |
| 8 | cups cauliflower florets and stems (about 2 small heads) |
| 6¾ | cups chicken broth, divided |
| 1 | cup half-and-half |
| ½ | teaspoon salt |
| ¼ | teaspoon ground white pepper |

Garnishes: croutons, fresh chives

Melt butter in a Dutch oven over medium heat. Add leeks, celery, and garlic; sauté 10 minutes or until vegetables are tender, but not brown. Add cauliflower; sauté 2 minutes. Add 6 cups broth; bring to a boil. Reduce heat, and simmer, uncovered, 20 minutes, or until vegetables are very tender. Cool slightly.

Puree vegetables, in batches, in a blender or food processor until very smooth and creamy. Return pureed vegetables to pan. Stir in half-and-half, salt, and pepper. Bring soup to a simmer over medium heat. Stir in remaining ¾ cup broth, and cook 5 minutes or until thoroughly heated. Garnish, if desired. Yield: about 10 cups.

## Use your glitzy ornaments as place card holders.

Roast Turkey with Cider-Rosemary Gravy,
Roasted Garlic and Herb Potatoes,
Green Beans with Roasted Shallots,
Ginger-Rum Carrots

## Green Salad with Cranberry-Champagne Vinaigrette

*The savory nuts that top these greens can be made up to a week in advance and kept in an airtight container.*

**Prep: 8 min.   Cook: 15 min.**

| | |
|---|---|
| 2 | cups pecan halves |
| 3 | tablespoons butter, melted |
| 1 | teaspoon paprika |
| 1 | teaspoon garlic powder |
| 1 | teaspoon onion powder |
| 1 | teaspoon salt |
| 1 | cup whole-berry cranberry sauce |
| ½ | cup cranberry juice |
| 2 | tablespoons champagne vinegar |
| ½ | teaspoon salt |
| ¼ | teaspoon freshly ground black pepper |
| ½ | cup extra-virgin olive oil |
| 3 | (5-ounce) packages mixed salad greens (we tested with Dole Spring Mix) |
| ⅓ | cup chopped fresh flat-leaf parsley |
| 1 | small red onion, thinly sliced |
| 2 | navel oranges, peeled and sectioned, or 1 cup drained mandarin oranges |

Combine first 6 ingredients in a small bowl; toss well. Arrange pecans in a single layer on a foil-lined baking sheet. Bake at 350° for 15 minutes or until toasted; set aside.

Combine cranberry sauce and next 4 ingredients in a jar with a tight-fitting lid; shake well until cranberry sauce dissolves. Add oil; shake well.

Combine greens, parsley, onion, and oranges; toss well. Sprinkle with reserved pecans, and serve with desired amount of vinaigrette. Yield: 10 servings.

---

*editor's favorite*

## Roast Turkey with Cider-Rosemary Gravy

*This turkey gets basted in apple cider, giving it a wonderfully caramelized skin.*

**Prep: 39 min.   Cook: 3 hr., 15 min.**

| | |
|---|---|
| 1 | (16-pound) fresh or frozen turkey, thawed |
| 1 | teaspoon salt |
| 1 | teaspoon pepper |
| 1 | large onion, coarsely chopped |
| 2 | celery ribs, coarsely chopped |
| 1 | Golden Delicious apple, coarsely chopped |
| 3 | fresh rosemary sprigs |
| 2 | tablespoons butter, softened |
| 6 | center-cut bacon slices |
| 1¼ | cups apple cider, divided |
| 2 | tablespoons finely chopped onion |
| 1 | garlic clove, minced |
| 2 | teaspoons minced fresh rosemary |
| 2 | tablespoons all-purpose flour |
| ¼ | teaspoon salt |
| ¼ | teaspoon pepper |

Garnish: rosemary sprigs

Remove giblets and neck, and rinse turkey with cold water; pat dry. Sprinkle cavity with 1 teaspoon salt and 1 teaspoon pepper. Place turkey, breast side up, in a roasting pan. Lightly stuff turkey body cavity with coarsely chopped onion, celery, apple, and 3 rosemary sprigs. Rub turkey with butter.

Loosen skin from turkey breast without totally detaching skin; carefully slip bacon slices under skin. Replace skin, using wooden picks to fasten skin over breast meat. Tie ends of legs together with heavy string, or tuck under flap of skin. Lift wing tips up and over back, and tuck under bird. Pour ¾ cup apple cider over turkey.

Bake turkey, uncovered, at 450° for 20 minutes. Reduce heat to 350°; bake 2 hours and 45 minutes or until a meat thermometer inserted into meaty part of thigh registers 180°, basting often with pan juices. Shield turkey with heavy-duty aluminum foil during cooking, if necessary, to prevent over-browning.

Transfer turkey to a serving platter; cover loosely with foil. Scrape roasting pan to remove browned bits; pour pan drippings into a gravy separator. Discard fat, reserving 2 tablespoons.

Heat reserved 2 tablespoons fat in a small saucepan over medium-high heat. Add finely chopped onion, garlic, and 2 teaspoons rosemary; sauté 2 minutes or until tender. Reduce heat to medium; add flour, and cook 1 minute. Whisk in pan drippings and remaining ½ cup cider. Bring to a boil; reduce heat, and simmer 2 to 3 minutes or until gravy thickens. Stir in ¼ teaspoon salt and ¼ teaspoon pepper. Serve gravy with turkey. Garnish, if desired. Yield: 16 servings.

**Note:** For ease in removing hot turkey from roasting pan, wear clean heat-resistant rubber gloves. They shield the heat and enable you to get a firm grip on the bird.

## Roasted Garlic and Herb Potatoes

*Roasted garlic can be made ahead for this dish and stored in a zip-top plastic bag in the refrigerator up to a week.*

Prep: 47 min.   Cook: 2 hr., 30 min.   Other: 10 min.

5     large garlic bulbs
2     tablespoons olive oil
1½   cups milk
1½   cups heavy whipping cream
1     tablespoon salt
2     teaspoons freshly ground black pepper
¼     teaspoon ground nutmeg
4½   pounds baking potatoes
⅓     cup chopped fresh sage leaves
½     cup chopped fresh oregano
1½   cups freshly grated Parmesan cheese

Cut off pointed end of each garlic bulb; place garlic on a piece of aluminum foil, and drizzle with oil. Fold foil to seal. Bake at 350° for 1 hour or until very soft; cool. Squeeze pulp from garlic bulbs to measure ¾ cup. Reserve any remaining garlic for another use. Process ¾ cup garlic, milk, and next 4 ingredients in a blender or food processor until smooth; transfer to a large bowl.

Peel potatoes and slice very thinly. Add potatoes to milk mixture as they are sliced. (This keeps potatoes from changing color.) Layer one-third each of potato mixture, herbs, and cheese in a greased 13" x 9" baking dish. Repeat layers twice, ending with cheese. Bake, covered, at 350° for 45 minutes. Uncover and bake 45 more minutes or until browned and bubbly. Let stand 10 minutes before serving. Yield: 12 servings.

## Green Beans with Roasted Shallots

Prep: 29 min.   Cook: 44 min.

2½   pounds fresh green beans, trimmed
1     pound shallots, peeled and halved (about 4 cups)
¼     cup olive oil
1½   teaspoons kosher salt
1     teaspoon freshly ground pepper

Cook green beans in boiling, salted water 7 to 9 minutes or until crisp-tender. Plunge beans into ice water to stop the cooking process; drain and set aside.

Spread shallots in a single layer on an ungreased jelly-roll pan. Drizzle with olive oil; toss well to coat. Bake at 450° for 35 minutes or until shallots are roasted, stirring twice.

Combine beans, salt, and pepper in a large serving bowl; add roasted shallots and pan drippings; toss well. Serve warm or at room temperature. Yield: 10 servings.

**Fix it Faster:** You can find trimmed ready-to-eat green beans in the produce section of your grocery store.

*editor's favorite*
## Ginger-Rum Carrots

*A splash of rum and ginger-infused broth make these thick-sliced carrots some of the best we've tried.*

Prep: 35 min.   Cook: 27 min.

7     cups chicken broth
½     cup sugar
1     (2-inch) piece fresh ginger, peeled and sliced into 6 pieces
4     pounds carrots, cut diagonally into ½" slices
½     cup butter
¼     cup finely chopped onion
2     tablespoons minced fresh ginger
2     teaspoons minced garlic
½     teaspoon salt
¼     teaspoon freshly ground black pepper
¼     cup spiced rum or dark rum (optional)
½     teaspoon vanilla extract

Combine first 3 ingredients in a Dutch oven; bring to a boil. Add carrots; reduce heat, and simmer, uncovered, 12 minutes or until almost tender. Drain; discard ginger slices. Set carrots aside.

Melt butter in a large skillet over medium heat. Add onion, minced ginger, and garlic; sauté 2 to 3 minutes or until onion is tender. Add reserved carrot, salt, and pepper; sauté 3 more minutes. Stir in rum, if desired, and vanilla; cook 1 minute. Yield: 10 servings.

**Make Ahead:** Place sliced carrots in a zip-top plastic bag, and store in refrigerator up to 2 days. Or for extra convenience, use packaged baby carrots.

**Caramel Chess Tart**

*editor's favorite • make ahead*

# Caramel Chess Tart

*Brown sugar and butter come together in this recipe to create a sublime caramel. This dessert's made of simple ingredients, yet it received our Test Kitchens highest marks.*

Prep: 17 min. Cook: 54 min.

| | |
|---|---|
| ½ | (15-ounce) package refrigerated piecrusts |
| ½ | cup butter, softened |
| 1½ | cups firmly packed light brown sugar |
| 3 | large eggs |
| 1 | tablespoon all-purpose flour |
| ¼ | cup buttermilk |
| 2 | teaspoons vanilla extract |

Powdered sugar (optional)
Whipped cream

Fit piecrust into a 10" tart pan with a removable bottom according to package directions. Line pastry with aluminum foil, and fill with dried beans. Bake at 450° for 7 minutes. Remove dried beans and foil, and bake piecrust 2 more minutes; cool on a wire rack. Reduce oven temperature to 350°.

Beat butter and brown sugar in a large bowl at medium speed with an electric mixer until fluffy; add eggs, 1 at a time, beating well after each addition. Stir in flour and buttermilk. Add vanilla, stirring well. Pour filling into prepared crust.

Bake at 350° for 45 minutes or until almost set. Cool completely on wire rack. Remove tart pan rim and transfer tart to a serving platter. Dust with powdered sugar, if desired. Dollop each serving with whipped cream. Yield: 1 (10") tart.

**Caramel Chess Tassies:** To make 3 dozen tassies, prepare filling as directed above. You'll need 1½ (15-ounce) packages refrigerated piecrusts. Using a 2¾" round cutter, cut 36 circles out of piecrusts. Place in ungreased miniature muffin pans, crimping edges. Spoon filling evenly into crusts. Bake at 350° for 25 minutes. Remove from pans, and cool completely on wire racks. Yield: 3 dozen.

# An English Feast

Potato-Leek Soup

Prime Rib with Horseradish Cream

Blue Cheese Yorkshire Puddings

Carrot Puree with Browned Butter and Ginger

Chocolate Bread Pudding

**serves 8 to 10**

## menu prep plan

**1 day ahead:**

• Prepare Chocolate Bread Pudding, but do not bake.

• Prepare Potato-Leek Soup; chill.

• Prepare Carrot Puree with Browned Butter and Ginger; chill.

**3 hours ahead:**

• Prepare Prime Rib; keep warm.

• Prepare Horseradish Cream; chill.

**1 hour ahead:**

• Prepare Blue Cheese Yorkshire Puddings.

• Reheat Potato-Leek Soup in microwave.

• Reheat Carrot Puree with Browned Butter and Ginger in microwave.

**last minute:**

• Carve Prime Rib; arrange on serving platter with Yorkshire Puddings.

**during dinner:**

• Sprinkle chocolate morsels and chopped pecans over Chocolate Bread Pudding; bake.

Prime Rib with Horseradish Cream

Blue Cheese Yorkshire Puddings

## Potato-Leek Soup

*For easy cleanup, use an immersion blender to puree soup right in the pan.*

Prep: 10 min.    Cook: 1 hr., 25 min.

1    tablespoon butter
3    large leeks, trimmed and thinly sliced
2    large russet potatoes, peeled and cubed
     (about 2¼ pounds)
¾    cup dry white wine, divided
4    cups chicken broth
1    bay leaf
2    fresh thyme sprigs
2    fresh parsley sprigs
1    cup whipping cream
¾    teaspoon salt
¾    teaspoon freshly ground black pepper
2    tablespoons chopped fresh chives
Garnishes: fresh thyme or parsley sprigs

Melt butter in a large Dutch oven over medium-high heat; add leeks, and sauté 10 minutes or until tender. Add potato, ½ cup wine, and broth. Using a piece of kitchen twine, tie bay leaf, 2 thyme sprigs, and 2 parsley sprigs into a bundle; add to pan. Bring to a boil; reduce heat, and simmer, uncovered, 1 hour and 15 minutes or until potatoes are very tender. Discard herb bundle.

Process potato mixture, in batches, in a blender or food processor until smooth, stopping to scrape down sides. Return puree to Dutch oven. Add remaining ¼ cup wine, cream, and next 3 ingredients. Garnish, if desired. Yield: 8 cups.

# Prime Rib with Horseradish Cream

*English mustard is an extremely hot condiment containing ground mustard seeds and turmeric. It contributes high flavor to the coating that bakes on the prime rib.*

Prep: 5 min.  Cook: 2 hr., 35 min.  Other: 10 min.

2    tablespoons prepared English mustard (we tested with Colman's)
2    tablespoons prepared horseradish
1    tablespoon chopped fresh thyme
1    teaspoon salt
1    teaspoon pepper
1    (8½-pound) prime rib roast
Horseradish Cream
Garnishes: lady apples, kumquats, pecans

Combine first 5 ingredients; rub on all surfaces of roast. Place roast on a rack in a roasting pan.

Bake, uncovered, at 450° for 20 minutes. Reduce heat to 300°, and bake 2 hours and 15 minutes or until a meat thermometer inserted in thickest portion registers 145° (medium rare) or 160° (medium). Let stand 10 minutes before slicing. Transfer roast to a serving platter, reserving ¼ cup drippings for Blue Cheese Yorkshire Puddings; keep warm. Serve with Horseradish Cream. Garnish, if desired. Yield: 10 servings.

# Horseradish Cream

Prep: 7 min.

1    cup heavy whipping cream
2    tablespoons finely chopped chives
2    tablespoons prepared horseradish
2    teaspoons prepared English mustard
½    teaspoon salt

Beat whipping cream at medium-high speed with an electric mixer until soft peaks form. Fold in chives and remaining ingredients. Cover and chill until ready to serve. Serve with Prime Rib. Yield: 2 cups.

# Blue Cheese Yorkshire Puddings

Prep: 14 min.  Cook: 40 min.

2    cups all-purpose flour
2    cups milk
1    teaspoon salt
5    large eggs, lightly beaten
4    ounces Stilton cheese, crumbled
¼    cup pan drippings from Prime Rib with Horseradish Cream

Preheat oven to 400°.

Whisk together first 4 ingredients until smooth; stir in crumbled cheese.

Place ungreased popover pans in preheated oven for 5 minutes. Brush bottom and sides of pans with pan drippings. Pour batter evenly into pans using a ladle. Bake at 400° for 35 minutes or until puffed and brown. Yield: 1 dozen.

# Carrot Puree with Browned Butter and Ginger

Prep: 13 min.  Cook: 28 min.

2½   pounds carrots, peeled and coarsely chopped
1    medium baking potato, peeled and coarsely chopped
¼    cup butter
⅔    cup half-and-half
1    teaspoon salt
1    teaspoon ground ginger
¼    teaspoon pepper
1    tablespoon white wine vinegar

Place carrot and potato in a large saucepan; add water to cover. Bring to a boil; cover, reduce heat, and simmer 25 minutes or until very tender. Drain well. Process half of potato and carrot in a food processor until smooth.

Place butter in a small skillet. Cook over medium heat 3 minutes or until butter solids turn light brown, stirring often. Add brown butter and half-and-half to carrot puree. Add remaining half of carrot and potato, salt, and remaining ingredients; process until smooth. Yield: 8 to 10 servings.

**Note:** *Beurre noisette* is French meaning " browned butter." Don't be tempted to substitute margarine; it won't have the same flavor or consistency. Cook carefully to develop the light hazelnut (*noisette*) color.

**Chocolate Bread Pudding**

*make ahead*

# Chocolate Bread Pudding

Prep: 12 min.   Cook: 1 hr., 20 min.   Other: 8 hr., 10 min.

- 1   pound challah bread, torn into bite-size pieces*
- 3   tablespoons butter, softened and divided
- 4   cups half-and-half
- 1   (12-ounce) package semisweet chocolate morsels, divided
- ½   cup unsweetened cocoa
- 1½  cups sugar
- ½   teaspoon salt
- 5   large eggs, lightly beaten
- ¾   cup bourbon, half-and-half, or brewed coffee
- 1   cup coarsely chopped pecans

Place bread on 2 baking sheets, and bake at 325° for 12 minutes. Transfer bread to a large bowl, and set aside.

Butter a 13" x 9" baking dish with 1 tablespoon butter.

Bring half-and-half and remaining 2 tablespoons butter to a simmer in a large saucepan over medium-high heat. Remove from heat; add 1 cup chocolate morsels, stirring until melted. Whisk in cocoa and next 4 ingredients. Pour over bread, tossing to coat; transfer to baking dish. Cover and chill 8 hours.

Sprinkle with remaining chocolate morsels and pecans. Bake, uncovered, at 350° for 1 hour or until set. Let stand 10 minutes. Yield: 12 servings.

*You can use French bread as a substitute for challah.

**Note:** You can also bake bread pudding in 8 (8-ounce) ramekins or 12 (6-ounce) ramekins or custard cups. Prepare as directed above, and after chilling 8 hours, spoon pudding evenly into ramekins. Sprinkle with morsels and pecans. Bake, uncovered, at 350° for 35 minutes (for 6 ounce) to 40 minutes (for 8 ounce).

# Roasted Lamb Dinner

Cornmeal-Crusted Oysters with Red Pepper Romesco

Roasted Mushroom Salad

Sage-Crusted Leg of Lamb with Pineapple-Pecan Salsa

Lemon Orzo

Wilted Kale with Roasted Garlic

Almond Torte with Cranberry Jam

**serves 8**

## menu prep plan

**3 days ahead:**
- Prepare Red Pepper Romesco; chill.
- Prepare vinaigrette for mushroom salad; chill.

**1 to 2 days ahead:**
- Roast garlic; trim and slice kale for Wilted Kale with Roasted Garlic; chill separately.
- Prepare Pineapple-Pecan Salsa, but do not add pecans; chill.
- Cook orzo for Lemon Orzo; chill.
- Prepare Cranberry Jam and Almond Torte, but do not dust with powdered sugar; chill both.

**2 to 3 hours ahead:**
- Prepare Sage-Crusted Leg of Lamb; bake 2 hours before serving. Keep warm.

**1½ hours ahead:**
- Prepare Wilted Kale with Roasted Garlic; stir in roasted garlic and seasonings just before serving.
- Roast mushrooms for salad; cool to room temperature.

**1 hour ahead:**
- Slice lemons and fry Cornmeal-Crusted Oysters; keep warm.
- Complete preparation of Lemon Orzo.
- Place Red Pepper Romesco in serving dish.

**last minute:**
- Assemble Roasted Mushroom Salad on salad plates; whisk vinaigrette and serve.
- Stir pecans into Pineapple-Pecan Salsa.
- Carve lamb.
- Dust Almond Torte with powdered sugar before serving.

Sage-Crusted Leg of Lamb with Pineapple-Pecan Salsa, Wilted Kale with Roasted Garlic, Lemon Orzo

## Cornmeal-Crusted Oysters with Red Pepper Romesco

*Romesco, the classic Spanish sauce of tomatoes and red peppers, focuses solely on red peppers here and replaces the typical almonds with pecans, the South's prized nut. It's a perfect accompaniment with crusty fried oysters.*

Prep: 19 min.   Cook: 15 min.

Peanut oil
1     cup yellow cornmeal
2½   teaspoons paprika
24   large fresh Select oysters, drained
1½   teaspoons salt
Red Pepper Romesco
Lemon wedges

Pour oil to a depth of 1" into a large skillet; heat to 375°.

Meanwhile, combine cornmeal and paprika in a shallow dish. Sprinkle oysters with salt. Dip oysters in cornmeal mixture, pressing gently to coat.

Fry oysters, 4 to 6 at a time, 30 seconds on each side or until golden brown. Drain on paper towels. Serve oysters with Red Pepper Romesco and lemon wedges. Yield: 8 servings.

## Red Pepper Romesco

Prep: 10 min.

¾ cup chopped pecans
6 garlic cloves
1 ancho chile, seeded and coarsely chopped
1 (12-ounce) jar roasted red bell peppers, drained
2 tablespoons red wine vinegar
2 tablespoons fresh flat-leaf parsley
½ teaspoon salt
¼ cup olive oil

Process first 3 ingredients in a food processor 30 seconds or until finely chopped. Add peppers and next 3 ingredients. With processor running, slowly pour oil through food chute in a thin stream. Pour into a bowl; cover and chill up to 3 days. Serve at room temperature. Yield: 1⅔ cups.

## Roasted Mushroom Salad

Prep: 37 min.  Cook: 45 min.

2 (8-ounce) packages fresh mushrooms, quartered
2 (8-ounce) packages fresh crimini mushrooms, quartered
4 (3.5-ounce) packages fresh shiitake mushrooms, stemmed and quartered
3 tablespoons olive oil
½ teaspoon salt
⅓ cup sherry vinegar
2 tablespoons minced shallot
1 small garlic clove, pressed
2 teaspoons Dijon mustard
½ teaspoon salt
¼ teaspoon freshly ground pepper
⅔ cup olive oil
1 (5-ounce) package fresh baby spinach (about 6 cups)
1 small head fresh radicchio, torn (about 4 cups)
8 ounces crumbled blue cheese

Combine first 5 ingredients in a large roasting pan. Roast at 450° for 45 minutes or until liquid evaporates; stir twice.

Meanwhile, combine vinegar and next 5 ingredients in a small bowl with a wire whisk; slowly whisk in ⅔ cup oil.

Combine mushrooms and ¼ cup vinaigrette; cool to room temperature. Divide spinach and radicchio among serving plates; top with mushrooms and cheese. Drizzle with remaining dressing. Serve immediately. Yield: 8 servings.

**Make Ahead:** Chill the vinaigrette in a jar up to 3 days; whisk well before serving.

## Sage-Crusted Leg of Lamb with Pineapple-Pecan Salsa

*Kosher salt is a coarse-grained salt. Many prefer its chunky texture over regular table salt.*

Prep: 10 min.  Cook: 1 hr., 30 min.  Other: 10 min.

2 tablespoons chopped fresh sage
2 tablespoons olive oil
1 teaspoon kosher salt
½ teaspoon freshly ground pepper
1 (5- to 6-pound) bone-in leg of lamb
4 garlic cloves, thinly sliced
Pineapple-Pecan Salsa

Combine first 4 ingredients in a small bowl.

Cut about 16 slits (about ½" deep) into lamb; insert garlic slices and a small amount of seasoned oil into each slit. Rub remaining oil over entire surface of lamb.

Place lamb on a rack in a roasting pan. Insert a meat thermometer into thickest part of roast, making sure it does not touch bone or fat.

Bake at 500° for 20 minutes; reduce temperature to 300°, and bake 1 hour and 10 minutes or until thermometer registers 150° (medium rare) or 160° (medium). Let stand 10 minutes. Slice lamb diagonally across the grain. Serve with Pineapple-Pecan Salsa. Yield: 8 servings.

## Pineapple-Pecan Salsa

Prep: 19 min.  Cook: 10 min.

½ cup chopped onion
2 tablespoons olive oil
2 garlic cloves, minced
½ cup pineapple juice
4 cups finely chopped fresh pineapple
2 tablespoons chopped fresh sage
¼ teaspoon dried crushed red pepper (optional)
Pinch of salt
¾ cup chopped pecans, toasted

Sauté onion in olive oil in a medium skillet over medium heat 5 minutes or until tender. Add garlic; cook 1 minute, stirring constantly. Add pineapple juice; cook over medium-high heat until liquid is reduced by half (about 3 minutes).

Combine pineapple and next 3 ingredients in a large bowl; stir in onion mixture. Cover and chill up to 24 hours. Stir in pecans just before serving. Yield: 4 cups.

**Fix it Faster:** Start with a cored fresh pineapple to speed things up when making this salsa.

# Lemon Orzo

*Greek pasta is tossed with a warm, buttery blend of lemon and Parmesan.*

Prep: 5 min.  Cook: 18 min.

| | |
|---|---|
| 6 | cups chicken broth |
| 16 | ounces uncooked orzo (rice-shaped pasta) |
| ¼ | cup butter or margarine |
| 2 | tablespoons grated fresh lemon rind |
| 2 | tablespoons fresh lemon juice |
| 1½ | cups freshly grated Parmesan cheese |
| ½ | teaspoon freshly ground pepper |

Garnish: freshly grated Parmesan cheese

Bring broth to a boil in a Dutch oven. Stir in orzo; cook, uncovered, 9 to 11 minutes or until tender, stirring occasionally to prevent sticking. Drain.

Melt butter in same pan over medium heat. Add hot cooked orzo, lemon rind, and next 3 ingredients. Stir gently just until cheese melts. Serve hot. Garnish, if desired. Yield: about 7 cups.

**Fix it Faster:** Use refrigerated shredded Parmesan cheese.

# Wilted Kale with Roasted Garlic

Prep: 21 min.  Cook: 1 hr.

| | |
|---|---|
| 1 | large garlic bulb |
| 4 | pounds kale, coarse stems removed (about 6 bunches) |
| ¼ | cup olive oil |
| ¾ | cup chicken broth |
| ½ | teaspoon salt |
| ¼ | teaspoon pepper |

Cut off pointed end of garlic bulb. Place on a piece of aluminum foil, and coat generously with cooking spray. Fold foil to seal. Bake at 350° for 1 hour or until garlic is tender. Remove garlic from oven, and let cool. Squeeze pulp from garlic bulb, and mash with a fork until smooth. Set aside.

Meanwhile, slice kale leaves into ¼" strips. Heat olive oil in a large Dutch oven over medium heat. Gradually add kale, and cook 12 minutes or until kale wilts, stirring often. Add broth. Reduce heat to low; cover and simmer 20 to 25 minutes or until greens are tender and liquid evaporates. Stir in garlic, salt, and pepper. Yield: 8 servings.

**Make Ahead:** Roast garlic, and trim and slice kale up to 2 days ahead. Chill in separate zip-top plastic bags.

# Almond Torte with Cranberry Jam

*This moist, dense European-style cake is rich enough to serve without the jam, but don't forget the coffee.*

Prep: 12 min.  Cook: 1 hr.

| | |
|---|---|
| 12 | ounces pure almond paste, crumbled (we tested with Odense) |
| ¾ | cup butter, softened |
| 1¼ | cups granulated sugar |
| 4 | large eggs |
| 2 | tablespoons almond liqueur |
| 1¼ | cups all-purpose flour |
| 1 | teaspoon baking powder |

Powdered sugar
Cranberry Jam

Lightly grease and line bottom of a 9" springform pan with parchment paper; set aside.

Beat almond paste, butter, and granulated sugar at medium speed with a heavy-duty stand mixer until blended. Add eggs, 1 at a time, beating until blended after each addition. Beat in liqueur.

Combine flour and baking powder; add to butter mixture, beating at low speed just until blended. Spread batter into prepared pan.

Bake at 325° for 1 hour or until cake is golden and edges spring back when lightly touched. Cool completely in pan on a wire rack. Dust cake with powdered sugar, and serve with Cranberry Jam. Yield: 1 (9") cake.

# Cranberry Jam

*This jewel-toned jam can dress up vanilla ice cream, too.*

Prep: 3 min.  Cook: 10 min.

| | |
|---|---|
| 1 | (12-ounce) package fresh cranberries |
| 1 | cup firmly packed light brown sugar |
| 1 | tablespoon orange zest |
| ¼ | cup fresh orange juice |
| 2 | tablespoons almond liqueur |

Combine first 4 ingredients in a medium saucepan. Cook over medium heat 10 minutes or until thickened; stir in liqueur. Cool completely. Serve at room temperature or chilled. Yield: 1½ cups.

**Make Ahead:** Both the torte and the cranberry jam can be made a day ahead and chilled until ready to serve.

Almond Torte with Cranberry Jam

# A Southern Holiday Supper

Oyster Stew with Rosemary Croutons

Brined Pork Roast with Chestnut and
Red Cabbage Sauté

Maple Mashed Squash with Candied Pecans

Lima Beans with Ham and Cream

Apple-Cheddar Cornbread

White Chocolate Rice Pudding with
Dried Cherry Sauce

**serves 8**

## menu prep plan

**1 day ahead:**

- Marinate pork loin in refrigerator.
- Prepare Rosemary Croutons; store at room temperature in airtight container.
- Chop cabbage and mushrooms and dice onion for Chestnut and Red Cabbage Sauté; chill.
- Cook squash and candied pecans for Maple Mashed Squash with Candied Pecans; chill.
- Prepare Dried Cherry Sauce; chill. Toast almonds; store in airtight container.
- Dice bacon, celery, and onion for Oyster Stew; chill.

**morning of:**

- Prepare Apple-Cheddar Cornbread.
- Prepare White Chocolate Rice Pudding, but do not add topping; cover and chill.
- Assemble Lima Beans with Ham and Cream, but do not bake; cover and chill.

**2 hours ahead:**

- Bake Brined Pork Roast; keep warm.
- Bake Lima Beans with Ham and Cream; keep warm.
- Reheat mashed squash and complete preparation of Maple Mashed Squash with Candied Pecans.
- Prepare Oyster Stew; keep warm.

**30 minutes ahead:**

- Cook Chestnut and Red Cabbage Sauté.

**last minute:**

- Carve Brined Pork Roast.
- Reheat cornbread.
- Spoon rice pudding into serving dishes; top with sauce and almonds.

Brined Pork Roast with Chestnut and Red Cabbage Sauté, Maple Mashed Squash with Candied Pecans, Apple-Cheddar Cornbread, Lima Beans with Ham and Cream

*editor's favorite*

## Oyster Stew with Rosemary Croutons

*Here's a thick, rich, and comforting stew that will warm you up after holiday shopping.*

Prep: 12 min.   Cook: 22 min.

| | |
|---|---|
| 2 | bacon slices, diced |
| 1 | cup finely diced celery |
| 1 | cup finely diced onion |
| ½ | cup vermouth |
| 2 | pints fresh oysters, undrained |
| 2 | tablespoons all-purpose flour |
| 2 | (8-ounce) bottles clam juice |
| 3 | cups half-and-half |
| 1 | teaspoon salt |
| ¼ | teaspoon pepper |
| 2 | teaspoons chopped fresh thyme |
| 2 | tablespoons chopped fresh parsley |

Rosemary Croutons

Cook first 3 ingredients in a Dutch oven over medium heat 12 minutes or until onion and celery are tender. Add vermouth, and simmer 1 minute. Add oysters.

Whisk together flour and clam juice in a small bowl; whisk into soup. Bring to a simmer over medium heat. Simmer 1 minute or until oyster edges begin to curl. Reduce heat to medium-low; add half-and-half and next 4 ingredients. Cook over medium-low heat until thoroughly heated. (Do not boil.) Serve with Rosemary Croutons. Yield: 10½ cups.

**Fix it Faster:** Use prechopped fresh celery and onion that's now available in most grocery store produce departments.

## Rosemary Croutons

*Sprinkle these garlic-and-herb croutons over salads, too.*

Prep: 4 min.   Cook: 16 min.

⅓   cup butter or margarine
2    garlic cloves, minced
2    teaspoons chopped fresh rosemary
¼    teaspoon salt
⅛    teaspoon pepper
4    cups (1-inch) French bread cubes

Melt butter in a large nonstick skillet; add garlic and next 3 ingredients. Sauté 1 minute over medium heat. Add bread cubes, tossing gently to coat.

Cook over medium heat, stirring occasionally, 15 minutes or until bread is lightly toasted. Yield: 4 cups.

*editor's favorite*
## Brined Pork Roast with Chestnut and Red Cabbage Sauté

*Brining, soaking lean cuts of meat in a solution of water and salt, is a technique used to achieve moist, juicy meat. Our recipe replaces water with apple cider. Mustard, sugar, and molasses are added for flavor.*

Prep: 7 min.   Cook: 1 hr., 21 min.   Other: 24 hr., 10 min.

5    cups apple cider
½    cup firmly packed dark brown sugar
2    tablespoons salt
2    tablespoons prepared mustard
2    tablespoons molasses
2    bay leaves, crumbled
1    (4-pound) boneless pork loin roast
1    tablespoon olive oil
Chestnut and Red Cabbage Sauté

Combine first 6 ingredients, stirring until sugar dissolves. Place pork in a large zip-top freezer bag; add cider mixture. Seal bag, and chill 24 hours.

Remove pork from brine, and pat dry with paper towels; discard brine. Heat oil in a large skillet over medium-high heat; add pork. Cook 6 minutes or until browned on all sides,

turning meat occasionally. Place pork on a rack in a lightly greased shallow roasting pan.

Bake at 300° for 1 hour and 15 minutes or until a meat thermometer inserted into thickest portion registers 150°. Remove from oven; cover and let rest 10 minutes or until thermometer reaches 160° before slicing. Serve with Chestnut and Red Cabbage Sauté. Yield: 8 to 10 servings.

## Chestnut and Red Cabbage Sauté

*Serve a hefty ¼ cup of this savory accompaniment over each slice of Brined Pork Roast.*

Prep: 9 min.   Cook: 17 min.

2    tablespoons butter
1    small onion, diced
1    cup coarsely chopped mushrooms
2    cups coarsely chopped red cabbage
1    cup diced chestnuts from a jar*
2    teaspoons sugar
½    teaspoon salt
1    teaspoon cider vinegar

Melt butter in a large skillet over medium heat; add onion, and sauté 3 minutes or until tender. Add mushrooms; sauté 2 minutes. Add cabbage and chestnuts; sauté 2 minutes. Stir in sugar and salt; cover and simmer 10 minutes or until cabbage is tender. Stir in vinegar. Yield: 2½ cups.

*Look for whole chestnuts sold in jars at Williams-Sonoma or other cook stores.

Whimsical snow globes serve as place card holders and set a casual tone to your table.

## Maple Mashed Squash with Candied Pecans

*Serve this delectable squash as an alternative to sweet potatoes.*

**Prep: 19 min.  Cook: 37 min.**

1     (4-pound) butternut squash
5     tablespoons butter, divided
7     tablespoons maple syrup, divided
1½   teaspoons maple flavoring
1¼   teaspoons salt, divided
1     cup chopped pecans

Microwave squash on HIGH 2 minutes to soften. Cut in half. Peel squash; remove and discard seeds. Cut squash into 1" squares.

Cook squash in water in a large Dutch oven 30 minutes or until tender; drain.

Combine squash, 3 tablespoons butter, 3 tablespoons syrup, maple flavoring, and ¾ teaspoon salt in a large bowl; mash with a potato masher until smooth.

Cook pecans, remaining 2 tablespoons butter, remaining ¼ cup maple syrup, and ½ teaspoon salt in a medium skillet over medium-low heat 7 minutes or until syrup caramelizes and pecans begin to brown; cool in a single layer on a plate.

Sprinkle pecans over squash. Serve warm. Yield: 8 servings.

*editor's favorite*
## Lima Beans with Ham and Cream

*Maple-honey ham imparts a smoky sweetness to these baby beans simmered in cream.*

**Prep: 10 min.  Cook: 1 hr.**

1     tablespoon butter
2     (10-ounce) packages frozen baby lima beans, thawed
½     pound maple-honey ham, diced (we tested with Boar's Head)
1     cup finely diced onion
1     teaspoon salt
¼     teaspoon freshly ground pepper
⅛     teaspoon ground nutmeg
1     cup whipping cream
¼     to ⅓ cup chicken broth

Butter a 2-quart shallow baking dish, and set aside.

Stir together lima beans and remaining ingredients in a large bowl; spoon into prepared dish.

Bake, covered, at 375° for 30 minutes. Uncover; stir and bake 30 more minutes or until bubbly and browned. Serve

with a slotted spoon, if desired. Beans will thicken as they begin to cool. Yield: 6 to 8 servings.

## Apple-Cheddar Cornbread

*Tidbits of tangy green apple are a nice surprise that balance the cheese in this crusty cast-iron favorite.*

**Prep: 13 min.  Cook: 28 min.**

1     tablespoon butter
1     Granny Smith apple, peeled and diced (1 cup)
1     tablespoon shortening
1½   cups yellow cornmeal
½     cup all-purpose flour
1     tablespoon baking powder
½     teaspoon salt
1½   cups milk
1     large egg, lightly beaten
6     tablespoons butter, melted
1     cup (4 ounces) shredded extra-sharp Cheddar cheese

Heat 1 tablespoon butter in a large skillet over medium-high heat until melted. Add apple, and sauté 3 minutes or until just tender. Remove from heat, and set aside.

Preheat oven to 425°. Heat shortening in a 9" cast-iron skillet in oven 5 minutes.

Meanwhile, stir together cornmeal and next 3 ingredients. Whisk together milk and egg; add to dry ingredients, stirring just until moistened. Stir in 6 tablespoons melted butter. Add sautéed apple and cheese, stirring just until combined.

Pour batter into hot skillet. Bake at 425° for 25 minutes or until golden. Cut into wedges. Yield: 8 servings.

*editor's favorite*
## White Chocolate Rice Pudding with Dried Cherry Sauce

*The seeds and pod of a vanilla bean simmer in this rich rice pudding. Be sure to stir it often so it doesn't scorch.*

**Prep: 10 min.  Cook: 45 min.  Other: 5 min.**

1½   cups hot water
¾     cup medium-grain rice
1     vanilla bean, split lengthwise
½     cup sugar
4     cups half-and-half
¼     teaspoon salt
¾     cup white chocolate morsels
Dried Cherry Sauce
½     cup sliced almonds, toasted

White Chocolate Rice Pudding
with Dried Cherry Sauce

Combine water and rice in a large saucepan. Bring to a boil. Cover, reduce heat, and simmer 15 minutes or until liquid is absorbed and rice is tender.

Scrape seeds from vanilla bean into pan. Stir seeds, pod, sugar, half-and-half, and salt into rice. Cook over medium-low heat 30 minutes, stirring often. Remove vanilla bean pod. Add white chocolate morsels, stirring until melted. Let cool 5 minutes. Spoon rice pudding into 8 individual serving dishes. If not serving immediately, cover and chill. When ready to serve, top with Dried Cherry Sauce, and sprinkle with almonds. Yield: 8 servings.

*quick & easy*

## Dried Cherry Sauce

**Prep: 6 min.  Cook: 27 min.**

½   cup dried cherries or cranberries
2    cups Merlot
¾   cup sugar
1    teaspoon grated fresh orange rind
1    teaspoon grated fresh ginger

Combine all ingredients in a medium saucepan. Bring to a boil; reduce heat, and cook, uncovered, 27 minutes or until sauce coats a spoon and is reduced to 1 cup, stirring occasionally. Cool completely. Yield: 1 cup.

# Mother-Daughter Holiday Tea

Turkey Finger Sandwiches

PB and J Cutouts

Ginger-Honey Bread

Citrus Curd

Buttery Scones    Pink Princess Spread

Fresh strawberries

Instant Spiced Tea Mix    Pink lemonade

**serves 12 to 16**

## menu prep plan

**Up to a month ahead**
• Prepare Instant Spiced Tea Mix; store in airtight container.

**1 day ahead**
• Prepare Turkey Finger Sandwiches; cover with a damp paper towel and then plastic wrap, and chill.
• Grate citrus rinds, and squeeze juices for Citrus Curd; cover and chill.
• Prepare Pink Princess Spread; cover and chill.
• Prepare Citrus Curd; cover and chill.

**Morning of**
• Bake Ginger-Honey Bread; wrap in plastic wrap once cooled.
• Prepare lemonade.

**1 hour ahead**
• Bake Buttery Scones.
• Let Pink Princess Spread come to room temperature.
• Prepare PB and J Cutouts.
• Wash strawberries, and arrange on platter.

**Last minute**
• Boil water for tea; place tea mix in a serving bowl.
• Slice Ginger-Honey Bread; serve with Citrus Curd.

Turkey Finger Sandwiches, Buttery Scones,
Pink Princess Spread, Fresh strawberries,
Instant Spiced Tea, Pink lemonade

*make ahead*

# Turkey Finger Sandwiches

*Garnish half of these dainty sandwiches for the grown-ups at your party, leaving the other half plain for little ones.*

**Prep: 58 min.**

| | |
|---|---|
| ½ | pound smoked turkey breast, cut into 1-inch cubes |
| ½ | cup unsalted butter, cut into pieces and softened |
| 2 | teaspoons honey mustard |
| 1 | tablespoon orange marmalade |
| 2 | teaspoons lemon juice |
| ¼ | cup chopped fresh parsley |
| 3 | tablespoons chopped fresh chives |
| ¼ | teaspoon salt |
| 1 | (24-ounce) package sliced firm white bread (we tested with Pepperidge Farm Hearty White) |

Fresh whole chives

| | |
|---|---|
| ¼ | cup unsalted butter, softened |
| ¼ | cup chopped fresh parsley |

Process turkey in a food processor until chopped. Add ½ cup butter and next 3 ingredients; process until almost smooth, stopping to scrape down sides. Transfer turkey spread to a medium bowl. Stir in ¼ cup parsley, 3 tablespoons chives, and salt.

Trim crusts from bread, using a serrated or an electric knife.

Spread about ¼ cup turkey spread on 8 bread slices. Top with remaining 8 bread slices; pressing lightly to adhere. Cut each sandwich into 4 fingers, using a serrated knife or an electric knife.

To garnish, tie a whole chive around each finger sandwich, and knot; or spread cut sides of sandwiches with ¼ cup softened butter, and dip lightly into ¼ cup chopped parsley. Arrange on a serving platter. Yield: 32 finger sandwiches.

**Note:** You can make sandwiches up to 1 day ahead. Just lay a damp paper towel over sandwiches before covering with plastic wrap. Store in refrigerator.

## pb and j cutouts

Using your bread of choice and holiday-shaped cutters, cut shapes from bread. (Discard trimmings, or use to make breadcrumbs.) Make peanut butter and jelly sandwiches. Arrange cutouts on a serving platter (see photo on following page).

## PB and J Cutouts will delight the daughters at the tea.

(directions previous page)

(directions previous page)

*editor's favorite • gift idea • make ahead*
## Ginger-Honey Bread

**Prep: 12 min.   Cook: 30 min.**

½   cup unsalted butter, softened
½   cup firmly packed light brown sugar
1    large egg
½   cup honey
½   cup light molasses
1¾  cups all-purpose flour
1    tablespoon ground ginger
½   teaspoon baking soda
1    teaspoon ground cinnamon
½   teaspoon ground allspice
¼   teaspoon salt
½   cup hot water

Beat butter and sugar in a large bowl at medium speed with an electric mixer until fluffy. Add egg, honey, and molasses, beating until blended. Combine flour and next 5 ingredients; add to butter mixture alternately with water, beginning and ending with flour mixture. Pour batter into a lightly greased and floured 9" square pan.

Bake at 350° for 30 minutes or until a wooden pick inserted in center comes out clean. Cool completely in pan on a wire rack. Cut into 20 rectangles. Yield: 20 servings.

*editor's favorite • gift idea • make ahead*
## Citrus Curd

*A thick-skinned navel orange will yield the best rind for this recipe. Spoon this refreshing curd over Ginger-Honey Bread or fresh fruit.*

**Prep: 6 min.   Cook: 25 min.**

2    cups sugar
1    cup butter
2    tablespoons lemon zest (about 3 lemons)
1    tablespoon lime zest (about 3 limes)
1    tablespoon orange zest (1 large orange)
⅓   cup fresh lemon juice
⅓   cup fresh lime juice
4    large eggs, lightly beaten

Combine first 7 ingredients in a heavy nonaluminum saucepan. Cook, whisking constantly, over medium heat 8 to 10 minutes or until butter melts and sugar dissolves.

Gradually whisk about one-fourth of hot sugar syrup into beaten eggs; add to remaining hot syrup, whisking constantly. Reduce heat to medium-low; cook 12 to 15 minutes, stirring gently, or until curd thickens and coats a spoon; let cool. Cover and chill overnight. Yield: 3½ cups.

## Buttery Scones

*These crusty scones are best right out of the oven.*

**Prep: 14 min.   Cook: 21 min.**

3½  cups unbleached all-purpose flour
¼   cup sugar
2¼  teaspoons baking powder
¼   teaspoon salt
1    cup cold unsalted butter, cut into pieces
1    cup half-and-half
2    large eggs, divided
1    teaspoon water
1    tablespoon sugar
Pink Princess Spread (optional)

Combine first 4 ingredients in a large bowl; cut in butter with a pastry blender until crumbly.

Whisk together half-and-half and 1 egg in a bowl; add to dry ingredients, stirring with a fork just until dry ingredients are moistened. Turn dough out onto a lightly floured surface, and knead 3 or 4 times.

Divide dough in half; shape each into a ball. Pat each into a 5½" circle on a lightly greased baking sheet. Cut each circle into 6 wedges, using a sharp knife (do not separate wedges).

Whisk together remaining egg with 1 teaspoon water in a small bowl; brush egg wash over dough. Sprinkle 1 tablespoon sugar evenly over dough.

Bake at 425° for 19 to 21 minutes or until golden. Serve warm. Serve with Pink Princess Spread, if desired. Yield: 1 dozen.

## Pink Princess Spread

Prep: 8 min.

1    (8-ounce) package cream cheese, softened
¼    cup butter or margarine, softened
2    teaspoons powdered sugar
¼    cup squeezable strawberry spread (we tested with Welch's)

Beat cream cheese, butter, and powdered sugar at medium speed with an electric mixer until smooth. Stir in strawberry spread. Cover and chill. Yield: 1½ cups.

*gift idea • make ahead*
## Instant Spiced Tea Mix

*Serve this tea mix in a sugar bowl next to a teapot of boiling water. Make an extra batch, and give small jars of the mix as party favors.*

Prep: 5 min.

1    cup lemonade-flavored iced tea (we tested with Country Time)
1    cup orange-flavored breakfast drink mix
1    teaspoon ground cinnamon
½    teaspoon ground cloves
¼    teaspoon ground nutmeg
¼    teaspoon ground ginger

Combine all ingredients in a large zip-top plastic bag.

To make 1 serving, place 2 heaping tablespoons spiced tea mix in a cup; add 1 cup boiling water, and stir gently. Yield: 2 cups mix.

Instant Spiced Tea Mix, Citrus Curd

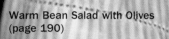

Warm Bean Salad with Olives
(page 190)

# Tuscan Dinner Party

Warm Bean Salad with Olives

Chicken with 40 Cloves of Garlic

Herb-Parmesan Smashed Potatoes

Broccoli with Balsamic Butter

Chocolate-Espresso Pots de Crème or

Chocolate Panini

**serves 6 to 8**

## menu prep plan

**6 hours ahead:**

- Cook cauliflower, dice celery and onion, and mince garlic for Warm Bean Salad with Olives; chill.
- Cut broccoli into florets; chill.
- Prepare Chocolate-Espresso Pots de Crème; cover and chill.

**2½ hours ahead:**

- Prepare Chicken with 40 Cloves of Garlic for roasting; bake and keep warm.
- Complete preparation of Warm Bean Salad with Olives.

**1 hour ahead:**

- Prepare Broccoli with Balsamic Butter.
- Microwave potatoes; prepare Herb-Parmesan Smashed Potatoes. Keep warm.

**last minute:**

- Carve chicken.

**just after dinner:**

- Prepare Chocolate Panini, or serve Chocolate-Espresso Pots de Crème.

Warm Bean Salad with Olives

Chicken with 40 Cloves of Garlic, Herb-Parmesan Smashed Potatoes, Broccoli with Balsamic Butter

## Warm Bean Salad with Olives

Prep: 23 min.   Cook: 11 min.

2     cups small fresh cauliflower florets (about 1 [10-ounce] package)
½     cup extra-virgin olive oil, divided
1     cup diced celery
1     cup diced red onion
2     garlic cloves, minced
⅓     cup white wine vinegar
1     tablespoon honey
2     (15.5-ounce) cans cannellini beans, rinsed and drained
1     (7-ounce) jar pitted kalamata olives, halved
2     tablespoons chopped fresh parsley
1     tablespoon chopped fresh sage
1     teaspoon salt
¼     teaspoon freshly ground pepper
Garnish: fresh sage

Cook cauliflower in boiling water to cover 5 to 6 minutes or until crisp-tender. Plunge into ice water to stop the cooking process; drain and set aside.

Heat ¼ cup olive oil in a large skillet over medium-high heat until hot. Add celery and onion; sauté 3 minutes or until almost tender. Add garlic; sauté 30 seconds. Stir in vinegar and honey, stirring to dissolve honey.

Combine cauliflower and sautéed vegetables in a large bowl. Add remaining ¼ cup olive oil, beans, and next 5 ingredients; stir well to combine. Serve warm or at room temperature. Garnish, if desired. Yield: 6 to 8 servings.

## Chicken with 40 Cloves of Garlic

*The abundance of garlic mellows in flavor during roasting.*

Prep: 10 min.   Cook: 1 hr., 45 min.

2    (3-pound) whole chickens
8    fresh thyme sprigs
¼    cup butter, softened
1    lemon, halved
2    teaspoons salt
1    teaspoon freshly ground pepper
40   garlic cloves, unpeeled (about 3 bulbs)
1    to 2 tablespoons olive oil
Garnish: fresh thyme

Rinse chickens, and pat dry with paper towels. Place 4 thyme sprigs in cavity of each bird. Rub each chicken with 2 tablespoons softened butter. Squeeze a lemon half over each chicken. Sprinkle with salt and pepper.

Tie ends of legs together with string; tuck wing tips under. Place chickens, breast side up, in a well-greased shallow roasting pan.

Toss garlic with olive oil in a bowl. Scatter garlic cloves around chickens, snuggling them close to chickens.

Bake at 375° for 1 hour and 45 minutes or until a meat thermometer inserted into thigh registers 180°.

Remove chickens and garlic to a serving platter. Garnish, if desired. Yield: 6 to 8 servings.

*editor's favorite • quick & easy*

## Herb-Parmesan Smashed Potatoes

*This dish can be prepared at the last minute and doesn't take up any space on the cooktop.*

Prep: 18 min.   Cook: 15 min.

| | |
|---|---|
| 5 | russet potatoes (about 3 pounds) |
| 3 | tablespoons butter |
| ½ | cup half-and-half |
| 1 | cup freshly grated Parmigiano-Reggiano cheese |
| 2 | teaspoons chopped fresh rosemary |
| 2 | tablespoons chopped fresh flat-leaf parsley |
| 1 | teaspoon salt |
| ½ | teaspoon freshly ground pepper |

Pierce potatoes with a fork. Microwave on HIGH 13 to 15 minutes or until tender; let cool slightly. Peel potatoes; mash with a potato masher. Add butter and remaining ingredients, mashing until blended. Serve warm. Yield: 6 to 8 servings.

Chocolate-Espresso
Pots de Crème

*quick & easy*

## Broccoli with Balsamic Butter

Prep: 19 min.   Cook: 14 min.

| | |
|---|---|
| 3 | pounds broccoli, cut into large florets |
| ½ | cup white balsamic vinegar |
| ¼ | cup minced shallots |
| ½ | cup cold butter, cut into ½" pieces |
| 1 | tablespoon chopped fresh parsley |
| ½ | teaspoon salt |
| ⅛ | teaspoon pepper |

Place broccoli florets in a steamer basket over boiling water, and cook 7 minutes or until crisp-tender.

Meanwhile, in a medium skillet, bring vinegar and shallots to a boil; reduce heat, simmer 7 minutes or until vinegar is almost absorbed. Remove from heat; add butter, a few pieces at a time, stirring constantly with a wire whisk until butter melts and sauce thickens. Stir in parsley, salt, and pepper. Toss with steamed broccoli. Yield: 8 servings.

**Fix it Faster:** Buy broccoli crowns to save a step in the kitchen.

*editor's favorite • make ahead*

## Chocolate-Espresso Pots de Crème

*Using premium chocolate guarantees velvety texture for this decadent dessert. Look for chocolate (below) in specialty grocery stores.*

Prep: 10 min.   Cook: 24 min.   Other: 4 hr.

| | |
|---|---|
| 2 | cups half-and-half |
| ½ | cup sugar |
| 2 | large eggs, lightly beaten |
| 1 | tablespoon instant espresso powder |
| ¼ | cup unsweetened cocoa |
| ¼ | cup brandy |
| 8 | ounces semisweet chocolate, cut into chunks (we tested with Scharffen Berger) |

Garnishes: unsweetened whipped cream, lavender

Whisk together first 6 ingredients in top of a double boiler; add chocolate. Bring water to a boil. Reduce heat to medium-low; cook, whisking constantly, 24 minutes or until mixture reaches 160° (mixture will be moderately thickened).

Remove from heat. Spoon chocolate into demitasse cups, chocolate pots, or 4- or 6-ounce ramekins. Cover and chill at least 4 hours. Garnish, if desired. Yield: 6 to 8 servings.

**Note:** Demitasse cups or chocolate pots will yield smaller servings than ramekins, which is a good option for such a rich dessert.

# Chocolate Panini

*A slender loaf of rustic Italian bread is the ideal shape to use for these little dessert sandwiches. Get your dinner guests involved in making and serving these hot off the press.*

Prep: 3 min.   Cook: 1 min. per batch

1   (8-ounce) loaf ciabatta bread
2   to 3 tablespoons olive oil
1   (4-ounce) bittersweet chocolate baking bar, coarsely
    chopped (we tested with Ghirardelli)

Preheat panini press according to manufacturer's instructions.

Slice bread into 10 (1") pieces; slice each piece in half. Brush crust sides of each piece of bread with olive oil. Turn bottoms of bread, oiled side down. Place chocolate evenly on bottom pieces of bread; cover with tops of bread, oiled side up.

Place 5 sandwiches in panini press; cook 1 minute or just until chocolate begins to melt and bread is toasted. Repeat procedure with remaining sandwiches. Serve hot. Yield: 10 sandwiches.

Chocolate Panini

# Vegetarian Night

Caramelized Onion and Mushroom Bisque

Black-eyed Pea Cakes with Cranberry-Red Pepper Salsa

Autumn Succotash with Gruyère Grits

Pumpkin-Pecan Layer Cake

**serves 6**

## menu prep plan

**2 or 3 days ahead:**

• Prepare Cranberry-Red Pepper Salsa; chill.

**1 day ahead:**

• Make Pumpkin-Pecan Layer Cake; chill overnight.
• Cook onions for Caramelized Onion and Mushroom Bisque up to the point of adding 2 cups broth; chill.
• Cut bell peppers, fennel, and onion for Autumn Succotash; chill.
• Prepare Black-eyed Pea Cakes, but do not cook; chill overnight.

**2 hours ahead:**

• Slice mushrooms and complete preparation of Caramelized Onion and Mushroom Bisque; keep warm.
• Prepare Autumn Succotash; keep warm.

**1 hour ahead:**

• Prepare Gruyère Grits; keep warm.
• Fry Black-eyed Pea Cakes; keep warm.

**last minute:**

• Spoon Cranberry-Red Pepper Salsa into serving dish.
• Ladle Caramelized Onion and Mushroom Bisque into bowls.

**Pumpkin-Pecan Layer Cake**

---

*editor's favorite*

## Caramelized Onion and Mushroom Bisque

Prep: 15 min.   Cook: 52 min.   Other: 30 min.

| | |
|---|---|
| 2 | tablespoons butter |
| 3 | pounds onions, sliced and separated into rings |
| 2 | garlic cloves, chopped |
| 4½ | cups vegetable broth, divided |
| 2 | tablespoons olive oil |
| 4 | (3.5-ounce) packages shiitake mushrooms, stems removed and sliced |
| ½ | teaspoon salt |
| ½ | cup whipping cream |
| 2 | tablespoons dry sherry |
| 1 | tablespoon fresh lemon juice |
| ¼ | teaspoon salt |
| ⅛ | teaspoon ground white pepper |

Sour cream (optional)

Melt butter in a Dutch oven over medium heat; add onions. Cook over medium heat, stirring occasionally, 35 minutes or until onion is lightly browned and very tender. Add garlic, and cook 1 minute. Add 1 cup broth, stirring to loosen browned bits from bottom of pan (can make ahead to this point. Remove onions from heat; cover and chill until ready to prepare remainder of soup). Stir in 2 cups broth; bring to a boil. Cover, reduce heat, and simmer 10 minutes. Remove from heat, and let cool 30 minutes.

Meanwhile, heat oil in a large skillet over medium-high heat. Add mushrooms, and cook 8 to 10 minutes, stirring once or twice, until mushrooms are lightly browned and liquid has evaporated; stir in ½ teaspoon salt. Remove from heat, and set aside.

Process soup, in batches, in a blender or food processor 2 minutes or until smooth, stopping to scrape down sides. Return to Dutch oven. Stir in remaining 1½ cups broth and whipping cream; bring to a boil. Remove from heat; stir in sherry, lemon juice, ¼ teaspoon salt, and pepper.

To serve, ladle soup into individual bowls, and top evenly with mushrooms; dollop each with sour cream, if desired. Yield: 7 cups.

**Make Ahead:** To jump-start this recipe, begin a day ahead and caramelize the onions up to the point of adding 2 cups of broth.

Black-eyed Pea Cakes with
Cranberry-Red Pepper Salsa

*make ahead*

# Black-eyed Pea Cakes with Cranberry-Red Pepper Salsa

*Here's a knife and fork appetizer with pizzazz; serve two patties as a meatless entrée.*

Prep: 27 min.    Cook: 3 min. per batch    Other: 8 hr.

2    (15.83-ounce) cans black-eyed peas, rinsed and drained
1    large egg
1    teaspoon ground cumin
¾    teaspoon salt
1¼    cups Japanese breadcrumbs (panko), divided
½    cup bottled roasted red peppers, drained and chopped
⅓    cup chopped red onion
⅓    cup chopped fresh cilantro
3    tablespoons all-purpose flour
2    garlic cloves, minced
Peanut oil for frying
Cranberry-Red Pepper Salsa

Process 1½ cups black-eyed peas in a food processor until coarsely chopped.

Whisk together egg, cumin, and salt in a large bowl. Add chopped peas, remaining whole peas, ¾ cup breadcrumbs, and next 5 ingredients; stir well to combine.

Place remaining ½ cup breadcrumbs in a shallow dish.

Using a ¼ cup measure, shape pea mixture into a cake; dredge in breadcrumbs. Repeat with remaining mixture and breadcrumbs. Place cakes on a baking sheet lined with plastic wrap; cover and chill overnight.

Pour oil to a depth of 1" into a large skillet; heat to 350°.

Fry cakes, in batches, 3 minutes or until golden. Drain well on paper towels. Serve immediately with Cranberry-Red Pepper Salsa. Yield: 12 appetizer or 6 entrée servings.

**Freezer Note**: If you won't be serving all the Black-eyed Pea Cakes at once, freeze uncooked cakes; then thaw before dredging in breadcrumbs and frying.

*make ahead • quick & easy*

# Cranberry-Red Pepper Salsa

*This pretty salsa can be made up to three days before serving.*

Prep: 15 min.

1½    cups fresh or frozen cranberries, thawed
½    cup bottled roasted red bell peppers, drained and chopped
3    tablespoons honey
½    teaspoon lime zest
2    tablespoons lime juice
1    green onion, chopped
1    jalapeño pepper, seeded and minced
2    tablespoons chopped fresh cilantro

Process cranberries in a food processor until coarsely chopped; transfer to a bowl. Add bell peppers and remaining ingredients, stirring well to combine. Cover and chill until ready to serve. Serve cold or at room temperature. Yield: 2 cups.

Autumn Succotash with
Gruyère Grits

# Autumn Succotash with Gruyère Grits

*Grits are a versatile base for this rustic blend of corn, onion, garlic, and fennel.*

**Prep: 18 min.   Cook: 26 min.**

2   tablespoons butter or margarine
1   large fennel bulb, cut into thin 2" strips
1   medium onion, cut into ¼" wedges
2   garlic cloves, minced
1   large red bell pepper, cut into thin 2" strips
1   large yellow bell pepper, cut into thin 2" strips
1   (16-ounce) bag frozen whole kernel corn, thawed
1   (10-ounce) package baby lima beans, thawed
½   cup heavy whipping cream
⅓   cup chopped flat-leaf parsley
2   tablespoons fresh lemon juice
1   teaspoon salt
½   teaspoon freshly ground black pepper
Gruyère Grits
4   medium plum tomatoes, chopped (about 1 cup)

Melt butter in a large nonstick skillet over medium heat. Add fennel, onion, and garlic; cook 9 to 11 minutes or until lightly browned, stirring often.

Add peppers; cook 10 minutes, stirring occasionally. Add corn, lima beans, and whipping cream; cook 5 minutes or until thoroughly heated, stirring often. Remove from heat; stir in parsley and next 3 ingredients. Serve over Gruyère Grits. Sprinkle with chopped tomato. Yield: 6 to 8 servings.

## Gruyère Grits

**Prep: 5 min.   Cook: 15 min.**

4   cups vegetable broth
1½   cups uncooked regular grits
1   cup (4 ounces) shredded Gruyère cheese
3   tablespoons butter
½   teaspoon salt
½   teaspoon freshly ground pepper

Bring broth to a boil in a large saucepan. Gradually stir in grits. Cover, reduce heat, and simmer 15 minutes or until tender, stirring occasionally. Remove from heat; stir in cheese and remaining ingredients. Serve immediately. Yield: 6 to 8 servings.

# Pumpkin-Pecan Layer Cake

**Prep: 30 min.   Cook: 20 min.   Other: 8 hr., 10 min.**

½   cup butter, softened
1½   cups firmly packed light brown sugar
2   large eggs
1   cup canned pumpkin
2   cups all-purpose flour
2   teaspoons baking powder
2   teaspoons pumpkin pie spice
½   teaspoon baking soda
½   teaspoon salt
½   cup buttermilk
2   teaspoons vanilla extract
2   teaspoons minced fresh ginger
1   cup chopped pecans, toasted
Ginger-Cream Cheese Frosting

Beat butter and sugar at medium speed with an electric mixer until light and fluffy. Add eggs, 1 at a time, beating until blended after each addition. Add pumpkin, beating until blended.

Combine flour and next 4 ingredients. Combine buttermilk, vanilla, and ginger. Add flour mixture to butter mixture alternately with gingered buttermilk, beginning and ending with flour mixture. Beat at low speed after each addition. Fold in chopped pecans. Pour batter into 2 greased, parchment paper-lined 9" round cakepans.

Bake at 350° for 18 to 20 minutes or until a wooden pick inserted in center comes out clean. Cool in pans on wire racks 10 minutes; remove from pans, and cool completely on wire racks.

Spread Ginger-Cream Cheese Frosting between layers and on top and sides of cake. Cover and chill overnight. Yield: 1 (2-layer) cake.

## Ginger-Cream Cheese Frosting

**Prep: 7 min.   Other: 30 min.**

1½   (8-ounce) packages cream cheese, softened
½   cup butter, softened
1   tablespoon minced fresh ginger
4   cups powdered sugar
1   teaspoon vanilla extract

Beat first 3 ingredients at medium speed with an electric mixer until light and fluffy. Gradually add powdered sugar, beating until smooth. Add vanilla, beating until smooth. Chill 30 minutes or until spreading consistency. Yield: 2¼ cups.

# Brunch Buffet

Hearts of Romaine Salad with
Walnut-Champagne Vinaigrette

Spinach and Gruyère Tarts

Rosemary Biscuits and Fresh Pork Sausage Patties

Ham-and-Hash Brown Breakfast Casserole

Banana Nut and Dulce de Leche Coffee Cake

Tropical Fruit with Ginger Syrup

Berry Fizz    Coffee    Orange juice

**serves 12**

## menu prep plan

**2 days ahead:**

• Prepare Walnut-Champagne Vinaigrette; chill.
• Make dough for Rosemary Biscuits; freeze unbaked biscuits.
• Chill Champagne.

**1 day ahead:**

• Wash romaine hearts and trim stems; chill. Toast walnuts for salad.
• Fill tart shells with spinach and cheese; prepare egg mixture for Spinach and Gruyère Tarts. Cover both, and chill overnight.
• Prepare Ham-and-Hash Brown Breakfast Casserole, but do not bake; chill overnight.
• Process all ingredients for Fresh Pork Sausage Patties; chill overnight.
• Bake Banana Nut and Dulce de Leche Coffee Cake; cover and store at room temperature.
• Cut fruit and prepare Ginger Syrup for Tropical Fruit; chill separately. Toast coconut, and store in airtight container.

**3 hours ahead:**

• Combine cranberry juice and liqueur for Berry Fizz; chill.

**1 to 2 hours ahead:**

• Bake Ham-and-Hash Brown Breakfast Casserole.
• Cook Fresh Pork Sausage Patties; keep warm.
• Add egg mixture to tart shells, and bake Spinach and Gruyère Tarts.
• Assemble Tropical Fruit with Ginger Syrup.
• Bake frozen biscuits at 425° for 15 minutes; keep warm.

**last minute:**

• Arrange Hearts of Romaine Salad on serving plates.
• Reheat Banana Nut and Dulce de Leche Coffee Cake.
• Stir Champagne into Berry Fizz.

Tropical Fruit with Ginger Syrup, Banana Nut and Dulce de Leche Coffee Cake, Spinach and Gruyère Tarts, Ham-and-Hash Brown Breakfast Casserole

*editor's favorite • make ahead*

## Hearts of Romaine Salad with Walnut-Champagne Vinaigrette

Prep: 10 min.

| | |
|---|---|
| ⅓ | cup champagne vinegar |
| ⅓ | cup walnut oil or extra-virgin olive oil |
| 2 | tablespoons minced shallot (about 1 large) |
| 2 | tablespoons chopped fresh flat-leaf parsley |
| 1 | tablespoon chopped fresh thyme |
| ¾ | teaspoon salt |
| ½ | teaspoon freshly ground pepper |
| 4 | romaine hearts* |
| ½ | cup chopped walnuts, toasted |

Whisk together first 7 ingredients.

Remove lower 3" of romaine stems. Arrange leaves on a large serving platter. Drizzle evenly with Walnut-Champagne Vinaigrette. Sprinkle with walnuts. Yield: 10 to 12 servings.

**Make Ahead:** You can make Walnut-Champagne Vinaigrette up to 2 days ahead.

*You can find washed, ready-to-serve romaine hearts at most grocery stores.

# Spinach and Gruyère Tarts

Prep: 15 min.   Cook: 35 min.   Other: 5 min.

2   (10-ounce) packages frozen tart shells (we tested with Dutch Ann)
1   (10-ounce) package frozen chopped spinach, thawed and squeezed dry
1½  cups (6 ounces) shredded Gruyère cheese
4   large eggs
1½  cups half-and-half
½   teaspoon salt
½   teaspoon freshly ground pepper
Ground nutmeg

Arrange tart shells on a baking sheet. Fill each shell with about 1 tablespoon each spinach and cheese.

Whisk together eggs and next 3 ingredients. Spoon egg mixture evenly into tart shells. Sprinkle lightly with nutmeg.

Bake at 375° for 30 to 35 minutes or until tarts are puffed and crust is lightly browned. Let stand 5 minutes before removing from foil pans. Yield: 16 tarts.

**Make Ahead:** To make ahead, simply fill the pastry with the spinach and cheese, and prepare the egg mixture. Cover both, and chill overnight. Next day, fill tarts with egg mixture, and bake.

*editor's favorite • make ahead*
# Rosemary Biscuits

Prep: 25 min.   Cook: 10 min.

3   cups self-rising soft-wheat flour
¼   cup sugar
½   teaspoon salt
½   cup shortening, chilled
1   cup buttermilk
½   cup whipping cream
1½  tablespoons chopped fresh rosemary
Fresh Pork Sausage Patties
Garnish: rosemary sprigs

Combine first 3 ingredients in a large bowl. Cut shortening into flour mixture with a pastry blender until mixture resembles coarse meal. Add buttermilk, whipping cream, and rosemary, stirring with a fork until all ingredients are moistened. (Dough with be soft.)

Turn dough out onto a generously floured surface; knead 3 or 4 times. Pat or roll dough to 1" thickness; cut with a floured 2" biscuit cutter, and place biscuits 1" apart on ungreased baking sheets.

Bake at 450° for 10 minutes or until lightly browned. Transfer to a wire rack, and cool slightly. Split biscuits with a fork, and fill with warm Fresh Pork Sausage Patties. Serve hot. Garnish, if desired. Yield: 20 biscuits.

**Make Ahead:** Make the biscuit dough several days in advance, and freeze unbaked biscuits in a single layer on a baking sheet until frozen solid. Transfer to a large zip-top freezer bag. Seal and store in freezer. Arrange frozen biscuits on an ungreased baking sheet. Bake at 425° for 15 minutes or until golden.

*editor's favorite • make ahead*
# Fresh Pork Sausage Patties

*This homemade sausage is best when made in advance, giving it more time to develop flavor. The patties can also be cooked in advance and refrigerated or frozen. Simply reheat them in the microwave when ready to serve.*

Prep: 30 min.   Cook: 4 min. per batch   Other: 4 hr.

6   bacon slices, frozen and coarsely chopped
2   garlic cloves
1   shallot
2   teaspoons fresh rosemary leaves
1½  teaspoons ground sage
¾   teaspoon salt
½   teaspoon freshly ground black pepper
¼   teaspoon ground red pepper
1½  pounds ground pork

Process first 8 ingredients in a food processor until finely minced. Add ground pork; process until mixture begins to form a ball. Cover and chill at least 4 hours or overnight.

Shape sausage into 20 (3 x ¼") patties. Cook in several batches in a large nonstick skillet over medium-high heat 2 minutes per side or until lightly browned and a thermometer inserted into the thickest portion registers 160°. Keep warm until ready to serve. Yield: 20 patties.

**Turkey Sausage Patties:** You can make this recipe using 1½ pounds ground turkey (white and dark meat). Follow above procedure, except blend ground turkey with seasonings by hand instead of using a processor. This will keep the turkey from becoming too finely ground.

Tropical Fruit with Ginger Syrup,
Banana Nut and Dulce de Leche Coffee Cake, Berry
Fizz, Rosemary Biscuits and Fresh Pork Sausage
Patties

*make ahead*

## Ham-and-Hash Brown Breakfast Casserole

*Make breakfast a breeze by preparing this casserole the day before. Simply spoon potato mixture into a dish, cover, and chill overnight. Next morning, place casserole directly into the oven, and add 15 minutes to the initial bake time.*

**Prep: 15 min.   Cook: 1 hr., 10 min.   Other: 10 min.**

| | |
|---|---|
| 8 | bacon slices |
| ¾ | cup chopped sweet onion |
| ⅓ | cup butter |
| 1 | (30-ounce) package frozen country-style hash brown potatoes, thawed |
| 1 | (10¾-ounce) can cream of chicken soup |
| 1 | (16-ounce) container sour cream |
| 2 | cups (8 ounces) shredded Colby Jack cheese |
| 1 | (8-ounce) package diced ham |
| 1 | (4-ounce) jar diced pimiento, drained |
| 2 | tablespoons coarse-grained Dijon mustard |
| ½ | teaspoon salt |
| ½ | teaspoon freshly ground pepper |

Cook bacon in a large nonstick skillet over medium heat until very crisp. Remove bacon from pan, reserving 2 tablespoons drippings in pan. Crumble bacon; set aside.

Add onion to reserved drippings; cook over medium-high heat 6 minutes or until tender and golden. Reduce heat to medium-low, and swirl in butter until melted; remove pan from heat.

Squeeze excess moisture from potatoes. Stir in potatoes, soup, and remaining ingredients. Spoon into a greased 13" x 9" baking dish.

Bake, covered, at 350° for 45 minutes. Uncover and sprinkle with crumbled bacon. Bake 15 more minutes or until browned on top. Let stand 10 minutes before serving. Yield: 12 servings.

# Banana Nut and Dulce de Leche Coffee Cake

*While best served warm, this cake can be made a day ahead and reheated.*

**Prep: 35 min.   Cook: 39 min.**

2¾   cups all-purpose flour, divided
1   cup granulated sugar
1½   teaspoons baking powder
½   teaspoon baking soda
½   teaspoon salt
1   cup cold unsalted butter, cut into pieces and divided
2   large eggs
1   cup mashed banana
½   cup sour cream
1   tablespoon vanilla extract
¼   cup firmly packed light brown sugar
1   cup pecan pieces
1   (13.4-ounce) can dulce de leche (we tested with Nestlé)*

Combine 2¼ cups flour and next 4 ingredients in a large bowl. Cut ¾ cup butter into flour mixture with a pastry blender until crumbly. Whisk together eggs and next 3 ingredients; add to flour mixture, stirring just until dry ingredients are moistened.

Spread batter into a greased 13" x 9" pan.

Combine remaining ½ cup flour and brown sugar in a small bowl. Cut remaining ¼ cup butter into flour mixture with pastry blender. Add pecans, pressing streusel mixture between fingers until large clumps form. Sprinkle streusel over batter in pan.

Microwave dulce de leche in a small glass bowl on HIGH 1 minute or until drizzling consistency, stirring once; drizzle over streusel topping.

Bake at 350° for 35 to 38 minutes or until streusel topping begins to brown and center of cake puffs slightly. Cool slightly. Yield: 12 to 16 servings.

*Find dulce de leche in the ethnic section or on the baking aisle of your grocery store.

---

*make ahead*
# Tropical Fruit with Ginger Syrup

*Purchase tropical fruit several days in advance to allow time for ripening to optimal flavor and sweetness. Leave it at room temperature until ripened; then chill until ready to use.*

**Prep: 30 min.   Cook: 8 min.**

¾   cup water
½   cup sugar
5   thin slices peeled fresh ginger
2   tablespoons fresh lime juice
6   kiwifruit, peeled and sliced
3   mangoes, peeled and cubed
3   star fruit, sliced
1   pineapple, peeled, cored, and cubed
½   (3-pound) Caribbean Red papaya, peeled, seeded, and cubed
Sweetened flaked coconut, toasted

Simmer water, sugar, and ginger in a small saucepan 5 minutes. Remove from heat; pour liquid through a wire-mesh strainer into a small bowl, discarding ginger. Stir in lime juice; cover and chill syrup.

Combine kiwifruit and next 4 ingredients in a trifle bowl or large serving bowl. Drizzle cooled syrup over fruit; toss gently. Sprinkle with toasted coconut. Yield: 20 servings.

---

*editor's favorite • make ahead • quick & easy*
# Berry Fizz

*Float a few fresh raspberries in each Champagne flute when serving this holiday alternative to mimosas.*

**Prep: 5 min.**

6   cups cranberry-raspberry juice drink, chilled (we tested with Ocean Spray)
¼   cup Chambord or other raspberry liqueur
1   (750-milliliter) bottle Champagne, chilled
Garnish: fresh raspberries

Stir together juice and liqueur; chill. Stir in Champagne just before serving. Garnish, if desired. Yield: 10 cups.

# Country Dinner

Butter Lettuces with Chutney Vinaigrette

Walnut Chicken with Dijon Cream Sauce

Brussels Sprouts with Marmalade Glaze

Cheddar and Green Onion Muffins

Butterscotch Pudding with Bourbon-Brown Sugar Meringue

Molasses Cigarillos

**serves 6**

## menu prep plan

**1 day ahead:**
- Prepare Butterscotch Pudding; cover and chill.
- Flatten chicken breasts using meat mallet; chill.
- Wash Brussels sprouts and trim stem ends; chill.

**4 to 5 hours ahead:**
- Bake Cheddar and Green Onion Muffins.
- Prepare Chutney Vinaigrette; chill. Combine lettuce, celery, cucumber, and raisins for salad; chill.
- Top Butterscotch Pudding with Bourbon-Brown Sugar Meringue.

**2 to 3 hours ahead:**
- Prepare Molasses Cigarillos.
- Prepare Brussels Sprouts with Marmalade Glaze; keep warm.

**1 hour ahead:**
- Prepare Walnut Chicken with Dijon Cream Sauce.

**last minute:**
- Toss Butter Lettuces with Chutney Vinaigrette.
- Reheat muffins.

Walnut Chicken with Dijon Cream Sauce, Butter Lettuces with Chutney Vinaigrette, Cheddar and Green Onion Muffins, Brussels Sprouts with Marmalade Glaze

*quick & easy*

## Butter Lettuces with Chutney Vinaigrette

*Using a prepackaged salad blend makes this a super-quick accompaniment with dinner. If you prefer, use 6 cups of torn Boston or Bibb lettuce.*

Prep: 11 min.

½ cup mango chutney
2 tablespoons cider vinegar
2½ teaspoons curry powder
1½ teaspoons coarse-grained Dijon mustard
1 teaspoon salt
½ teaspoon pepper
½ cup olive oil
1 (7-ounce) package butter lettuce and radicchio salad blend (we tested with Fresh Express Riviera Salad blend)
2 celery ribs with leaves, thinly sliced diagonally
¾ cup peeled, seeded, and thinly sliced cucumber
½ cup golden raisins

Whisk together first 6 ingredients in a small bowl; gradually whisk in oil until blended.

Combine lettuce, celery, cucumber, and raisins in a salad bowl; toss well. Just before serving, pour desired amount of dressing over salad, and toss well. Refrigerate any remaining dressing for other uses. Yield: 6 servings.

# Walnut Chicken with Dijon Cream Sauce

*Substitute pecans for walnuts to give this chicken a Southern accent.*

Prep: 26 min.    Cook: 24 min.

¼ cup butter or margarine, melted
½ teaspoon garlic powder
½ cup Japanese or fine, dry breadcrumbs (we tested with panko)
¼ cup all-purpose flour
½ cup finely chopped walnuts
¼ cup sesame seeds
1 teaspoon salt
½ teaspoon freshly ground pepper
6 skinned and boned chicken breasts
2 tablespoons butter or margarine, divided
2 tablespoons olive oil, divided
1 cup heavy whipping cream
2 tablespoons Dijon mustard
2 tablespoons dry sherry
¼ teaspoon salt
⅛ teaspoon freshly ground pepper

Combine ¼ cup butter and garlic powder in a small bowl, stirring well; set aside.

Combine breadcrumbs and next 5 ingredients in a shallow dish, stirring well.

Place each chicken breast between 2 sheets of heavy-duty plastic wrap; flatten to ½" thickness using a meat mallet or rolling pin.

Brush both sides of chicken with garlic butter; dredge in breadcrumbs.

Heat 1 tablespoon butter and 1 tablespoon olive oil in a large skillet over medium heat until butter melts. Add 3 chicken breasts; cook 4 to 6 minutes on each side or until lightly browned and done. Transfer to a serving platter; repeat procedure with remaining chicken, butter, and olive oil.

Meanwhile, combine whipping cream and remaining 4 ingredients in a small saucepan; whisk until blended. Bring to a simmer; cook 10 minutes or until mixture thickens slightly and coats the back of a spoon. Serve sauce with chicken. Yield: 6 servings.

# Brussels Sprouts with Marmalade Glaze

*Fresh Brussels sprouts are best during the winter months. Choose small sprouts that are firm and bright green.*

Prep: 10 min.    Cook: 36 min.

2 pounds fresh Brussels sprouts
1 (32-ounce) container chicken broth
2 tablespoons butter or margarine
½ cup minced onion
2 garlic cloves, minced
½ cup orange marmalade
¼ teaspoon salt
¼ teaspoon pepper

Wash Brussels sprouts thoroughly, and remove any discolored leaves. Trim stem ends. Place Brussels sprouts in a large saucepan; add broth. Bring to a boil over medium-high heat; reduce heat, and simmer 5 minutes or until desired tenderness.

Drain Brussels sprouts, reserving 1 cup chicken broth. Melt butter in saucepan; add onion and garlic. Sauté over medium-high heat 2 minutes or until tender. Add reserved broth and marmalade; bring to a simmer. Cook, stirring often, 15 minutes or until glaze reduces and thickens. Add Brussels sprouts, salt, and pepper; toss well until thoroughly heated. Serve warm. Yield: 6 servings.

*quick & easy*
# Cheddar and Green Onion Muffins

Prep: 10 min.    Cook: 22 min.

2 cups all-purpose flour
1 tablespoon baking powder
1 teaspoon salt
¼ teaspoon garlic powder
¼ teaspoon ground red pepper
1 cup (4 ounces) shredded extra-sharp Cheddar cheese
⅓ cup finely chopped green onions
1 large egg, lightly beaten
1 cup milk
⅓ cup butter, melted

Combine first 5 ingredients in a large bowl; stir well. Stir in cheese and green onions. Make a well in center of mixture.

Whisk together egg, milk, and butter; add to dry ingredients, stirring just until moistened. Spoon into lightly greased muffin pans, filling three-fourths full.

Bake at 375° for 22 minutes or until a wooden pick inserted in center comes out clean. Remove from pans immediately, and serve warm. Yield: 1 dozen.

## Butterscotch Pudding with Bourbon-Brown Sugar Meringue

*If you prefer a subtle molasses flavor, use the lesser amount of molasses in the pudding. For entertaining, serve the pudding with Molasses Cigarillos.*

**Prep: 12 min.   Cook: 40 min.   Other: 8 hr.**

¼   cup butter
¾   cup firmly packed light brown sugar
2    to 3 tablespoons molasses
2¼  cups milk, divided
1    cup heavy whipping cream
½   vanilla bean
3    egg yolks
3    tablespoons cornstarch
2    teaspoons vanilla extract
¼   teaspoon salt
½   cup firmly packed light brown sugar
1    tablespoon bourbon
2    tablespoons water
3    egg whites
¼   teaspoon cream of tartar

Butterscotch Pudding with
Bourbon-Brown Sugar Meringue

Combine butter, ¾ cup brown sugar, and molasses in a medium saucepan. Cook over medium heat, stirring constantly, 5 minutes or until sugar dissolves.

Combine 1¾ cups milk and whipping cream in a separate saucepan. Split vanilla bean lengthwise. Scrape seeds from vanilla bean into saucepan; stir in bean pod. Bring just to a simmer over medium heat. Remove and discard vanilla bean pod. Slowly whisk milk mixture into sugar mixture.

Whisk together egg yolks, remaining ½ cup milk, cornstarch, vanilla, and salt in a small bowl. Gradually stir about one-fourth of hot mixture into yolk mixture; add yolk mixture to remaining hot mixture, stirring constantly. Cook over medium heat, stirring constantly, 20 minutes or until thickened. Remove from heat; pour into a 1-quart baking dish. Place plastic wrap directly on surface of pudding; chill at least 8 hours.

Combine ½ cup brown sugar, bourbon, and water in a small saucepan. Cook over medium-low heat 7 minutes or until a candy thermometer reaches 235°.

Meanwhile, beat egg whites and cream of tartar at high speed with an electric mixer until stiff peaks form. Gradually drizzle in hot brown sugar syrup, beating at high speed 2 minutes or until thick and glossy. Mound meringue over chilled pudding, forming peaks with the back of a spoon. Broil 8 inches from heat 2 minutes or until meringue is browned. Yield: 6 servings.

## Molasses Cigarillos

*These buttery, crisp cookies are a tasty complement to any pudding or ice cream.*

**Prep: 23 min.   Cook: 66 min.   Other: 16 min.**

¼   cup butter
6    tablespoons light brown sugar
3    tablespoons molasses
1    teaspoon vanilla extract
¾   cup ground pecans
¼   cup all-purpose flour

Combine first 3 ingredients in a small saucepan. Cook over medium-low heat 1 to 2 minutes or until butter melts and sugar dissolves, whisking constantly. Remove from heat. Stir in vanilla.

Combine ground pecans and flour; add to molasses mixture, stirring until blended.

Working in batches, making 2 cookies at a time, drop batter by 1 tablespoonful onto a lightly greased aluminum foil-lined baking sheet (keep remaining batter covered with a damp cloth).

Bake at 350° for 8 minutes or until golden. Let stand 2 minutes (no longer). Working quickly, carefully roll each delicate cookie into a tight cigarette shape. Cool completely on wire racks. Serve within 3 hours. Yield: 16 cookies.

# Ham Dinner

Shrimp and Benne Seed Tartlets

Baked Ham with Mustard-Peach Glaze

Fennel, Apple, and Celery Slaw

Sweet Potato Salad with Bacon Vinaigrette

Bakery rolls

Dark Chocolate Layer Cake

**serves 8**

## menu prep plan

1 day ahead:

• Make and bake tart shells; store in an airtight container.

• Peel and devein shrimp; chill.

morning of:

• Prepare White Chocolate Frosting; chill.

• Bake and assemble Dark Chocolate Layer Cake.

• Bake sweet potato and onion, toast pecans, and prepare Bacon Vinaigrette.

• Cook shrimp, and make shrimp salad; chill.

3 hours ahead:

• Prepare Baked Ham with Mustard-Peach Glaze; keep warm.

• Prepare Fennel, Apple, and Celery Slaw; chill.

1 hour ahead:

• Complete preparation of Sweet Potato Salad with Bacon Vinaigrette.

• Prepare peach nectar sauce for ham.

• Carve ham, and place on serving platter; keep warm.

last minute:

• Assemble Shrimp and Benne Seed Tartlets.

• Heat rolls.

## Shrimp and Benne Seed Tartlets

Prep: 17 min.   Cook: 8 min.

Tartlet Shells
| | |
|---|---|
| 1 | pound unpeeled, medium-size fresh shrimp |
| 3 | cups water |
| ¼ | cup mayonnaise |
| ¼ | cup sour cream |
| 1 | tablespoon lemon zest |
| 2 | teaspoons fresh lemon juice |
| 2 | teaspoons Creole seasoning |
| ⅓ | cup diced celery |
| 2 | tablespoons thinly sliced green onions |

Garnish: thinly sliced green onions

Prepare and bake Tartlet Shells.

Peel and devein shrimp. Bring water to a boil; add shrimp. Cook 3 to 5 minutes or until shrimp turn pink; drain. Coarsely chop shrimp, and pat dry with a paper towel.

Stir together mayonnaise and next 4 ingredients in a large bowl. Add shrimp, celery, and 2 tablespoons green onions.

Fill each Tartlet Shell with 1 heaping tablespoonful shrimp salad. Garnish, if desired. Serve immediately. Yield: 2 dozen.

**Make Ahead:** Tartlet shells can be baked up to 24 hours ahead. Store in an airtight container.

## Tartlet Shells

Prep: 6 min.   Cook: 10 min.   Other: 35 min.

| | |
|---|---|
| 1 | cup all-purpose flour |
| ¾ | teaspoon salt |
| 5 | tablespoons cold butter, cut into pieces |
| 2 | tablespoons sesame seeds |
| 1 | to 2 tablespoons cold water |
| ½ | teaspoon cider vinegar |

Place flour and salt in a food processor; pulse until blended. Add butter and sesame seeds; pulse until blended. With processor running, add 1 tablespoon water and vinegar; process until mixture forms a ball, adding more water, if needed. Shape dough into a log; cover and chill 30 minutes.

Place 1½ teaspoons of dough into each ungreased miniature (1¾") muffin cup, pressing gently up sides of cup. Prick sides and bottom of dough with a fork. Bake at 400° for 10 minutes or until edges are lightly browned. Cool in pan on wire racks 5 minutes. Remove from pans, and cool completely on wire rack. Yield: 2 dozen.

Baked Ham with Mustard-Peach Glaze;
Fennel, Apple, and Celery Slaw; bakery roll;
Sweet Potato Salad with Bacon Vinaigrette

Baked Ham with
Mustard-Peach
Glaze

Small and shapely Seckel pears with
stems make a striking garnish.

*editor's favorite*

# Baked Ham with Mustard-Peach Glaze

*Basting this ham with peach preserves and mustard creates a glistening entrée that tastes as good as it looks.*

Prep: 13 min.   Cook: 2 hr., 20 min.   Other: 15 min.

1   (8-pound) fully cooked shank portion
    hardwood-smoked ham
1   cup peach preserves
1   (7.3-ounce) jar coarse-grained Dijon mustard
    (we tested with Maille)
2   cups peach nectar, divided
Garnish: Seckel pears

Remove and discard skin from ham. Using a boning knife, score fat on ham ⅛" deep in a diamond pattern. Place ham, fat side up, on a lightly greased rack in a shallow roasting pan. Insert a meat thermometer, making sure it does not touch fat or bone.

Stir together preserves, mustard, and 1 cup peach nectar in a large bowl; pour over ham.

Bake ham, uncovered, at 350° for 2 hours and 20 minutes or until meat thermometer registers 140°, basting with pan juices every 20 minutes.

Transfer ham to a serving platter. Let stand 15 minutes before carving.

Pour pan drippings into a large saucepan. Add remaining 1 cup peach nectar; bring to a boil. Serve sauce with ham. Garnish, if desired. Yield: 8 to 10 servings.

*make ahead*

# Fennel, Apple, and Celery Slaw

*Fennel has a delicate licorice flavor and adds a pleasant note in this tangy slaw with apples.*

Prep: 27 min.   Other: 4 hr.

1   tablespoon cider vinegar
1   tablespoon molasses
1   teaspoon Dijon mustard
½   teaspoon salt
¼   teaspoon freshly ground pepper
¼   cup olive oil
1   large fennel bulb
2   unpeeled Granny Smith apples, julienned
2   unpeeled Gala apples, julienned
2   celery ribs, thinly sliced

Whisk together first 5 ingredients in a large bowl; slowly pour in oil, whisking constantly.

Rinse fennel. Trim stalks to within 1" of end. Discard hard outside stalks. Remove tough core from bottom of bulb. Starting at 1 side, cut bulb vertically into thin shreds.

Add fennel, apple, and celery to dressing, tossing to combine. Cover and chill up to 4 hours. Toss well just before serving. Yield: 8 servings.

# Sweet Potato Salad with Bacon Vinaigrette

*With a nutty, sweet, and roasted flavor, this salad is the ideal side for baked ham.*

Prep: 26 min.   Cook: 35 min.

4   pounds sweet potatoes, peeled and cut into
    ¾" pieces
1   small red onion, cut into thin wedges
6   tablespoons olive oil, divided
1½  teaspoons salt, divided
4   thick-cut bacon slices
1   tablespoon cider vinegar
2   teaspoons Dijon mustard
½   teaspoon freshly ground pepper
¾   cup pecan pieces, toasted
½   cup golden raisins

Combine sweet potato, onion, 2 tablespoons olive oil, and ¾ teaspoon salt in a large bowl; toss to coat. Arrange vegetables in a single layer on 2 lightly greased baking sheets.

Bake at 450° for 35 minutes or until browned, removing onion after 25 minutes, and stirring sweet potato.

Meanwhile, cook bacon in a large nonstick skillet over medium heat 12 minutes or until crisp. Drain bacon, reserving 2 tablespoons drippings in pan.

Add remaining ¼ cup olive oil, remaining ¾ teaspoon salt, vinegar, mustard, and pepper to drippings in skillet. Stir well. Transfer vinaigrette to a large bowl. Add roasted sweet potato, onion, pecans, and raisins, tossing gently to coat. Cool. Yield: 8 servings.

**Note:** If you have only one oven, place 1 baking sheet on the lower oven rack and 1 on the upper rack; switch positions after 25 minutes. Bake 5 to 10 more minutes or until potatoes are browned.

# Dark Chocolate Layer Cake

*A cake to please all chocolate lovers—dark chocolate layers under a blanket of creamy white chocolate frosting.*

**Prep: 37 min.   Cook: 22 min.   Other: 10 min.**

| | |
|---|---|
| 1 | cup butter, softened |
| ¾ | cup granulated sugar |
| ¾ | cup firmly packed dark brown sugar |
| 2 | large eggs |
| 2 | ounces sweet dark chocolate, melted and cooled |
| 1 | tablespoon vanilla extract |
| 2 | cups all-purpose flour |
| ½ | cup unsweetened cocoa powder |
| 1½ | teaspoons baking soda |
| ¼ | teaspoon salt |
| 1½ | cups buttermilk |

White Chocolate Frosting

Beat butter and sugars at medium speed with an electric mixer until fluffy. Add eggs, 1 at a time, beating until blended after each addition. Add cooled chocolate and vanilla, beating until blended.

Combine flour and next 3 ingredients; add to butter mixture alternately with buttermilk, beginning and ending with flour mixture. Beat at low speed after each addition. Pour batter into 2 greased parchment paper-lined 9" round cakepans.

Bake at 350° for 22 minutes or until a wooden pick inserted in center comes out clean. Cool in pans on wire racks 10 minutes; remove from pans, and cool completely on wire racks.

Spread White Chocolate Frosting between layers and on top and sides of cake. Yield: 1 (2-layer) cake.

## White Chocolate Frosting

**Prep: 8 min.   Other: 45 min.**

| | |
|---|---|
| 1½ | (8-ounce) packages cream cheese, softened |
| ½ | cup butter, softened |
| 2 | (4-ounce) white chocolate baking bars, melted and cooled (we tested with Ghirardelli) |
| 1½ | cups powdered sugar |
| 2 | teaspoons vanilla extract |
| 2 | teaspoons fresh lemon juice |

Beat cream cheese and butter at medium speed with an electric mixer until fluffy. Add cooled chocolate, beating until blended. Gradually add powdered sugar, beating until smooth. Add vanilla and lemon juice, beating until blended. Cover and chill 45 minutes or until spreading consistency. Yield: 3½ cups.

# Office Party

Take one of these savory or sweet holiday offerings to your next office party, or surprise your coworkers and make all of them. All the recipes have make-ahead merit.

Pomegranate Margaritas

Easy Mushroom Puffs

Scallop Ceviche    Taro chips

Beef and Blue Sandwiches with Caramelized Onions

Asian Chicken Won Ton Cups

Bittersweet Chocolate Fondue

Gingerbread Petits Fours    Pumpkin Pie Truffles

**serves 20 to 24**

## menu prep plan

Up to 1 week ahead:
• Prepare Pumpkin Pie Truffles; chill.

1 day ahead:
• Prepare Gingerbread Petit Fours; store in airtight container in refrigerator.
• Combine ingredients for Pomegranate Margaritas; freeze.
• Prepare sandwich ingredients; bake rolls and store in airtight container, caramelize onions and chill, and make cheese spread and chill.
• Prepare filling for Easy Mushroom Puffs; chill.
• Prepare Scallop Ceviche; chill.
• Prepare chicken mixture, cabbage, and won ton cups for Asian Chicken Won Ton Cups; chill chicken mixture and cabbage separately, and store cups in airtight bag at room temperature.

3 hours ahead:
• Prepare and bake Easy Mushroom Puffs; store in airtight container.

2 hours ahead:
• Reheat onions in microwave; assemble Beef and Blue Sandwiches with Caramelized Onions.
• Arrange fruit and other dippers on platter for Bittersweet Chocolate Fondue.

last minute:
• Prepare rims of Margarita glasses.
• Assemble Asian Chicken Won Ton Cups.
• Arrange Scallop Ceviche and taro chips in serving dishes.
• Microwave Bittersweet Chocolate Fondue; keep warm.

**Pomegranate Margaritas**

*editor's favorite • make ahead*

## Pomegranate Margaritas

*Pomegranate and cranberry juices mingle to make this slushy drink a crowd-pleaser.*

Prep: 9 min.   Other: 24 hr.

6   cups white tequila
12  cups water
4   cups cranberry juice cocktail
2   cups pomegranate juice (we tested with POM)*
1½ cups Triple Sec
2   (10-ounce) cans frozen margarita mix, thawed
2   (11.5-ounce) cans frozen cranberry juice cocktail, thawed and undiluted
2   (12-ounce) cans frozen limeade concentrate, thawed and undiluted
Light corn syrup
Coarse sparkling sugar

Combine first 8 ingredients in a very large plastic container. Cover and freeze at least 24 hours or until slushy.

Pour a small amount of corn syrup onto a flat plate. Pour coarse sugar onto another plate. Dip rims of margarita glasses in corn syrup; dip each glass into sugar. Pour margaritas into prepared glasses. Yield: about 32 cups.

**Freezer Note:** For more convenient storage, divide Pomegranate Margaritas among zip-top freezer bags.

*Find pomegranate juice year-round in the produce section of your local grocery store.

# Easy Mushroom Puffs

*Simple ingredients come together in a quick and delicious appetizer that will have everyone asking for the recipe.*

Prep: 32 min.   Cook: 15 min. per batch   Other: 1 hr.

1   (8-ounce) container garlic-and-herb cream cheese (we tested with Philadelphia Swirls)
2   (4.5-ounce) jars sliced mushrooms, drained
½   cup chopped onion
¼   cup grated Parmesan cheese
1   teaspoon dried chives
¼   teaspoon hot sauce
1   (17.3-ounce) package frozen puff pastry sheets, thawed
1   large egg
1   tablespoon water
Freshly ground pepper (optional)

Combine first 6 ingredients in a medium bowl; cover and chill 1 hour.

Roll 1 sheet puff pastry into a 16" x 10" rectangle. Cut pastry in half lengthwise. Spread one-fourth of filling (about ½ cup) down center of each rectangle. Whisk together egg and water, and brush edges of pastry with egg wash. Fold pastry in half lengthwise over filling; seal edges of pastry with a fork. Cut each pastry into 10 pieces, and place on a parchment-lined baking sheet.

Repeat procedure with remaining sheet puff pastry and filling. Brush remaining egg wash over top of pastries and, if desired, sprinkle with pepper.

Bake at 400° for 15 minutes or until lightly browned. Yield: 40 puffs.

**Make Ahead:** Filling can be made up to 2 days ahead and chilled.

*make ahead*
# Scallop Ceviche

*Ceviche typically consists of raw fish marinated in citrus juices, which "cook" the fish. We chose to sear our scallops for color and flavor. Find taro (a potatolike root) chips in the organic section or the chip aisle of your grocer.*

Prep: 20 min.   Cook: 2 min. per batch   Other: 4 hr., 15 min.

1   pound sea scallops
1   teaspoon ground cumin
½   teaspoon salt
2   plum tomatoes, finely chopped
½   cup finely chopped red onion
½   cup finely chopped yellow bell pepper
¼   cup chopped fresh cilantro
½   cup fresh lime juice
1   jalapeño pepper, seeded and minced
¼   teaspoon black pepper

Pat scallops dry; sprinkle with cumin and salt.

Heat a large skillet over high heat. Add scallops, and cook, in 2 batches, 1 minute on each side or until browned. Remove from heat, and let cool 15 minutes. Finely chop scallops, and place in a bowl. Stir in tomato and next 6 ingredients. Cover and chill at least 4 hours or up to 24 hours. Serve with taro chips. Yield: 4 cups.

# Beef and Blue Sandwiches with Caramelized Onions

*(pictured on following page)*

Prep: 27 min.   Cook: 17 min.

2   (25-ounce) packages frozen roll dough (we tested with Rich's)
Blue Cheese Spread (on following page)
1½   pounds premium sandwich-sliced deli roast beef (we tested with Boar's Head)
Caramelized Onions (on following page)

Prepare rolls, and bake according to package directions; cool completely.

Slice rolls in half; spread tops and bottoms of rolls with Blue Cheese Spread. Place roast beef on bottoms of rolls; top beef with Caramelized Onions. Cover with tops. Yield: 4 dozen rolls.

**Make Ahead:** Rolls, Blue Cheese Spread, and Caramelized Onions can be made a day ahead. Assemble sandwiches no more than 2 hours before serving.

Beef and Blue Sandwiches with Caramelized Onions

## Blue Cheese Spread

*Choose your "blues." Make your selection from blue-veined cheeses that range in flavor from mildest Maytag, to medium Gorgonzola, to strongest Stilton.*

Prep: 7 min.   Other: 2 hr.

1½   (8-ounce) packages cream cheese, softened
1   (8-ounce) container sour cream
2   teaspoons Worcestershire sauce
1   teaspoon hot sauce
6   ounces blue cheese, crumbled (we tested with Danish blue cheese)
½   cup walnut halves, toasted and chopped

Beat cream cheese at medium speed with an electric mixer until creamy. Add sour cream, Worcestershire sauce, and hot sauce; stir until blended. Stir in blue cheese and walnuts. Cover and chill at least 2 hours. Yield: 3 cups.

**Note about Leftovers:** Spoon extra spread over steak, or add a splash of milk to transform it into salad dressing.

## Caramelized Onions

Prep: 8 min.   Cook: 30 min.

3   tablespoons olive oil
3   large sweet onions, thinly sliced
1½   tablespoons balsamic vinegar
¼   teaspoon freshly ground pepper

Heat oil in a Dutch oven over medium heat; add onions. Cook, stirring often, 30 minutes or until caramelized. Stir in vinegar and pepper. Remove from heat; cool slightly. Yield: 1½ cups.

## Asian Chicken Won Ton Cups

Prep: 24 min.   Cook: 14 min.

Vegetable cooking spray
24   won ton wrappers (we tested with Frieda's Asian Specialties)
3   tablespoons creamy peanut butter
3   tablespoons water
2   tablespoons fresh lime juice
1   tablespoon rice wine vinegar
1   tablespoon honey
2   teaspoons chili sauce with garlic  (we tested with Hokan)
2   teaspoons dark sesame oil
½   cup sliced almonds, toasted
2   green onions, sliced
1   cup chopped cooked chicken
½   cup shredded napa cabbage

Coat 24 miniature muffin cups with cooking spray. Carefully press 1 won ton wrapper into each muffin cup; spray lightly with cooking spray (wrapper will extend above rim). Bake at 375° for 8 to 10 minutes or until lightly browned and crisp. Remove from pan; cool completely on a wire rack. Store in airtight container until ready to assemble cups.

Meanwhile, whisk together peanut butter and next 6 ingredients. Add sliced almonds, sliced green onions, and chicken; toss to coat. Cover and chill chicken until ready to assemble cups.

Fill won ton cups evenly with cabbage (about 1 teaspoon) and chicken mixture (about 2½ teaspoons) just before serving. Yield: 2 dozen.

**Make Ahead:** Won ton cups can be baked a day ahead and stored in an airtight container. Chicken filling and cabbage can be prepared a day ahead and chilled separately.

# Bittersweet Chocolate Fondue

*Arrange fresh strawberries, cubed pineapple, and pear slices on a serving platter as healthy dippers. For more decadent dippers, serve pretzel rods, large marshmallows, biscotti, or cream-filled chocolate sandwich cookies.*

Prep: 2 min.   Cook: 2 min.

| | |
|---|---|
| 1 | (11.5-ounce) package double chocolate chips (we tested with Ghirardelli) or 3 (4-ounce) bars bittersweet or dark sweet chocolate |
| 1½ | cups whipping cream |
| 2 | teaspoons vanilla extract |

Combine all ingredients in a microwave-safe bowl; microwave on HIGH for 1½ to 2 minutes, stirring once. Let stand 2 minutes. Stir with a wire whisk until smooth. Keep warm in a fondue pot. Yield: 3 cups.

*make ahead*

# Gingerbread Petits Fours

*Traditional petits fours take a holiday turn with home-made gingerbread, spiced cream cheese filling, and a finishing drench in cream cheese frosting.*

Prep: 47 min.   Cook: 42 min.   Other: 8 hr., 10 min

| | |
|---|---|
| 1½ | cups all-purpose flour |
| ½ | teaspoon baking soda |
| 1½ | teaspoons ground ginger |
| ½ | teaspoon ground cinnamon |
| ½ | teaspoon ground allspice |
| ½ | cup butter or margarine, softened |
| ½ | cup firmly packed dark brown sugar |
| 1 | large egg |
| ½ | cup light molasses |
| 1 | tablespoon grated fresh ginger |
| ½ | cup buttermilk |
| ½ | (8-ounce) package cream cheese, softened |
| ¼ | cup powdered sugar |
| ⅛ | teaspoon ground ginger |
| 1 | pinch of ground cinnamon |
| 1 | pinch of ground allspice |
| 2 | (16-ounce) containers ready-to-spread cream cheese frosting (we tested with Duncan Hines) |

Whisk together first 5 ingredients in a bowl; set aside.

Beat butter and brown sugar in a large bowl at medium-high speed with an electric mixer until creamy. Add egg; beat until blended. Add molasses and grated ginger; beat until well blended. Add flour mixture and buttermilk alternately, beginning and ending with dry ingredients. Spread batter into a greased and floured 8" pan.

Bake at 350° for 40 to 42 minutes or until a wooden pick inserted in center comes out clean. Cool in pan on a wire rack 10 minutes. Carefully transfer cake to cooling rack; cool completely. Wrap cake in plastic wrap; chill 8 hours or overnight.

Beat cream cheese and powdered sugar at medium speed until fluffy. Stir in ⅛ teaspoon ginger, pinch of cinnamon, and pinch of allspice. Cut cake in half horizontally, making 2 equal layers. Spread frosting evenly over bottom cake layer. Carefully place remaining cake layer on frosting. Cut cake into 25 squares, using a serrated or an electric knife. Place squares on a rack over a baking sheet.

Remove foil cover from frosting containers. Microwave frosting at HIGH 30 seconds or until melted, stirring once. Pour or spoon frosting over petits fours, coating top and sides completely. If additional frosting is needed, scrape excess frosting from baking sheet and return to container, and microwave on HIGH 15 seconds or until melted. Place petits fours in large candy cups, if desired. Store in an airtight container in refrigerator. Yield: 25 petits fours.

*make ahead*

# Pumpkin Pie Truffles

Prep: 30 min.   Cook: 1 min.   Other: 6 hr.

| | |
|---|---|
| 1 | cup chopped pecans |
| 1 | tablespoon butter |
| 2 | (4-ounce) white chocolate baking bars, chopped |
| 2 | tablespoons butter |
| ¼ | cup canned unsweetened pumpkin |
| ½ | cup powdered sugar |
| ½ | teaspoon ground cinnamon |
| ½ | teaspoon vanilla extract |
| ¼ | teaspoon ground ginger |
| ⅛ | teaspoon salt |
| 9 | gingersnaps, coarsely crushed (we tested with Nabisco) |

Sauté pecans in 1 tablespoon butter in a large nonstick skillet over medium heat until toasted. Cool completely. Pulse pecans in a food processor until finely chopped.

Combine chocolate and 2 tablespoons butter in a glass bowl. Microwave on HIGH 1 minute; stir until smooth. Stir in pumpkin, next 5 ingredients, and ½ cup pecans. Chill 3 hours or until almost firm.

Combine remaining ½ cup pecans and crushed gingersnaps in shallow dish. Shape pumpkin mixture into 1" balls; roll in pecan mixture. Cover and chill at least 3 hours. Store in refrigerator up to 1 week. Yield: 2½ dozen.

# Christmas Party *in the Kitchen*

**Many parties end up in the kitchen, so go ahead and declare it party headquarters. Make it a casual holiday get-together and involve your friends in the cooking.**

Open-Faced Chile-Cheese Quesadillas

Roasted Tomato Salsa     Orange, Red Onion, and Mint Salad

Steak Fajitas with Sautéed Onions and Peppers

Mexican Rice and Cheese Casserole

Deep, Rich Mexican Hot Chocolate     Chipotle-Chocolate Toffee (page 358)

**serves 10**

# game plan

**1 day ahead:**
- Prepare Roasted Tomato Salsa.
- Marinate beef.
- Assemble Mexican Rice and Cheese Casserole; refrigerate.
- Prepare Chipotle-Chocolate Toffee (page 358), if serving.

**1 to 4 hours ahead:**
- Prepare ingredients and dressing for salad; chill separately.

**1 hour ahead:**
- Sauté onions and peppers for fajitas, and keep warm.

**½ hour ahead:**
- Bake Mexican Rice and Cheese Casserole.

**Last minute:**
- Get everybody working on quesadillas.
- Grill steak, and slice.
- Dress salad.

**Just after dinner:**
- Prepare dessert drinks.

*quick & easy*

## Open-Faced Chile-Cheese Quesadillas

*These quesadillas make an easy party hors d'oeuvre. The topping can be prepared a day ahead and kept covered in the refrigerator. The flour tortillas can be baked several hours ahead and kept at room temperature until ready to top. Let your guests help top the tortillas before baking and cut them up for serving.*

**Prep: 7 min.   Cook: 14 min.**

| | |
|---|---|
| 5 | (8") flour tortillas |
| | Olive oil |
| 2 | cups (8 ounces) shredded Monterey Jack cheese with peppers or Monterey Jack cheese |
| ½ | cup bottled roasted red bell peppers, drained and finely chopped |
| ½ | cup pitted ripe olives, drained and chopped |
| 1 | to 2 chipotle chiles in adobo sauce, chopped |
| 1 | teaspoon adobo sauce |
| ¼ | cup minced fresh cilantro |

Open-Faced Chile-Cheese Quesadillas,
Roasted Tomato Salsa

Brush tortillas lightly with olive oil; prick each tortilla several times with a fork. Place tortillas on 2 large baking sheets. Bake at 400° for 6 minutes or until lightly browned and puffed. Let tortillas cool before topping.

Combine cheese and next 5 ingredients. Sprinkle cheese mixture evenly over tortillas.

Bake at 400° for 6 to 8 minutes or until cheese melts. Cut each tortilla into 6 wedges; arrange wedges on a serving platter. Yield: 30 appetizer servings.

## make ahead
## Roasted Tomato Salsa

*Roasting the tomatoes and vegetables for this salsa gives it a wonderful depth of flavor. Unlike fresh tomato salsas, which are generally eaten soon after preparation, this salsa can be prepared several days ahead.*

**Prep: 18 min.  Cook: 28 min.  Other: 10 min.**

| | |
|---|---|
| 2 | pounds plum tomatoes |
| 2 | to 3 large jalapeño peppers |
| 1 | small onion, sliced |
| 6 | garlic cloves, peeled |
| 1 | tablespoon olive oil |
| ¼ | cup tomato juice |
| ¼ | cup minced fresh cilantro |
| 1 | teaspoon salt |
| 2 | tablespoons cider vinegar |

Arrange tomatoes and jalapeños on a lightly greased baking sheet; broil 5½" from heat 10 to 15 minutes or until lightly charred and blistered, turning once or twice. Transfer jalapeños to a bowl, and let cool. Place tomatoes in a large zip-top plastic bag; seal and let stand 10 minutes.

Combine onion, garlic, and olive oil in a bowl; transfer to a baking sheet. Bake at 450° for 10 minutes, stirring once, until golden and soft.

Remove stems from jalapeños, and transfer whole peppers to a food processor. Add onion and garlic; process until finely chopped, scraping down sides of bowl. Transfer mixture to a bowl.

Peel tomatoes over a bowl to catch juices. (Do not seed.) Transfer peeled tomatoes to food processor; process until coarsely chopped. Add to jalapeño mixture, stirring well. Stir in tomato juice and remaining ingredients. Store in an airtight container in refrigerator up to 2 days. Serve salsa at room temperature. Yield: 3¾ cups.

Orange, Red Onion, and Mint Salad

## make ahead • quick & easy
## Orange, Red Onion, and Mint Salad

*Prepare and chill this colorful salad up to three hours ahead. Lightly dress and toss greens right before serving. Use Valencia oranges; they're both sweet and tart with an intense citrus flavor.*

**Prep: 16 min.**

| | |
|---|---|
| 2 | heads romaine lettuce, chopped |
| 5 | Valencia or navel oranges, peeled and sectioned or sliced |
| 1 | small red onion, thinly sliced, separated into rings, and halved |
| 2 | avocados, sliced |
| 2 | tablespoons lime juice |
| 1 | tablespoon white or red wine vinegar |
| ½ | teaspoon salt |
| ½ | teaspoon ground cumin |
| ¼ | teaspoon freshly ground black pepper |
| Pinch of sugar | |
| ⅓ | cup olive oil |
| 3 | tablespoons minced fresh mint |
| 8 | fresh mint leaves |

Combine first 4 ingredients in a salad bowl.

Combine lime juice and next 5 ingredients in a small bowl; slowly add oil in a thin stream, whisking constantly. Drizzle dressing over salad; sprinkle with minced mint, and toss. Top with mint leaves. Yield: 10 servings.

*make ahead*

## Steak Fajitas with Sautéed Onions and Peppers

*Skirt steak is the traditional cut used to make beef fajitas. Aside from being full of flavor, it's a relatively inexpensive cut of meat, perfect for large gatherings. Marinating the steak overnight only improves its flavor and tenderness.*

**Prep: 27 min.   Cook: 25 min.   Other: 8 hr.**

½    cup olive oil
12   garlic cloves, minced
¼    cup lime juice
4    teaspoons ground cumin
1    teaspoon salt
½    teaspoon freshly ground black pepper
3    pounds skirt steak or flank steak
3    tablespoons olive oil
1    large red bell pepper, cut lengthwise into ½" strips
1    large yellow bell pepper, cut lengthwise into ½" strips
1    large orange bell pepper, cut lengthwise into ½" strips
2    large onions, sliced and separated into rings
1½   teaspoons dried oregano
4    garlic cloves, minced
¼    cup minced fresh cilantro
10   (10") flour tortillas
Toppings: Roasted Tomato Salsa (page 219), guacamole, sour cream

Combine first 6 ingredients in a shallow dish. Add steak, turning to coat with marinade. Cover and chill 8 hours.

Heat 3 tablespoons oil in a large cast-iron skillet over medium-high heat. Add bell peppers, onions, and oregano. Cook 12 minutes or until tender, stirring often.

▲ Thinly slice grilled steak for serving.

Add remaining minced garlic, and cook 2 minutes, stirring often. Stir in cilantro. Keep warm.

Warm tortillas according to package directions.

Remove steak from marinade, discarding marinade. Grill steak, covered with grill lid, over medium-high heat (350° to 400°) 5 minutes on each side or to desired degree of doneness. Transfer steak to a cutting board, and let stand 10 minutes. Cut steak diagonally across the grain into thin strips. Serve with tortillas, onions and peppers, and desired toppings. Yield: 10 servings.

*editor's favorite • make ahead*

## Mexican Rice and Cheese Casserole

**Prep: 12 min.   Cook: 45 min.**

2    (8-ounce) packages Mexican Rice (we tested with Vigo)
2    cups (8 ounces) shredded Monterey Jack cheese, divided
1    cup thinly sliced green onions
1    (8-ounce) container sour cream
1    teaspoon salt
¼    teaspoon ground red pepper
¼    teaspoon smoked or sweet paprika

Prepare rice according to package directions.

Combine hot cooked rice, 1½ cups shredded cheese, and next 4 ingredients in a large bowl; stir until combined.

Transfer seasoned rice mixture to a greased 13" x 9" baking dish; sprinkle with remaining ½ cup cheese and paprika.

Bake, uncovered, at 350° for 25 to 30 minutes or until thoroughly heated. Yield: 10 servings.

*editor's favorite • quick & easy*

## Deep, Rich Mexican Hot Chocolate

*For a special touch, add a split vanilla bean to each mug as a stirrer stick—vanilla "seeds" will permeate the hot chocolate as you stir. (pictured on page 216)*

**Prep: 6 min.   Cook: 10 min.**

9    cups milk
½    cup firmly packed dark brown sugar
2    (3.5-ounce) bars bittersweet chocolate, finely chopped
⅓    cup Dutch process or unsweetened cocoa
3    tablespoons instant espresso powder
1½   teaspoons ground cinnamon
⅔    cup coffee liqueur (optional)
Garnishes: sweetened whipped cream*, ground cinnamon
Vanilla beans (optional)

Combine first 6 ingredients in a Dutch oven. Cook over medium heat 10 minutes or until chocolate melts and sugar dissolves, stirring occasionally. Remove from heat, and whisk vigorously until hot chocolate is frothy.

Immediately pour into mugs; stir a splash of coffee liqueur into each serving, if desired. Top with whipped cream, and sprinkle with cinnamon, if desired. Add a vanilla bean to each mug as a stirrer stick, if desired. Yield: 11 cups.

*We tested with canned Reddi-wip topping. For party fun, it's quick and easy, and fun to squirt.

# Healthy
# Holiday Meals

**These recipes show that you can hold the fat and calories at bay
and still enjoy a grand holiday meal. Each recipe includes a nutrient
analysis—as well as a great flavor profile.**

# Elegant Dinner for Eight

Peppered Beef Tenderloin Medallions with
Olive-Herb Relish

Sun-dried Tomato and Garlic Whipped Potatoes

Green Beans with Roasted Mushrooms

Cran-Ginger Granita

## game plan

**1 week ahead:**
• Prepare and freeze Cran-Ginger Granita.

**1 day ahead:**
• Steam green beans; cover and chill.
• Prepare Sun-dried Tomato and Garlic Whipped Potatoes; cover and chill.
• Make Olive-Herb Relish; cover and chill.

**2 hours ahead:**
• Roast mushrooms.

**15 minutes ahead:**
• Roast beef medallions.

**Last Minute:**
• Reheat whipped potatoes in microwave.
• Toss together green beans and mushrooms, and reheat in microwave.

**After Dinner:**
• Scrape frozen granita until fluffy. Spoon into serving dishes.

*editor's favorite • low calorie • low carb*

## Peppered Beef Tenderloin Medallions with Olive-Herb Relish

*A pair of these mouthwatering tender little medallions topped with tangy olives makes a luxurious entrée.*

**Prep: 6 min.   Cook: 14 min.**

16   (3-ounce) beef tenderloin fillets*
2    teaspoons crushed black peppercorns
2    teaspoons crushed pink peppercorns
1    teaspoon kosher salt
¼    cup olive oil
Olive-Herb Relish

Sprinkle fillets with peppercorns and salt.

Heat 2 tablespoons oil in each of 2 large skillets (preferably cast iron) over medium-high heat. Sear fillets in hot oil over medium-high heat 2 minutes on each side. Arrange beef medallions in a single layer on a large baking sheet lined with aluminum foil.

Bake at 400° for 6 to 10 minutes or until desired degree of doneness. Serve with Olive-Herb Relish. Yield: 8 servings.

Per serving and 2 tablespoon relish: Calories 315 (62% from fat); Fat 21.6g (sat 5.6g, mono 12g, poly 1.6g); Protein 27.2g, Carb 1.8g; Fiber 0.6g; Chol 80mg; Iron 3.9mg, Sodium 543mg; Calc 18mg

*Ask your butcher to cut 3-ounce petit beef fillets (medallions) from the slender end of several tenderloins. This will ensure that you end up with 16 medallions not over 3 ounces each.

## Olive-Herb Relish

**Prep: 8 min.   Other: 2 hr.**

½    cup pitted kalamata olives, chopped
½    cup pitted Manzanilla green olives, chopped
½    cup roasted red bell peppers, diced
2    tablespoons chopped fresh tarragon
2    tablespoons capers, drained
1    tablespoon extra-virgin olive oil

Combine all ingredients in a small bowl; stir well. Cover and chill at least 2 hours. Yield: 1½ cups.

Per tablespoon: Calories 19 (85% from fat); Fat 1.8g (sat 0.2g, mono 1.4g, poly 0.2g); Protein 0.1g; Carb 0.6g; Fiber 0.1g; Chol 0mg; Iron 0.1mg; Sodium 124mg; Calc 4mg *low cholesterol • low fat • make ahead*

## Sun-dried Tomato and Garlic Whipped Potatoes

*Tangy tomato bits and a subtle garlic flavor enhance these fluffy spuds.*

Prep: 12 min.   Cook: 20 min.

| | |
|---|---|
| 3 | pounds Yukon gold potatoes, peeled and cut into chunks |
| ¼ | cup dried tomatoes packed in oil, drained |
| 4 | large garlic cloves |
| 1½ | cups 2% reduced-fat milk |
| 2 | tablespoons light butter |
| 1 | teaspoon salt |
| 1 | teaspoon pepper |

Cook potatoes in boiling water to cover 15 to 20 minutes or until tender; drain well.

Meanwhile, place dried tomatoes and garlic cloves in a mini food processor; process until finely minced. Combine milk and butter in a glass bowl. Partially cover with heavy-duty plastic wrap, and microwave at HIGH 1½ to 2 minutes or until butter is melted. Combine potatoes, warm milk, and salt and pepper in a large bowl. Beat at medium speed with an electric mixer until potatoes are fluffy. Gently stir in dried tomatoes and garlic. Yield: 8 servings.

Per serving: Calories 183 (15% from fat); Fat 3g (sat 1.5g, mono 0.6g, poly 0.2g); Protein 4.6g; Carb 35.9g; Fiber 3.2g; Chol 7mg; Iron 0.7mg; Sodium 355mg; Calc 74mg

**Make Ahead:** Cover and chill prepared potatoes overnight. Microwave at HIGH 5 to 7 minutes to reheat.

*low calorie • low cholesterol • make ahead*

## Green Beans with Roasted Mushrooms

*The roasted mushrooms tossed with slender French green beans make a rich but light side dish. Regular green beans and button mushrooms can be substituted.*

Prep: 7 min.   Cook: 30 min.

| | |
|---|---|
| 2 | pounds haricots verts, trimmed |
| 1½ | pounds assorted mushrooms, quartered (we tested with 6 [4-ounce] packages of Gourmet Mushroom Blend) |
| 2 | tablespoons balsamic vinegar, divided |
| 2 | tablespoons extra-virgin olive oil |
| 1 | tablespoon chopped fresh thyme |
| ½ | teaspoon salt |
| ½ | teaspoon freshly ground black pepper |

Place green beans in a large pot of boiling water, and cook 3 to 4 minutes or until crisp-tender. Immediately plunge into ice water to stop the cooking process. Cover and chill up to 2 days.

Combine mushrooms, 1 tablespoon vinegar, and next 4 ingredients on a large rimmed baking sheet coated with cooking spray. Spread mushrooms in a single layer.

Roast at 425° for 20 to 25 minutes or until tender and browned, stirring once or twice. Reheat green beans in the microwave at HIGH 3 minutes or until hot. Combine green beans, roasted mushrooms, and remaining 1 tablespoon vinegar; toss well. Yield: 8 servings.

Per serving: Calories 84 (42% from fat); Fat 3.9g (sat 0.6g, mono 2.7g, poly 0.5g); Protein 4.5g; Carb 10.6g; Fiber 4.3g; Chol 0mg; Iron 1.6mg; Sodium 157mg; Calc 42mg

*low calorie • low cholesterol • low fat • make ahead*

## Cran-Ginger Granita

*(pictured on page 222)*

Prep: 6 min.   Other: 4 hr.

| | |
|---|---|
| 3 | cups cranberry-apple juice drink, divided |
| ½ | cup sugar |
| 1 | (12-ounce) can natural ginger ale (we tested with Natural Brew Outrageous Ginger Ale)* |

Combine 1 cup cranberry-apple juice drink and sugar in a 2-qt. saucepan. Cook over medium heat until sugar dissolves. Remove from heat and cool completely.

Combine cran-syrup, remaining 2 cups juice drink, and ginger ale. Pour into 3 ice cube trays, and freeze 1½ hours or until almost frozen. Transfer cubes to a blender or food processor, and pulse until slushy.

Pour slush into a 13" x 9" pan, and freeze 3½ hours or until frozen.

To serve, scrape granita in pan with tines of a fork until fluffy. Spoon into dessert glasses, and serve immediately. Yield: 8 cups.

Per 1-cup serving: Calories 124 (0% from fat); Fat 0g (sat 0g, mono 0g, poly 0g); Protein 0.1g; Carb 31.9g; Fiber 0.1g; Chol 0mg; Iron 0.1mg; Sodium 5mg; Calc 8mg

*Natural ginger ale has an intense gingery taste. Find it on the soft drink aisle or with beers, especially in upscale markets.

# Winter Harvest

Broccoli Pesto

Fennel and Parmesan Salad

Rosemary-Dijon Roast Pork with
Autumn Fruit Compote

Parsnip and Potato Mash

Lemon-Drenched Gingerbread Cake

**serves 8**

**2 days ahead:**

• Prepare Autumn Fruit Compote; cover and chill.

**1 day ahead:**

• Make Broccoli Pesto; cover and chill. Toast bread, and store in an
airtight container.

• Wash Bibb lettuce, grate cheese, and make dressing for Fennel
and Parmesan Salad; chill separately.

• Bake Lemon-Drenched Gingerbread Cake; store at room
temperature in an airtight container.

**1 hour ahead:**

• Bake pork roast.

• Make Parsnip and Potato Mash; keep warm.

**Last minute:**

• Assemble pesto and bread for serving.

• Toss Fennel and Parmesan Salad.

• Garnish cake for serving.

---

*editor's favorite • low calorie • low carb • quick & easy*

## Broccoli Pesto

*Traditional pesto is made with fresh basil. Broccoli replaces
basil in this version, giving the pesto the same beautiful
green color and an even healthier result. We served it on
baguette slices; it's also great tossed with hot cooked pasta.
It also makes a nice base for pizza.*

**Prep: 14 min.   Cook: 10 min.**

| | |
|---|---|
| 1 | (12-ounce) bag fresh broccoli florets, rinsed and drained |
| ⅓ | cup extra-virgin olive oil |
| 4 | garlic cloves, thinly sliced |
| ⅛ | teaspoon dried crushed red pepper |
| ⅓ | cup freshly grated Parmesan cheese |
| ¼ | cup pine nuts, toasted |
| ⅓ | cup chicken broth |
| 2 | tablespoons fresh lemon juice |
| ½ | teaspoon salt |

Garnish: toasted pine nuts
Toasted or grilled baguette slices

Place broccoli in a large bowl; cover with heavy-duty plastic wrap. Microwave at HIGH 8 minutes or until broccoli is
tender. Drain and transfer broccoli to a food processor.

While broccoli cooks, heat olive oil in a small skillet over
medium heat. Add garlic and crushed red pepper; sauté
2 minutes until garlic is lightly browned. Add garlic mixture,
Parmesan cheese, and next 4 ingredients to food processor;
process until smooth. Cover and refrigerate up to 2 days.
Garnish, if desired. Serve pesto with baguette slices. Yield:
2 cups.

**Per 1 tablespoon pesto and 1 (¼"-thick) baguette slice:** Calories 49 (62% from fat); Fat 3.4g
(sat 0.5g, mono 1.9g, poly 0.7g); Protein 1.3g; Carb 4.1g; Fiber 0.5g; Chol 1mg; Iron 0.3mg;
Sodium 103mg; Calc 15mg

# Fennel and Parmesan Salad

*Fresh lemon flavor carries this recipe. Buy the whole fennel, and use the feathery fronds, which look like dill, to add that herby punch to the salad.*

**Prep: 25 min.**

| | |
|---|---|
| 2 | fennel bulbs with stalks (about 2½ pounds) |
| 2 | teaspoons lemon zest |
| 2 | tablespoons fresh lemon juice (about 1 large) |
| 2 | tablespoons extra-virgin olive oil |
| ½ | teaspoon salt |
| ¼ | teaspoon freshly ground pepper |
| 1 | large head Bibb lettuce, torn (6 cups) |
| ¾ | cup freshly shredded Parmesan cheese |

Trim stalks from fennel, reserving feathery fronds. Quarter fennel bulbs vertically, discarding cores. Cut each quarter into ⅛" lengthwise slices. Chop fronds to measure ¼ cup, discarding remaining fronds.

Whisk together lemon zest and next 4 ingredients in a large bowl. Add fennel, fennel fronds, lettuce, and cheese; toss well. Divide salad among 8 serving plates. Serve immediately. Yield: 8 servings.

Per serving: Calories 100 (53% from fat); Fat 5.9g (sat 1.8g, mono 3.2g, poly 0.6g); Protein 4.7g; Carb 9.1g; Fiber 3.7g; Chol 5mg; Iron 1.3mg; Sodium 328mg; Calc 160mg

# Rosemary-Dijon Roast Pork with Autumn Fruit Compote

*Searing this roast in a hot skillet kick-starts that sought-after crusty, caramelized exterior.*

**Prep: 5 min.   Cook: 55 min.   Other: 10 min.**

| | |
|---|---|
| 1 | (2½-pounds) boneless pork loin roast, trimmed |
| ¾ | teaspoon salt |
| ½ | teaspoon freshly ground pepper |
| 1 | tablespoon olive oil |
| 3 | tablespoons Dijon mustard |
| 2 | tablespoons chopped fresh rosemary |
| | Autumn Fruit Compote |

Pat pork roast dry with paper towels. Sprinkle or rub roast with salt and pepper.

Heat oil in a large heavy skillet over medium-high heat. Brown pork roast on all sides, about 5 minutes total. Place roast on a rack in a lightly greased roasting pan.

Combine mustard and 2 tablespoons rosemary; spread onto browned pork.

Bake, uncovered, at 350° for 45 to 55 minutes or until a thermometer inserted in center of roast registers 155°. Cover with aluminum foil, and let stand 10 minutes or until thermometer registers 160° before slicing. Serve with Autumn Fruit Compote. Yield: 8 servings.

Per serving with ⅓ cup compote: Calories 290 (25% from fat); Fat 8.1g (sat 2.5g, mono 3.8g, poly 0.8g); Protein 29.3g; Carb 25g; Fiber 2.2g; Chol 81mg; Iron 2.1mg; Sodium 351mg; Calc 26mg

## Autumn Fruit Compote

**Prep: 12 min.   Cook: 16 min.   Other: 2 hr.**

| | |
|---|---|
| 4 | (3") fresh rosemary sprigs |
| ½ | teaspoon black peppercorns, crushed |
| 1 | cup orange juice |
| ¼ | cup firmly packed brown sugar |
| 2 | Bartlett pears, peeled and sliced |
| 2 | Granny Smith apples, peeled and sliced |
| ½ | cup dried apricots |
| ½ | cup golden raisins |
| ½ | cup fresh cranberries |

Place rosemary and crushed peppercorns in a small square of cheesecloth; tie to secure. Place cheesecloth bag, orange juice, and next 6 ingredients in a large saucepan; bring to a boil over medium-high heat. Reduce heat to medium-low; cover and simmer 8 minutes or until apple and pear are almost tender. Remove from heat, and let cool to room temperature. Remove and discard cheesecloth. Yield: 3¾ cups.

Per tablespoon: Calories 18 (0% from fat); Fat 0g (sat 0g, mono 0g, poly 0g); Protein 0.2g; Carb 4.6g; Fiber 0.4g; Chol 0mg; Iron 0.1mg; Sodium 1mg; Calc 3mg

**Make-Ahead Note:** Compote can be prepared at least 2 days in advance and stored in refrigerator. Bring to room temperature before serving.

# Parsnip and Potato Mash

*No more cold mashed potatoes—pour hot water in a serving bowl, and let sit for a minute or two before dinner. Drain the bowl, wipe it dry, and then add hot potatoes.*

**Prep: 16 min.   Cook: 32 min.**

- 2    pounds parsnips, peeled and cut into 1" pieces
- 2    pounds baking potatoes, peeled and cut into 1" pieces
- 2    tablespoons butter
- ½    cup 2% reduced-fat milk
- 1    teaspoon salt
- ¼    teaspoon freshly ground pepper

Place parsnips and potatoes in a Dutch oven; cover with 1" water. Bring to a boil; cover, reduce heat, and simmer 25 minutes or until vegetables are tender. Drain vegetables, and return to hot pan.

Add butter, and mash vegetables using a potato masher. Add milk, salt, and pepper. Mash. Serve warm. Yield: about 7 cups.

**Per ¾-cup serving:** Calories 175 (16% from fat); Fat 3.1g (sat 1.8g, mono 0.8g, poly 0.2g); Protein 3.1g; Carb 35.1g; Fiber 5.9g; Chol 8mg; Iron 0.8mg; Sodium 296mg; Calc 56mg

# Lemon-Drenched Gingerbread Cake

**Prep: 12 min.   Cook: 35 min.   Other: 15 min.**

- ¾    cup molasses
- ⅔    cup firmly packed light brown sugar
- ½    cup canola oil
- 1    large egg
- 2½    cups all-purpose flour
- 1    tablespoon ground ginger
- 2    teaspoons baking powder
- 1    teaspoon baking soda
- 1    teaspoon ground cinnamon
- 1    teaspoon ground cloves
- ½    teaspoon salt
- 1    cup hot water
- ½    cup granulated sugar
- ⅔    cup water
- 2    tablespoons fresh lemon juice
- ½    teaspoon lemon extract

Powdered sugar
Garnish: lemon and orange rind

Coat a 10-cup Bundt pan with cooking spray.

Beat first 4 ingredients at medium speed with an electric mixer until blended.

Combine flour and next 6 ingredients; add to molasses mixture alternately with hot water, beginning and ending with flour mixture. Beat at low speed after each addition. Pour batter into prepared pan.

Bake at 350° for 32 to 35 minutes or until a long wooden pick inserted in center comes out clean. Cool cake in pan on a wire rack 15 minutes.

Meanwhile, combine ½ cup sugar, ⅔ cup water, lemon juice, and lemon extract in a small saucepan; simmer over medium-low heat 5 minutes, stirring to dissolve sugar. Remove from heat, and let cool 10 minutes.

Poke holes in top of cake using a skewer. Pour syrup over cake. Cool completely. Invert cake onto a serving platter; lightly sprinkle with powdered sugar. Garnish, if desired. Yield: 12 servings.

**Per serving:** Calories 328 (28% from fat); Fat 10.1g (sat 0.9g, mono 5.7g, poly 3g); Protein 3.3g; Carb 57.2g; Fiber 0.9g; Chol 18mg; Iron 2.7mg; Sodium 302mg; Calc 108mg

This is not an indulgent cake—no butter and only one egg; however, you'll think it is because it soaks in a lemon syrup and becomes gooey good.

Lemon-Drenched Gingerbread Cake

# Holiday's Finest

Dried Fig and Blue Cheese Salad with Pomegranate Vinaigrette

Crab Cakes with Lemon-Parsley Slaw

Ambrosia with Meringues

**serves 6**

## game plan

**1 day ahead:**
• Prepare dried figs and pomegranate vinaigrette, and wash greens for Dried Fig and Blue Cheese Salad with Pomegranate Vinaigrette; chill.
• Make dressing for Lemon-Parsley Slaw; chill.
• Prepare fruit for ambrosia; chill.

**4 hours ahead:**
• Shape crab cakes, and place on a baking sheet; cover and chill.

**Last minute:**
• Slice fennel, and assemble Dried Fig and Blue Cheese Salad with Pomegranate Vinaigrette.
• Bake crab cakes.
• Toss together ingredients for Lemon-Parsley Slaw.

Crab Cakes with Lemon-Parsley Slaw

Ambrosia with Meringues

*editor's favorite • make ahead • quick & easy*

## Dried Fig and Blue Cheese Salad with Pomegranate Vinaigrette

*Not only is the vinaigrette good for you with antioxidants in the pomegranate juice, it's an impressive salad to serve guests.*

**Prep: 6 min.   Cook: 19 min.**

18   dried mission figs
1   (16-ounce) bottle pomegranate juice (2 cups)
2   tablespoons honey
1   teaspoon Dijon mustard
1/4   teaspoon salt
1/4   teaspoon freshly ground pepper
1/4   cup olive oil
9   cups mesclun salad greens
2   ounces blue cheese, crumbled

Place figs and pomegranate juice in a medium saucepan; bring to a boil. Reduce heat, cover, and simmer 10 minutes or until figs are softened. Remove figs with a slotted spoon; set aside.

Bring pomegranate juice to a boil over medium-high heat; boil 2 minutes or until syrupy and reduced to ⅓ cup. Transfer reduction to a bowl; let cool to room temperature.

Add honey and next 3 ingredients to pomegranate reduction; stir with a wire whisk. Gradually whisk in oil.

To serve, divide mesclun greens among 6 serving plates; top each salad with 3 figs. Drizzle evenly with vinaigrette, and sprinkle with blue cheese. Serve immediately. Yield: 6 servings.

**Per serving:** Calories 345 (33% from fat); Fat 12.8g (sat 3.4g, mono 7.5g, poly 1.2g); Protein 5.7g; Carb 58.2g; Fiber 7.6g; Chol 8mg; Iron 2.1mg; Sodium 311mg; Calc 166mg

**Make-Ahead Note:** Cooked figs and vinaigrette can be stored in refrigerator up to 2 days.

*low calorie • low carb • low fat*

# Crab Cakes with Lemon-Parsley Slaw

*Get the crispy brown crust on these crab cakes with our easy oven procedure.*

**Prep: 15 min.   Cook: 20 min.**

1½    pounds fresh crabmeat
½     cup panko or other breadcrumbs, divided
2     tablespoons reduced-fat mayonnaise
1     large egg
1     tablespoon minced chives
1     tablespoon Dijon mustard
1     teaspoon Old Bay seasoning
Vegetable cooking spray
Lemon wedges
Lemon-Parsley Slaw

Preheat oven to 450°.
Place a jelly-roll pan in oven 10 minutes to heat.
Drain and flake crabmeat, removing any bits of shell.
Combine ¼ cup breadcrumbs, mayonnaise, and next 4 ingredients; gently add crabmeat to mixture using hands to toss. Shape into 12 small patties. Dredge patties in remaining ¼ cup breadcrumbs.
Coat crab cakes well with cooking spray. Remove hot pan from oven; coat pan with cooking spray. Place crab cakes on hot pan in a single layer. Bake at 450° for 10 minutes; turn cakes over and bake 10 more minutes or until lightly browned. Serve with lemon wedges and Lemon-Parsley Slaw. Yield: 6 servings.

**Per 2 crab cakes and ¾ cup slaw:** Calories 187 (40% from fat); Fat 8.4g (sat 1.1g, mono 3.9g, poly 0.6g); Protein 18.9g; Carb 9.2g; Fiber 1.9g; Chol 137mg; Iron 1.5mg; Sodium 1037mg; Calc 61mg

## Lemon-Parsley Slaw

**Prep: 4 min.**

2     teaspoons lemon zest
1     teaspoon fresh lemon juice
½     teaspoon Dijon mustard
½     teaspoon salt
2     tablespoons extra-virgin olive oil
6     cups angel hair slaw or thinly sliced cabbage
1     cup chopped fresh flat-leaf parsley

Whisk together first 4 ingredients in a large bowl; gradually whisk in olive oil. Add slaw and parsley, tossing gently to coat. Serve immediately. Yield: 6 servings.

**Per ¾ cup slaw:** Calories 63 (69% from fat); Fat 4.8g (sat 0.7g, mono 3.6g, poly 0.4g); Protein 1g; Carb 4.2g; Fiber 1.7g; Chol 0mg; Iron 0.6mg; Sodium 218mg; Calc 15mg

*low calorie • low cholesterol • low fat • quick & easy*

# Ambrosia with Meringues

*Store-bought meringue kiss cookies provide a simple garnish and sweet crunch for holiday fruit.*

**Prep: 22 min.**

1     cup fresh cranberries
½     cup sugar
½     cup water
4     large navel oranges
2     cups fresh pineapple chunks (½" chunks)
⅓     cup sweetened flaked coconut
12    prebaked meringue cookies

Combine first 3 ingredients in a medium saucepan; cook, stirring often, over medium heat 6 to 8 minutes or until most of cranberries pop. Grate 1 tablespoon plus 1 teaspoon orange rind from oranges.

Remove cranberries from heat, and stir in 1 teaspoon orange rind. Let cranberries cool completely. Cover and refrigerate.

Section oranges over a large bowl, catching juices. Add pineapple and 1 tablespoon orange rind to orange sections in bowl. Cover and chill until ready to serve.

To serve, spoon oranges and pineapple into individual dessert dishes; top evenly with cranberry mixture. Sprinkle each serving with coconut. Serve with meringue cookies. Yield: 6 servings.

**Per serving:** Calories 216 (6% from fat); Fat 1.5g (sat 1.2g, mono 0.1g, poly 0.1g); Protein 1.5g; Carb 51.3g; Fiber 4.6g; Chol 0mg; Iron 0.5mg; Sodium 21mg; Calc 53mg

# Countdown to *Christmas Dinner*

'Tis the season for family gatherings and good food.
The plan on these pages will help you produce a dynamite-
tasting meal with time to spare. Take our make-ahead tips and
prepare the whole menu, or just pick a recipe or two to
add to your traditional meal.

Crab and Oyster Bisque

Cabbage and Apple Salad
with Roasted Onions

Coffee-Crusted Beef Wellingtons

Cast-Iron Herbed Potatoes Anna

Carrots with Country Bacon

Scalloped Greens

Chocolate Tiramisù Charlotte

Cardamom-Scented Sweet Potato Pie

Wine          Coffee

# the countdown

*It's the biggest holiday celebration of the year. Let our timeline help you organize your meal preparation.*

## 1 week to 1 month ahead:
- Make grocery list. Shop for nonperishables.
- Visit wine shop to select wines.
- Prepare Coffee-Crusted Beef Wellingtons; freeze.
- Plan centerpiece and other table decorations.

## 2 or 3 days ahead:
- Take inventory of china, serving dishes, and utensils. Gather whatever pieces you'll need. Polish silver.

## 1 day ahead:
- Prepare Chocolate Tiramisù Charlotte; refrigerate overnight.
- Blanch and peel pearl onions, and prepare dressing for salad; refrigerate overnight.
- Peel and slice carrots; refrigerate overnight.
- Prepare Scalloped Greens without breadcrumb topping, and refrigerate unbaked overnight.
- Set the table, complete with centerpiece.

## morning of the meal:
- Prepare and bake Cardamom-Scented Sweet Potato Pie.

*grace notes*

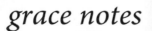

Offer a selection of red and white wines. ▶
▼ Write names on place cards.

▲ Label bowls and platters for specific recipes.
◀ Gather flatware and serving pieces.

### 3 hours before the meal:
• Prepare and bake Cast-Iron Herbed Potatoes Anna.

### 2 hours before the meal:
• Add breadcrumb topping to Scalloped Greens, and bake; cover with foil to keep warm.
• Prepare Cabbage and Apple Salad with Roasted Onions.
• Prepare Carrots with Country Bacon.

### 45 minutes before the meal:
• Prepare Crab and Oyster Bisque; keep warm over low heat.
• Bake beef Wellingtons (do not thaw); finish sauce, and keep warm over low heat.

### just before serving:
• Reheat side dishes in the oven and on stovetop as needed.
• Garnish beef Wellingtons with herbs.

### just after dinner:
• Brew coffee.
• Set out desserts for guests to sample.

Garnish each entrée simply with fresh herbs.▼

▲ Toast dinner guests with a blessing. Serve coffee. It never fails with rich desserts. ▶

▲ Pin pomander place cards to backs of chairs.

## get the look

*For the special touches of Christmastime, find our best ideas this season below.*

◀ Decorate with versatile fir pomanders. Use them as part of a centerpiece, or suspend them on chair backs as place card holders. To make pomanders, wrap Christmas tree clippings around 4" plastic craft foam balls, securing them with U-shape florist pins. For centerpiece, wrap each ball in ribbon, and tie with a bow. For place card holders, thread ribbon through hole-punched place cards. Attach ribbon to pomanders with florist pins. Attach ribbon to chairs with straight pins. If greenery is fresh, pomanders should last up to 2 weeks. Spritz pomanders occasionally to refresh greenery.

◀ Scout out antique or just unique salt and pepper cellars for each place setting.

◀ Present a menu handwritten on fabric at each place setting. Use pinking shears from a craft store to cut out linen fabric swatches; fray edges, if desired. Write the menu on each fabric cutout, using a fabric pen. Attach the fabric swatch to the napkin at each place setting, using a large safety pin. (Alternatively, you can *print* your menu on fabric using a home computer. Computer Printer Fabric™ feeds directly into your printer. All you do is input your menu and pick a font that suits your holiday style.)

## Crab and Oyster Bisque

*This rich seafood soup earned our Test Kitchens highest rating.*

Prep: 15 min.   Cook: 20 min.

¼  cup butter or margarine
4  garlic cloves, minced
2  shallots, finely chopped
3  tablespoons all-purpose flour
1  (8-ounce) bottle clam juice
1  cup dry white wine
1  tablespoon Worcestershire sauce
1  teaspoon Cajun seasoning
¼  teaspoon pepper
1  quart whipping cream
1  (12-ounce) container fresh oysters, drained
1  pound fresh lump crabmeat

Melt butter in a Dutch oven over medium heat; add garlic and shallot, and sauté until tender. Add flour; cook 1 minute, stirring constantly. Add clam juice and wine; cook 2 minutes or until thickened, stirring constantly.

Stir in Worcestershire sauce and next 3 ingredients. Cook until thoroughly heated, about 10 minutes. Stir in oysters and crabmeat; cook just until edges of oysters curl. Yield: 10 cups.

Serve **crab and oyster bisque** in little cups at the start of your meal.

*Cabbage and Apple Salad with Roasted Onions*

# Cabbage and Apple Salad with Roasted Onions

*It's worth the time to blanch and peel pearl onions for this salad. We don't recommend using frozen pearl onions.*

Prep: 38 min.   Cook: 33 min.

| | |
|---|---|
| 2 | (10-ounce) packages fresh pearl onions |
| 1 | head red cabbage, shredded |
| 2 | tablespoons salt |
| 2 | tablespoons olive oil |
| 6 | tablespoons white wine vinegar, divided |
| 6 | tablespoons maple syrup, divided |
| 2 | cups chopped pecans, toasted and divided |
| 1 | cup sour cream |
| ½ | teaspoon salt |
| 4 | Granny Smith apples, chopped |
| 1 | head curly endive, chopped |

Trim bottom ends of onions. Blanch unpeeled onions, in batches, in rapidly boiling water in a large saucepan 45 seconds. (It's important to blanch in batches so that the water remains at a boil.) Drain and peel onions; place in a large zip-top freezer bag, seal, and refrigerate overnight, if desired.

Combine cabbage and 2 tablespoons salt in a large bowl; let stand 30 minutes, tossing occasionally. Rinse thoroughly, and drain well.

Combine onions and oil in a shallow roasting pan or a large cast-iron skillet; toss to coat. Spread onions in a single layer. Roast at 450° for 25 minutes or until browned, stirring after 20 minutes.

Combine ¼ cup each vinegar and maple syrup; add to roasted onions. Roast 5 more minutes or until slightly thickened and onions are glazed. Set aside.

Combine remaining 2 tablespoons vinegar, 2 table-spoons maple syrup, 1 cup chopped pecans, sour cream, and ½ teaspoon salt in a food processor or blender; process 1 to 2 minutes or until smooth. Cover and chill dressing overnight, if desired.

Toss together chopped apple, cabbage, and endive in a large bowl. Drizzle each serving with dressing, and top with roasted onions; sprinkle with remaining 1 cup pecans. Yield: 8 servings.

**Make Ahead:** Blanch and peel pearl onions a day ahead; store in refrigerator. Prepare dressing up to a day ahead, and store in refrigerator.

## Coffee-Crusted Beef Wellingtons

*Coffee gives classic beef Wellington an intriguing new flavor dimension. For the pastry wrap, we found puff pastry shells easier to work with than sheets. Follow our make-ahead steps that make this fancy entrée easy. You can freeze filets up to a month ahead, and bake them without thawing.*

Prep: 58 min.   Cook: 1 hr., 11 min.   Other: 8 hr.

| | |
|---|---|
| 2 | teaspoons freshly ground coffee |
| 1 | teaspoon salt |
| ¾ | teaspoon pepper |
| ¾ | teaspoon garlic powder |
| 8 | (5- to 6-ounce) center-cut filet mignons (1½" thick) |
| 1 | tablespoon olive oil or vegetable oil |
| 3 | tablespoons butter or margarine |
| ¼ | cup finely chopped onion |
| ¼ | cup finely chopped carrot |
| ¼ | cup finely chopped celery |
| 2 | garlic cloves, minced |
| ¾ | cup Madeira |
| ¾ | cup freshly brewed coffee |
| ½ | cup beef broth |
| 2 | tablespoons butter or margarine |
| ½ | pound fresh mushrooms, minced |
| 2 | shallots, minced |
| ½ | teaspoon salt |
| ½ | teaspoon pepper |
| ½ | cup Madeira |
| 8 | frozen puff pastry shells, thawed (we tested with part of 2 Pepperidge Farm [10-ounce] packages) |
| 1 | large egg, lightly beaten |
| 2 | large eggs, lightly beaten |
| 2 | tablespoons butter |
| 2½ | tablespoons all-purpose flour |
| ½ | cup whipping cream |
| ½ | teaspoon salt |

Garnishes: fresh rosemary, flat-leaf parsley, and thyme

Combine first 4 ingredients; stir well. Pat filets dry. Coat both sides of filets with spice rub. Heat 1 tablespoon oil in a large skillet over medium-high heat until skillet is hot. Sear filets, in 2 batches, 1 to 1½ minutes on each side. Remove filets from skillet; place on a plate, and cover and chill until ready to assemble Wellingtons. (Don't clean skillet.)

While filets are chilling, melt 3 tablespoons butter in same skillet over medium-high heat. Add onion,

## wine advice

**Offer both red and white.** Put an assortment of bottles on your sideboard for guests to sample. Consider an Australian Shiraz or French Syrah; the full-bodied flavor of either partners well with this rich meal of beef Wellington. For a white wine, offer Gallo of Sonoma Chardonnay, lightly chilled.

**Serve wine in fashionable tumblers.** They're elegant, yet sturdier than stemmed glasses.

carrot, celery, and garlic; sauté 5 minutes or until very tender. Add ¾ cup Madeira, brewed coffee, and broth; simmer 5 minutes. Remove from heat, and let cool. Transfer sauce to a 4-cup glass measuring cup, and chill overnight, if desired, or pour cooled sauce into ice cube trays and freeze. Once frozen, seal frozen sauce cubes in zip-top freezer bags.

Melt 2 tablespoons butter in same skillet over medium-high heat. Add mushrooms, shallots, ½ teaspoon salt, and ½ teaspoon pepper; sauté until all liquid evaporates. Add ½ cup Madeira; cook over medium-high heat until all liquid evaporates. Remove from heat, and let cool. Cover and chill until ready to assemble Wellingtons.

Roll each of 8 puff pastry shells to about ⅛" thick on a lightly floured surface; spoon 1 heaping tablespoonful mushroom filling in center of each pastry. Top each with a chilled filet. Brush edges of each pastry square with 1 beaten egg. Wrap 2 opposite sides of pastry over each filet, overlapping them; seal seam with beaten egg. Wrap remaining 2 sides of pastry over filet, and seal with beaten egg. Seal any gaps with beaten egg, and press pastry around filet to enclose completely. Wrap Wellingtons individually in press-and-seal plastic wrap. Place wrapped Wellingtons in large zip-top freezer bags, and freeze overnight or up to 1 month.

To bake, place oven rack on lowest oven shelf; preheat oven to 425°. Place a broiler pan on oven rack; heat pan 5 minutes. Brush tops and sides of frozen Wellingtons with 2 beaten eggs. Carefully place frozen Wellingtons, seam side down, on preheated pan. Bake at 425° for 36 minutes.

While Wellingtons bake, melt 2 tablespoons butter in a saucepan over medium heat; add 2½ tablespoons flour and cook, stirring constantly, 1 minute. Add reserved Madeira sauce; cook, stirring constantly, over medium heat 6 to 8 minutes or until slightly thickened. (If using frozen Madeira sauce cubes, thaw cubes in a saucepan over medium heat before adding to flour mixture.) Stir in whipping cream; simmer 5 minutes or until desired thickness. Add ½ teaspoon salt. Remove from heat.

Arrange baked Wellingtons on a serving platter. Cut a small slit in top of each pastry, and tuck several sprigs of fresh herbs into each slit. Serve with Madeira sauce. Yield: 8 servings.

**Note**: You can bake beef Wellingtons the same day they're assembled. After wrapping beef filets in pastry, cover and chill Wellingtons 1 hour. Bake as directed above, reducing the baking time to 20 to 25 minutes.

## *worry-free Wellingtons*

*This update of a classic and time-consuming entrée has great merit for today's busy cook and host.*

- You can assemble the pastry-wrapped beef, make the sauce ahead, and freeze both up to 1 month. The sauce freezes well in ice cube trays. Wrap the Wellingtons in press-and-seal plastic wrap and then in zip-top freezer bags.
- We found that preheating a broiler pan for 5 minutes and baking Wellingtons on the lowest oven shelf produced the best baked results with golden, flaky pastry.
- There's no fussy pastry cutout garnish. Before serving, simply tuck fresh herbs into the pastry for each serving.

Crab and Oyster Bisque

Apple Salad

## Cast-Iron Herbed Potatoes Anna

*Last-minute stovetop cooking gets this classic potato dish browned and crispy on the bottom. A well-seasoned cast-iron skillet is the key to unmolding the dish.*

Prep: 27 min.   Cook: 1 hr., 17 min.

⅓   cup butter
6    garlic cloves, finely chopped
1    tablespoon finely chopped fresh rosemary
1    tablespoon finely chopped fresh thyme
2    tablespoons vegetable oil
2¼   pounds russet potatoes, peeled and thinly sliced (about ⅛" thick)
¾    teaspoon salt, divided
¾    teaspoon freshly ground pepper, divided

Melt butter in a small skillet over medium heat. Add garlic. Cook 2 minutes or just until garlic is lightly browned. Remove from heat, and stir in rosemary and thyme; set aside.

Brush bottom and sides of a 9" cast-iron skillet with 2 tablespoons oil. Arrange enough potato slices to cover bottom of skillet, overlapping slices; drizzle with one-third herbed garlic butter. Sprinkle with ¼ teaspoon salt and ¼ teaspoon pepper. Repeat procedure twice with remaining potato, herbed garlic butter, salt, and pepper. Brush a piece of aluminum foil with melted butter; press foil firmly, buttered side down, onto potato slices.

Bake at 400° for 1 hour and 10 minutes. Remove from oven, and using an oven mitt, press down firmly on the aluminum foil-covered potatoes. Remove aluminum foil, and place skillet on stovetop over medium heat. Cook 5 minutes. Remove from heat; let stand 2 minutes. Invert potatoes onto a plate, coaxing potatoes loose from skillet with a spatula. Yield: 6 to 8 servings.

**Make Ahead**: Bake Potatoes Anna earlier in the day; invert onto an ovenproof plate, and cover loosely with foil. Just before serving, uncover and reheat at 400° for 10 minutes.

Carrots with Country Bacon

## Carrots with Country Bacon

*Country bacon in this recipe refers to thick-sliced or wood-smoked bacon.*

Prep: 19 min.   Cook: 35 min.

4    thick bacon slices
2    pounds carrots, peeled and diagonally sliced into 1" pieces
2    cups water
¼    cup firmly packed light brown sugar
2    tablespoons butter or margarine
2    teaspoons chopped fresh thyme

Cook bacon in a large skillet over medium heat until crisp. Drain, reserving 1 tablespoon drippings in skillet. Crumble bacon, and set aside. Add carrots and next 3 ingredients to skillet. Bring to a boil. Cook over medium-high heat 30 to 35 minutes or until liquid is reduced to a glaze and carrots are tender. Sprinkle with thyme and reserved bacon. Yield: 6 to 8 servings.

**Make Ahead**: Peel and slice carrots up to a day ahead. Store in a zip-top plastic bag in refrigerator.

Keep your centerpiece low and simple.

## Scalloped Greens

*Greens have never tasted as good as they do in this crumb-topped casserole.*

Prep: 28 min.   Cook: 3 hr.   Other: 15 min.

| | |
|---|---|
| 1 | (1-pound) bag chopped collard greens |
| 1 | (1-pound) bag chopped turnip greens |
| 3 | cups water |
| ½ | cup all-purpose flour |
| ¼ | cup grated onion |
| 2 | large garlic cloves, minced |
| 3 | cups milk |
| 2 | cups half-and-half |
| 2 | large eggs |
| 1¼ | teaspoons salt, divided |
| ¼ | teaspoon pepper |
| 2 | cups (8 ounces) shredded sharp white Cheddar cheese |
| 2 | cups (8 ounces) shredded Havarti cheese |
| 3 | cups sourdough breadcrumbs (see Note) |
| 2 | tablespoons butter or margarine, melted |

Wash greens; remove coarse stems. Bring greens and water to a boil in a large Dutch oven. Cover, reduce heat, and simmer 1 hour and 45 minutes or until tender, stirring occasionally. Drain well. Return greens to pot.

Whisk together flour, next 5 ingredients, 1 teaspoon salt, and pepper. Add to greens in pot. Add cheeses; pour into a buttered 13" x 9" baking dish.

Combine breadcrumbs, 2 tablespoons melted butter, and remaining ¼ teaspoon salt, tossing until crumbs are coated. Sprinkle over greens.

Bake, uncovered, at 350° for 1 hour and 15 minutes or until golden. Let stand 15 minutes before serving. Yield: 15 servings.

**Note:** To make 3 cups sourdough breadcrumbs, we used ⅓ (10-ounce) round loaf sourdough bread, torn into pieces, and pulsed in a food processor.

**Make Ahead:** Cook greens, shred cheese, assemble casserole, and store in refrigerator, without breadcrumb topping, up to a day ahead. Prepare breadcrumb topping, and add just before baking. Bake casserole according to recipe up to 2 hours before serving. Reheat briefly before serving.

## Cardamom-Scented Sweet Potato Pie

*This delicately flavored custard pie is accented with freshly ground spices.*

Prep: 19 min.   Cook: 1 hr., 28 min.

| | |
|---|---|
| 1¼ | pounds sweet potatoes, peeled and cut into 1½" chunks |
| 1 | (3") cinnamon stick, broken |
| ¼ | teaspoon cardamom seeds |
| 4 | large eggs |
| 2 | cups half-and-half |
| 1 | cup sugar |
| 2 | teaspoons grated orange zest |
| 2 | teaspoons vanilla extract |
| ¼ | teaspoon salt |
| 1½ | cups all-purpose flour |
| ½ | teaspoon salt |
| ½ | cup chilled shortening |

5 to 6 tablespoons ice water
Garnishes: sweetened whipped cream, ground cinnamon

Arrange sweet potato in a steamer basket over boiling water. Cover and steam 20 minutes or until very tender.

While sweet potato cooks, process cinnamon and cardamom seeds in a coffee grinder or blender until finely ground; set aside, reserving ¼ teaspoon for top of pie.

When sweet potato is done, cool slightly, and process in a food processor until smooth. Whisk together spices (except for ¼ teaspoon), sweet potato, eggs, and next 5 ingredients in a large bowl.

Combine flour and ½ teaspoon salt. Cut in shortening with a pastry blender until the size of small peas. Sprinkle ice water, 1 tablespoon at a time, evenly over surface; stir with a fork until dry ingredients are moistened. Shape dough into a ball. Roll dough to about ¼" thickness on a lightly floured surface. Fit into an ungreased 9½" deep-dish fluted tart pan; trim off excess pastry along edges. Line tart shell with aluminum foil, pressing foil into the flutes. Trim foil to within ½" of top of pan. Fold foil down over top edge of crust to prevent overbrowning.

Bake at 425° for 15 minutes; remove foil, and bake 7 minutes or until pastry is golden. Reduce oven temperature to 350°. With tart pan still on oven rack, pull out rack; pour filling into pastry, and sprinkle with remaining ¼ teaspoon spices. Bake at 350° for 1 hour or until set. Cool completely before serving. Garnish, if desired. Store in refrigerator. Yield: 1 (9½") deep-dish pie.

*Cardamom-Scented Sweet Potato Pie*

**Note:** If you don't have a fluted tart pan, you can bake this pie in 2 (9") glass pieplates. Fit each piecrust (from a 15-ounce package refrigerated piecrusts) into a 9" pieplate according to package directions; fold edges under, and crimp. (No need to prebake crusts for these smaller pies.) Pour filling evenly into 2 prepared piecrusts. Sprinkle with remaining ¼ teaspoon spices.

Bake at 450° for 15 minutes. Reduce heat to 350°; bake 30 more minutes or until set. Cool on a wire rack. (Pies will be thin.) Or bake pies using 2 frozen piecrusts.

**Tip:** Use a meat mallet to break cinnamon stick before placing in coffee grinder. Tap cardamom pods lightly with mallet to release seeds.

Use a sideboard to keep wine bottles, bread, the entrée platter, desserts, dessert plates, and coffee cups during the meal.

*Chocolate Tiramisù Charlotte*

# Chocolate Tiramisù Charlotte

*Every holiday dinner needs a luscious chocolate dessert. This one can be made ahead and can sit out awhile before serving.*

Prep: 1 hr.   Cook: 14 min.   Other: 8 hr., 20 min.

| | |
|---|---|
| 1 | round bakery pound cake |
| 2 | tablespoons instant espresso granules |
| ¾ | cup boiling water |
| ½ | cup Kahlúa or sweet marsala wine, divided |
| 6 | large eggs, separated |
| 1¼ | cups sugar, divided |
| 2 | envelopes unflavored gelatin |
| ½ | cup cold water |
| ½ | cup whipping cream, divided |
| 1½ | (8-ounce) containers mascarpone cheese* |
| 1¼ | cups (8 ounces) double chocolate morsels, divided (we tested with Ghirardelli) |
| 2 | tablespoons butter |

Garnishes: sweetened whipped cream, coarsely
chopped chocolate-covered coffee beans

Slice enough pound cake to get 18 (⅓") slices. Line sides and bottom of an ungreased 9" springform pan with 12 to 14 slices of pound cake. Set remaining pound cake aside. Dissolve espresso in ¾ cup boiling water; stir in ¼ cup Kahlúa. Brush pound cake with ¾ cup espresso mixture, setting aside remaining ¼ cup espresso mixture.

Whisk together 6 egg whites and ¾ cup sugar in top of a double boiler; place over simmering water, and cook, whisking often, until mixture reaches 160°. Transfer egg white mixture to a large bowl; beat at high speed with an electric mixer until stiff peaks form. Set aside.

Sprinkle gelatin over ½ cup cold water in a saucepan; let soften 1 minute. Cook over medium heat, stirring until gelatin dissolves. Add ¼ cup whipping cream; set aside.

Whisk together 6 egg yolks, remaining ½ cup sugar, and remaining ¼ cup Kahlúa in top of double boiler. Place over simmering water, and cook, whisking often, until mixture reaches 160°. Remove bowl, and beat at medium speed with a handheld electric mixer until thick and pale. Add mascarpone cheese and gelatin mixture, beating until smooth. Fold in about 1 cup meringue; fold in remaining meringue. Spoon half of mascarpone mixture into springform pan. Top with remaining pound cake slices; brush pound cake slices with remaining ¼ cup espresso mixture.

Place half of chocolate morsels in a glass bowl. Microwave on HIGH 1½ minutes; stir until smooth and slightly cool. Add ½ cup mascarpone mixture, stirring until smooth; fold into remaining mascarpone mixture. Spoon chocolate mascarpone mixture into springform pan. Chill 20 minutes or until slightly firm on top.

Combine remaining chocolate morsels, remaining ¼ cup whipping cream, and butter in a small glass bowl. Microwave on HIGH 1½ minutes. Stir until chocolate melts and mixture is smooth. Spoon chocolate ganache over top of dessert, spreading to edges with a small offset spatula. Cover and chill at least 8 hours.

Before serving, run a knife around edge of pan to release sides. Remove Charlotte to a serving plate; let stand 20 minutes. Garnish, if desired. Yield: 12 servings.

*Substitute 12 ounces cream cheese if you can't find mascarpone cheese.

## helping hands

The heart of the holiday season is spending time with loved ones. If you're hosting the holiday dinner, don't be shy about asking for help. Guests will enjoy being asked to pitch in for last-minute tasks like lighting candles, stirring gravy, opening or pouring wine, or serving up side dishes.

# Christmas Fare: Grand Style Made Easy

**Host the holiday get-together with ease. Let our Foods staff walk you through the planning, from turkey basics to setting a pretty table. This classic Southern feast features both ham and turkey options, side dishes with make-ahead tips, and a simple fruit dessert as well as a luscious cake.**

Honey and Brown Sugar-Crusted Ham or
Marmalade-Glazed Turkey and Giblet Gravy

Shortcut Cornbread Dressing    Cranberry-Maple Sauce

Citrus Sweet Potato Rounds    Succotash    Seasoned Green Beans

Waldorf Salad Jubilee

Bakery dinner rolls

Spiced Ambrosia or

Pumpkin-Rum Cake with Brown Sugar Icing

Wine or Iced tea

**serves 10**

# game plan

## Before the Day

### As much as 3 months ahead:

• Purchase ingredients for Shortcut Cornbread Dressing; prepare, cover, and freeze it unbaked (or prepare dressing 1 day ahead and refrigerate).

### 2 weeks ahead:

• Make grocery list. Shop for nonperishables.
• Plan table centerpiece and/or decorations.

### 3 or 4 days ahead:

• Do remaining shopping.
• Place turkey in refrigerator to thaw, if frozen.

### 2 days ahead:

• Set table and organize serving pieces.
• Arrange table centerpiece.
• Toast pecans for Waldorf Salad Jubilee; store in a zip-top plastic bag.
• Hard-cook egg for Giblet Gravy. Store in refrigerator.
• Chop onion and celery for Giblet Gravy, Shortcut Cornbread Dressing, and Waldorf Salad Jubilee; label and store in airtight plastic bags. Or buy prechopped onion and celery.
• Prepare Cranberry-Maple Sauce; cover and refrigerate.
• Cook sweet potatoes for Citrus Sweet Potato Rounds; let cool, and refrigerate overnight.

### 1 day ahead:

• Thaw frozen Shortcut Cornbread Dressing in refrigerator, or prepare dressing, cover, and refrigerate.
• Bake Pumpkin-Rum Cake.
• Slice potatoes, and prepare recipe for Citrus Sweet Potato Rounds; cover and chill.
• Cook green beans; store in zip-top plastic bag in refrigerator.
• Combine apple mixture for Waldorf Salad Jubilee; cover and chill. Wash radicchio for salad; place in plastic bag, and refrigerate.
• Prepare fruit and syrup for Spiced Ambrosia; cover and chill in separate containers.
• Brew tea, if desired.

## The Day of

### 5 hours ahead:

• Review plan for the day, and get organized.
• Ready ham for baking; cover loosely, and refrigerate.

### 3 hours ahead:

• Prepare turkey, and bake; then cover with aluminum foil.
• Let ham come to room temperature.

### 2 hours ahead:

• Bake ham; then cover with aluminum foil.
• Simmer broth for Giblet Gravy.
• Let Shortcut Cornbread Dressing come to room temperature.

### 1 hour ahead:

• Prepare Succotash; hold out bacon, tomatoes, and seasonings.

• Let Citrus Sweet Potato Rounds stand at room temperature.
• Bake Shortcut Cornbread Dressing.

### 30 minutes ahead:

• Bake Citrus Sweet Potato Rounds.
• Finish preparing Seasoned Green Beans and Giblet Gravy.

### 10 minutes ahead:

• Heat rolls.
• Add pecans to Waldorf Salad Jubilee; serve in radicchio leaves.
• Heat Succotash; stir in bacon, tomatoes, basil, salt, and pepper.

### After dinner:

• Have dessert plates ready for Pumpkin-Rum Cake.
• Serve ambrosia in stemless tumblers; sprinkle with coconut.

## Apple and Calla Lily Centerpiece

▲ Core apples with an apple corer.

▲ Trim calla lilies and insert one into each cored apple. Add seeded eucalyptus.

◀ Insert a candle into center of each calla lily, and build a centerpiece around apples. We filled stemless wine tumblers with a little water, and added fresh cranberries and calla lilies.

## Place cards

◀ Tie small name cards around stems of wine glasses using ribbon or tuck name cards into calla lily apples as another option (below).

# Honey and Brown Sugar-Crusted Ham

*A dark brown sugar crust makes this ham incredibly yummy. Any leftover slices should make their way onto biscuits.*

**Prep: 6 min.  Cook: 2 hr., 15 min.  Other: 15 min.**

| | |
|---|---|
| 1 | (9- to 10-pounds) ready-to-cook, bone-in ham shank |
| ¾ | cup honey |
| 1 | cup firmly packed dark brown sugar |
| 1 | teaspoon ground nutmeg |
| 1 | teaspoon ground cinnamon |
| 1 | teaspoon ground cloves |

▲ Brush honey on partially baked ham. It serves as the "glue" for the brown sugar crust.

▲ Pat sugar and spice coating onto honeyed ham.

Ham ready for final baking

Slice away hard outer skin from ham with a sharp knife, leaving a thin layer of fat. Place ham, fat side up, on a rack in a shallow roasting pan. Score top of ham in a diamond pattern; insert a meat thermometer into ham, making sure it does not touch fat or bone.

Bake ham on lowest oven rack at 325° for 1½ hours. Remove ham from oven, leaving oven on. Brush ham with honey. Combine sugar and spices; pat over honey, coating ham well.

Return ham to oven, and continue to bake at 325° for 35 to 45 minutes or until thermometer registers 148°. (Cover ham with aluminum foil during the last 20 minutes, if necessary, to prevent excessive browning.) Let ham stand 15 minutes before carving. Yield: 10 servings.

# Marmalade-Glazed Turkey and Giblet Gravy

*Juicy meat and darkly glazed skin set this holiday bird apart. A wonderful orange marmalade and honey glaze gives this a sweet twist from grandma's traditional turkey. If your turkey is frozen, place turkey in its original wrapper in a pan, and refrigerate two to three days or until thawed.*

**Prep: 8 min.  Cook: 3 hr.  Other: 15 min.**

| | |
|---|---|
| 1 | (10- to 12-pound) fresh or frozen turkey, thawed |
| 1½ | teaspoons salt |
| 1 | teaspoon pepper |
| 1 | teaspoon dried whole savory, crumbled |
| 1 | teaspoon rubbed sage |
| ¼ | cup unsalted butter, softened |
| ½ | cup orange juice |
| ½ | cup orange marmalade |
| 1 | tablespoon honey |

Garnishes: oranges, fresh sage
Giblet Gravy (opposite)

Remove giblets and neck from turkey; place in refrigerator for use in Giblet Gravy. Rinse turkey with cold water; pat dry with paper towels. Place turkey, breast side up, on a rack in a lightly greased roasting pan. Lift wing tips up and over back, and tuck under bird.

Combine salt and next 3 ingredients in a small bowl; rub some of seasoning inside turkey cavity. Combine remaining herb mixture with softened butter, and rub all over outside of turkey, legs and all. Tie ends of legs together with heavy string or tuck under flap of skin around tail.

Bake, uncovered, at 325° for 1 hour and 30 minutes.

Combine orange juice, marmalade, and honey, stirring well. Brush half of orange glaze over turkey; bake 1 to 1½ hours or until a meat thermometer inserted into meaty part of thigh registers 170°, brushing with orange glaze every 30 minutes. Shield turkey with aluminum foil during cooking, if necessary, to prevent overbrowning.

Transfer turkey to a serving platter, reserving pan drippings for Giblet Gravy. Let turkey stand, covered with foil, 15 minutes before carving. Garnish platter, if desired. Serve turkey with Giblet Gravy. Yield: 10 to 12 servings.

## Giblet Gravy

**Prep: 5 min.   Cook: 1 hr., 51 min.**

Giblets and neck reserved from turkey
4    cups water
Pan drippings from roasted turkey
1    small onion, chopped
1    celery rib, chopped
1    teaspoon salt
½    teaspoon pepper
2    tablespoons cornstarch
¼    cup water
1    hard-cooked large egg, chopped
Salt and pepper to taste

Combine giblets, neck, and water in a saucepan. Bring to a boil; cover, reduce heat, and simmer 1 hour or until giblets are tender. Strain, reserving broth. Discard turkey neck. Coarsely chop giblets; set aside.

Skim and discard fat from reserved pan drippings of roasted turkey. Add reserved broth (at least 2½ cups) to pan drippings; stir until browned bits are loosened from bottom of roasting pan.

Transfer broth and drippings to a saucepan, if desired, or continue cooking in roasting pan over 2 burners on the stove. Stir in chopped giblets. Add onion and next 3 ingredients. Bring to a boil; reduce heat, and simmer, uncovered, 30 minutes.

Combine cornstarch and ¼ cup water, stirring well; gradually stir into gravy. Bring to a boil; boil 1 minute or until thickened. Stir in egg. Add salt and pepper to taste. Serve hot. Yield: 4 cups.

## Turkey Talk

In 2006, the USDA determined a new minimum doneness temperature of 165° for both white and dark meat poultry; however, this minimum internal temperature for food safety may not achieve the desired doneness for personal preferences and best quality. For this recipe, the turkey was best when baked to a slightly higher temperature of 170° that our taste panel preferred. And we recommend buying a fresh bird. If you buy a frozen bird, be sure it is completely thawed—especially in the center. Check it after you remove the giblets. Otherwise, the turkey may need to cook a bit longer to reach proper doneness.

▲ Lift wing tips up and over back, and tuck under bird.

▲ Rub herb butter all over bird.

▲ Brush some of orange marmalade glaze over partially roasted turkey.

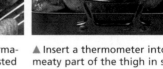

▲ Insert a thermometer into the meaty part of the thigh in search of 170° ideal doneness for this recipe.

▲ Using packaged cornbread and refrigerated biscuits shaves time off preparing this dressing. Look for prechopped onion and celery in the produce section of the grocery store.

*make ahead*
## Shortcut Cornbread Dressing

**Prep: 26 min.   Cook: 1 hr.**

2    (6-ounce) packages cornbread mix (we tested with Martha White)
1    (6-ounce) can refrigerated buttermilk biscuits
¼    cup butter or margarine
1    large onion, chopped (2 cups)
5    celery ribs, chopped (1½ cups)
5    cups chicken broth
4    large eggs, lightly beaten
2    teaspoons rubbed sage
1½   teaspoons pepper
¾    teaspoon salt

Prepare cornbread mix and biscuits according to package directions; let cool. Crumble cornbread and biscuits in a large bowl. Set aside.

Melt butter in a large skillet over medium-high heat; add onion and celery, and sauté until tender. Add sautéed vegetables, broth, and remaining ingredients to crumbled cornbread; stir well. Spoon dressing into a lightly greased 13" x 9" baking dish.

Bake, uncovered, at 350° for 55 minutes or until browned. Yield: 10 servings.

**Make-Ahead Note:** Prepare recipe as directed; do not bake. Cover and freeze dressing up to 3 months or refrigerate up to 24 hours. Remove from refrigerator; let stand 30 minutes. Uncover and bake as directed.

*gift idea • make ahead • quick & easy*
## Cranberry-Maple Sauce

*Aside from its traditional place on the holiday dinner plate, this sauce makes a great topping for waffles or pancakes, too.*

**Prep: 5 min.   Cook: 12 min.**

1    (12-ounce) package fresh or frozen cranberries (3 cups)
¾    cup pure maple syrup (not pancake syrup)
½    cup firmly packed light brown sugar
¼    cup water
½    teaspoon vanilla extract

Combine all ingredients in a heavy saucepan. Bring mixture to a boil; reduce heat, and simmer 8 minutes or just until cranberries begin to pop, stirring often. Pour sauce into a serving bowl, and let cool completely. Serve chilled, if desired. Yield: 2½ cups.

**Make-Ahead Note:** Sauce can be made up to 1 week ahead. Keep covered in refrigerator.

▲ Simmer just until cranberries start to pop. The sauce will thicken as it cools.

▲ Spoon orange glaze over sweet potatoes before baking. The glaze thickens in the oven and coats the sweet potatoes.

*make ahead*

## Citrus Sweet Potato Rounds

*Vanilla bean paste enhances the glaze for these sweet potatoes.*

Prep: 13 min.   Cook: 1 hr., 30 min.

7     medium sweet potatoes (about 4 pounds)
½     cup pecan halves
1     cup orange juice
⅔     cup firmly packed brown sugar
¼     cup butter, melted
1     tablespoon cornstarch
¼     teaspoon salt
1     teaspoon vanilla bean paste or vanilla extract

Place washed sweet potatoes on a baking sheet; prick each potato with a fork. Bake at 450° for 45 minutes or until almost tender. Let potatoes cool to the touch.

Peel potatoes, and cut into ½"-thick slices. Arrange potato slices in a lightly greased 13" x 9" baking dish or round 3-qt. casserole. Top with pecan halves.

Combine orange juice and next 4 ingredients in a small saucepan, stirring well. Bring glaze mixture to a boil; boil 1 minute or until thickened and bubbly. Stir in vanilla bean paste. Pour or spoon orange glaze over sweet potato slices.

Bake, uncovered, at 350° for 30 to 45 minutes or until glaze is thickened. Yield: 10 servings.

**Make-Ahead Note:** After baked sweet potatoes have cooled, cover and refrigerate up to 24 hours. The next day, peel and slice potatoes, and let come to room temperature before baking as directed above.

*make ahead • quick & easy*

## Succotash

*We especially liked this side dish paired with ham.*

Prep: 6 min.   Cook: 19 min.

5     bacon slices, coarsely chopped
2     green onions, chopped
4     cups frozen whole kernel corn, thawed
3½     cups frozen baby lima beans, thawed
¾     cup chicken broth
1     pint grape tomatoes, halved
2     teaspoons chopped fresh basil or ¾ teaspoon dried basil
½     teaspoon salt
½     teaspoon pepper

Cook bacon in a large skillet until crisp; remove bacon, and drain on paper towels, reserving 3 tablespoons drippings in skillet.

Sauté green onions in hot drippings 2 minutes. Stir in corn, lima beans, and broth. Cook, uncovered, 15 minutes or until beans are just tender and most of broth evaporates, stirring often. Stir in bacon, tomatoes, basil, salt, and pepper. Cook 1 to 2 minutes or until thoroughly heated. Yield: 10 servings.

▲ Have tomatoes prepped and ready to add to Succotash just before serving.

# Seasoned Green Beans

*Every busy holiday menu needs at least one easy side dish. Cook the beans and slice the onion a day ahead.*

Prep: 13 min.   Cook: 30 min.

2½  pounds green beans, trimmed
2   tablespoons olive oil
1   onion, vertically sliced
4   garlic cloves, minced
1   teaspoon salt
½   teaspoon pepper

Cook green beans in boiling salted water 5 to 7 minutes or until crisp-tender. Plunge beans in ice water to stop the cooking process; drain and set aside.

Heat oil in a large skillet or sauté pan over medium heat; add onion and garlic, and sauté 15 to 20 minutes or until tender and onion starts to caramelize. Stir in green beans, salt, and pepper; sauté 2 to 3 minutes or until beans are heated. Serve hot. Yield: 10 servings.

**Make-Ahead Note:** Place cooked green beans in a large zip-top plastic bag, and store in refrigerator up to 1 day. When ready to use, simply toss in with caramelized onions, and sauté until warm.

▲ Plunge crisp-tender beans in ice water to stop the cooking process. Seal beans in a zip-top bag and refrigerate for make-ahead ease.

*make ahead* • *quick & easy*
# Waldorf Salad Jubilee

*This vibrant salad will brighten your holiday table. For a slightly sweeter salad, use Gala or Fuji apples in place of Granny Smith.*

Prep: 26 min.

1   cup mayonnaise
1   teaspoon lemon juice
½   teaspoon salt
6   Granny Smith apples (about 2½ pounds), unpeeled and cut into ½" pieces
1½  cups chopped celery
1½  cups chopped radishes
¾   cup orange-flavored dried cranberries
½   cup finely chopped red onion
1½  cups pecan pieces, toasted
2   heads radicchio, washed, and leaves separated

Combine first 3 ingredients in a medium bowl, stirring well. Toss apples with next 4 ingredients in a large bowl. Add mayonnaise dressing, and toss to coat. (Salad can be prepared a day ahead; cover and refrigerate overnight).

Fold toasted pecans into salad. Line a serving bowl with radicchio leaves, and spoon in salad; or arrange radicchio leaves on each plate, and spoon salad into leaves. Yield: 10 servings.

# Spiced Ambrosia

**Prep: 37 min.   Cook: 4 min.   Other: 8 hr.**

½    cup water
½    cup sugar
1    (1" to 2") piece fresh ginger, peeled and thinly sliced
1    tablespoon grated orange rind
1    (3") cinnamon stick
3    black peppercorns
½    teaspoon vanilla extract
10   navel oranges, peeled and sectioned
1    (8-ounce) can pineapple tidbits in juice
¾    cup sweetened flaked coconut
¼    cup maraschino cherries with stems

Bring first 6 ingredients to a boil in a small saucepan over medium heat. Remove from heat; stir in vanilla.

Cover and let stand 30 minutes. Pour syrup through a wire-mesh strainer into a small bowl, discarding ginger and spices. Cool completely; chill.

Combine sectioned oranges and pineapple in a large bowl. Gently stir in chilled syrup. Spoon fruit and syrup into individual dessert dishes. Sprinkle with coconut, and top with cherries. Yield: 10 servings.

**Make-Ahead Note:** Prepare fruit. Seal in a zip-top freezer bag, and refrigerate overnight. Cover and chill ginger syrup overnight. Combine fruit and syrup before serving.

Spoon ambrosia into stemless wine tumblers for elegant yet casual flair.

Pumpkin-Rum Cake with
Brown Sugar Icing

# Pumpkin-Rum Cake with Brown Sugar Icing

*Pumpkin, a classic holiday flavor, gets blended with a yummy pecan streusel and doused with a fudgelike icing.*

**Prep: 21 min.   Cook: 1 hr., 28 min.   Other: 10 min.**

¾     cup chopped pecans, toasted
¾     cup firmly packed dark brown sugar
3     tablespoons all-purpose flour
1½    teaspoons ground cinnamon
¼     cup butter, melted
1     cup unsalted butter, softened
2     cups granulated sugar
2     cups firmly packed dark brown sugar
5     large eggs
2     cups canned unsweetened pumpkin
¼     cup dark rum
3     cups all-purpose flour
2     teaspoons baking powder
½     teaspoon baking soda
¾     teaspoon salt
2     teaspoons ground cinnamon
½     teaspoon ground ginger
½     teaspoon ground allspice
½     teaspoon ground nutmeg
¾     cup firmly packed dark brown sugar
½     cup whipping cream
¼     cup unsalted butter
1     teaspoon dark rum
1     cup plus 2 tablespoons sifted powdered sugar

Combine first 4 ingredients in a small bowl; stir in ¼ cup melted butter. Use fingers to pinch streusel into big clumps. Set aside.

Beat 1 cup butter at medium speed with an electric mixer about 2 minutes or until creamy. Gradually add 2 cups each granulated and dark brown sugar, beating at medium speed 5 to 7 minutes. Add eggs, 1 at a time, beating just until yellow disappears.

Stir together pumpkin and ¼ cup rum in a bowl. Combine flour and next 7 ingredients in a medium bowl. Add flour mixture to butter mixture alternately with pumpkin, beginning and ending with flour.

Pour half of batter into a well-greased and floured 12-cup Bundt pan. (We recommend greasing pan with shortening.) Sprinkle batter with streusel; top with remaining batter.

Bake at 325° for 1 hour and 28 minutes or until a long wooden pick inserted in center comes out clean. Cool in pan on a wire rack 10 minutes; remove from pan, and let cool completely.

Combine ¾ cup brown sugar, whipping cream, and ¼ cup unsalted butter in a medium saucepan. Cook, stirring constantly, over medium-low heat, until butter melts and sugar dissolves. Increase heat to medium-high, and bring to a boil. Boil 3 minutes. Remove from heat, and stir in 1 teaspoon rum.

Place powdered sugar in a bowl; pour brown sugar mixture over powdered sugar, stirring with a wire whisk 1 minute or until smooth. Let cool 20 to 25 minutes or until lukewarm. Spoon icing over cooled cake, and let stand until icing is firm. Yield: 12 servings.

A splash of dark rum enhances both this dreamy icing and moist cake.

# FAVORITE RECIPES

Welcome the holidays with these top-rated, kitchen-tested dishes. From appetizers to casseroles to slow-cooker sensations, you'll find everything you need for a season full of sweet and savory delights.

# 25 All-Time Favorite
## *Christmas Recipes*
*These holiday staff favorites are the recipes
we serve our families year after year.*

*Butter Coconut Pie, page 266*

*Grapefruit-Rosemary Daiquiris*

*editor's favorite*
## Grapefruit-Rosemary Daiquiris

*The surprising combo of citrus and herb tastes great in this slushy daiquiri. For a special effect, dip rims of glasses in coarse sugar before filling.*

Prep: 17 min.   Cook: 10 min.   Other: 8 hr.

| | |
|---|---|
| 3 | cups freshly squeezed ruby red grapefruit juice (about 7 grapefruit) |
| 1½ | cups water |
| ⅔ | cup sugar |
| 2 | large sprigs fresh rosemary |
| ⅓ | cup vodka (optional) |
| 1½ | teaspoons finely chopped fresh rosemary |

Sparkling white sugar (optional)
Garnish: fresh rosemary sprigs

Pour 2½ cups grapefruit juice into 2 ice cube trays; freeze until firm. Cover and chill remaining juice.

Stir together water, sugar, and 2 rosemary sprigs in a saucepan; bring to a boil. Cover, reduce heat, and simmer 10 minutes. Remove from heat; discard rosemary sprigs. Cool syrup; chill.

Process frozen juice cubes, remaining ½ cup grapefruit juice, rosemary syrup, vodka, if desired, and chopped rosemary in a 5-cup blender for 10 seconds or until slushy. Serve in sugar-rimmed glasses, and garnish, if desired. Yield: 5 cups.

**Fix it Faster:** Use 3 cups bottled ruby red grapefruit juice.

**Note:** For sugared rims, dip rims of stemmed glasses into a thin coating of light corn syrup or water, and then spin rims in a plateful of sparkling white sugar.

*Savory Kalamata*
*Cheesecake Squares*

*make ahead • editor's favorite*

## Savory Kalamata Cheesecake Squares

*Garnish your platter with herbs and olives so your guests will know this is an appetizer and not dessert. Serve a Pinot Noir with these rich squares.*

Prep: 29 min.  Cook: 32 min.  Other: 1 hr.

1¼ cups Italian-seasoned breadcrumbs
½ cup very finely chopped pecans
⅓ cup butter or margarine, melted
1 (8-ounce) package cream cheese, softened
1 (3-ounce) package cream cheese, softened
1 (8-ounce) container sour cream
1 tablespoon all-purpose flour
¼ teaspoon salt
¼ teaspoon pepper
1 large egg
1 egg yolk
½ cup pitted kalamata olives, sliced or chopped
1 tablespoon chopped fresh rosemary
Garnishes: fresh rosemary sprigs, kalamata olives

Combine first 3 ingredients; stir well. Press crumb mixture firmly into a lightly greased, foil-lined 9" square pan. Bake at 350° for 12 minutes; set aside to cool.

Meanwhile, beat cream cheese, sour cream, and next 3 ingredients at medium speed with an electric mixer until smooth. Add egg and egg yolk, beating just until blended. Stir in olives and rosemary; pour filling into baked crust.

Bake at 350° for 20 minutes or just until firm; cool to room temperature on a wire rack. Cover and chill at least 1 hour.

To serve, lift foil out of pan, and cut cheesecake into little squares. Garnish serving platter, if desired. Store in refrigerator. Yield: 3 dozen.

The **rich and fruity** flavor of a kalamata olive is hard to top.

*editor's favorite*

## Butternut Squash Spread on Cheese Croutons

*Baked butternut squash and Asiago cheese blend with herbs and toasted pecans for a fabulous-tasting spread.*

Prep: 22 min.   Cook: 1hr., 6 min.

1   medium butternut squash (about 2 pounds)
3   tablespoons butter or margarine
3   garlic cloves, minced
½   (8-ounce) package cream cheese, softened
1½  cups freshly grated Asiago cheese, divided
1   tablespoon sugar
½   cup toasted chopped pecans
2   teaspoons chopped fresh thyme
2   teaspoons chopped fresh rosemary
1   baguette, cut into 48 thin slices
½   cup olive oil
Salt and pepper
Garnish: small sprigs of fresh thyme

Microwave squash on HIGH 1 to 2 minutes. (This step softens squash for slicing.) Cut squash in half lengthwise; remove and discard seeds. Place squash, cut sides down, in a 13" x 9" baking dish. Add hot water to dish to depth of 1". Bake, uncovered, at 350° for 1 hour or until squash is very tender. Let cool slightly.

Scoop out squash pulp. Mash pulp, and place in a large bowl.

Melt butter in a small skillet over medium-high heat. Add garlic; sauté 1 minute. Add garlic butter to squash pulp in bowl. Add cream cheese, ½ cup Asiago cheese, and sugar; beat at medium speed with an electric mixer until smooth. Stir in pecans and chopped herbs.

Place baguette slices on 2 large ungreased baking sheets; brush or drizzle with olive oil. Sprinkle slices with salt and pepper. Bake at 400° for 4 minutes. Sprinkle slices with remaining 1 cup Asiago cheese. Bake 2 more minutes or until cheese melts.

Spoon 1 tablespoon squash mixture onto each cheese crouton. Garnish, if desired. Yield: 4 dozen.

*make ahead • editor's favorite*

## Florentine Artichoke Dip

*Make this dip ahead, and bake it just before serving. Crisp bagel chips make great dippers.*

Prep: 30 min.   Cook: 25 min.

1   (10-ounce) package frozen chopped spinach, thawed
2   (6-ounce) jars marinated artichoke hearts, drained and chopped
1½  (8-ounce) packages cream cheese, softened
1   cup freshly shredded Parmesan cheese
½   cup mayonnaise
3   large garlic cloves, pressed
2   tablespoons lemon juice
1½  cups French breadcrumbs (homemade; see Note)
2   tablespoons butter or margarine, melted

Drain spinach; press between layers of paper towels to remove excess moisture.

Combine spinach, artichoke hearts, and next 5 ingredients in a bowl, stirring well. Spoon into a greased 11" x 7" baking dish. Combine breadcrumbs and butter; sprinkle over spinach mixture.

Bake, uncovered, at 375° for 25 minutes or until browned. Serve with bagel chips, crackers, or breadsticks. Yield: 4 cups.

**Note:** To get 1½ cups French breadcrumbs, tear off a piece of a baguette. Pulse in a food processor until coarse crumbs form. Measure crumbs, tear off another chunk, and repeat procedure until you get 1½ cups.

*Butternut Squash Spread on Cheese Croutons*

## Grapefruit Compote in Rosemary Syrup

*If you have an abundance of grapefruit during the holidays, this recipe is a great use for it.*

Prep: 20 min.   Cook: 5 min.

1    cup sugar
½    cup water
3    tablespoons honey
3    sprigs fresh rosemary
6    large grapefruit
½    cup maraschino cherries with stems
Garnish: fresh rosemary sprigs

Combine first 4 ingredients in a saucepan; bring to a boil over medium heat. Boil 5 minutes. Remove from heat, and let cool completely. Remove and discard rosemary.

Section grapefruit over a large bowl, catching juices. Pour rosemary syrup over fruit in bowl. Add cherries. Cover and chill until ready to serve. Garnish, if desired. Yield: 8 to 10 servings.

Serve in compotes and enjoy the herb-kissed syrup with each spoonful.

*Grapefruit Compote in Rosemary Syrup*

*Rum Fudge Cakes*

# Rum Fudge Cakes

*A wooden spoon gets you from start to finish with this recipe. Rum flavor permeates these petite fudgy cakes that received our highest rating. Make and freeze them ahead.*

Prep: 21 min.   Cook: 22 min.   Other: 10 min.

1   cup butter
4   (1-ounce) unsweetened chocolate squares
4   (1-ounce) semisweet chocolate squares
1⅓ cups granulated sugar
⅓  cup heavy whipping cream
1½ teaspoons rum extract
3   large eggs
1   cup all-purpose flour
1   cup (6 ounces) semisweet chocolate mini-morsels
Powdered sugar

Melt butter and chocolate squares in a heavy saucepan over medium-low heat, stirring often. Remove from heat, and cool completely. Stir in granulated sugar, whipping cream, and rum extract until blended. Add eggs, 1 at a time, stirring until blended after each addition. Gently fold in flour. Stir in mini-morsels.

Spoon batter into lightly greased miniature (1¾") muffin pans, filling almost full.

Bake at 375° for 14 minutes or until a wooden pick inserted in center comes out almost clean. Let cool in pans on wire racks 10 minutes. Remove to wire racks to cool completely. Sprinkle cakes with powdered sugar before serving. Yield: 4 dozen.

*Coffee Lovers' Coffee Cake*

butter with a pastry blender until crumbly. Press half of crumb mixture into a lightly greased 9" square pan; set aside.

Combine sour cream and baking soda, stirring well. Add to remaining crumb mixture, stirring just until dry ingredients are moistened. Add egg, stirring gently to combine. Pour sour cream mixture over crumb crust in pan; sprinkle with pecans.

Bake at 350° for 45 minutes. Cool and cut into squares. Yield: 1 (9") coffee cake.

*editor's favorite . gift idea*
## Butter Coconut Pie

*This easy coconut pie makes a nice gift packaged in the disposable pan it's baked in. Crimp the store-bought crust's edges to make it look homemade. See photo on page 260.*

Prep: 15 min.   Cook: 50 min.   Other: 15 min.

| | |
|---|---|
| 1 | (9") frozen deep-dish pastry shell (we tested with Mrs. Smith's) |
| 1 | cup sugar |
| 1 | tablespoon all-purpose flour |
| 3 | large eggs, lightly beaten |
| 1 | (3.5-ounce) can sweetened flaked coconut |
| ½ | cup evaporated milk |
| ⅓ | cup butter, melted |
| 1 | teaspoon vanilla extract |

Garnish: toasted flaked coconut

Remove frozen pastry shell from package; let stand at room temperature 15 minutes. Smooth edges of pastry shell, and crimp.

Line pastry with aluminum foil or parchment paper, and fill with dried beans or pie weights. Bake at 400° for 8 to 10 minutes or until lightly browned. Remove weights and foil.

Combine sugar and flour in a large bowl; stir in eggs. Add 1 can coconut and next 3 ingredients, stirring well. Pour filling into prepared piecrust.

Bake at 325° for 40 minutes or until pie is just set (center will be slightly jiggly). Cool completely. Store in refrigerator. Garnish, if desired. Yield: 1 (9") pie.

**Note:** You can use half of a 15-ounce package of refrigerated piecrusts and a 9" pieplate instead of a frozen piecrust. The filling will be more shallow and crust may need shielding to prevent overbrowning.

*make ahead . editor's favorite*
## Coffee Lovers' Coffee Cake

*A buttery coffee crumb mixture makes a shortbreadlike crust for this easy snack cake.*

Prep: 17 min.   Cook: 45 min.

| | |
|---|---|
| 2 | cups all-purpose flour |
| 2 | teaspoons instant coffee granules |
| 2 | cups firmly packed light brown sugar |
| 1 | teaspoon ground cinnamon |
| ½ | teaspoon salt |
| ½ | cup butter or margarine, cut into pieces |
| 1 | (8-ounce) container sour cream |
| 1 | teaspoon baking soda |
| 1 | large egg, lightly beaten |
| 1 | cup chopped pecans or walnuts |

Combine flour and coffee granules in a large bowl. Add brown sugar, cinnamon, and salt; stir well. Cut in

# Eggnog Pie

Prep: 17 min.   Cook: 26 min.   Other: 4 hr., 6 min.

2   cups pecan shortbread cookie crumbs (about 18 cookies; we tested with Pecan Sandies)
¼   cup butter or margarine, melted
½   cup semisweet chocolate morsels
2¼  cups whipping cream
⅓   cup granulated sugar
½   cup bourbon or rum
½   teaspoon freshly grated nutmeg
1   envelope unflavored gelatin
¼   cup cold water
6   egg yolks, lightly beaten
1   tablespoon butter or margarine
Freshly grated nutmeg
Powdered sugar
Unsweetened whipped cream (optional)

Stir together cookie crumbs and ¼ cup melted butter; press firmly into a greased 9" deep-dish pieplate. Bake at 350° for 8 minutes. Remove crust from oven, and sprinkle chocolate morsels into warm crust. Let stand 5 minutes or until morsels melt; carefully spread chocolate over bottom of crust with a spatula. Set aside.

Stir together whipping cream and next 3 ingredients in top of a double boiler; bring water just to a simmer. Cook over simmering water 6 to 8 minutes or until thoroughly heated.

Meanwhile, sprinkle gelatin over cold water in a small bowl; let stand 1 minute.

Gradually whisk one-fourth of warm cream mixture into egg yolks. Add to remaining warm cream, whisking constantly. Whisk in softened gelatin. Cook over simmering water 3 to 5 minutes or until custard reaches 160°. Remove from heat; add 1 tablespoon butter, stirring gently until butter melts. Cool filling to room temperature.

Pour filling into prepared crust. Gently cover with plastic wrap, pressing directly on surface of filling. Chill pie at least 4 hours or until firm.

Sprinkle nutmeg and powdered sugar over pie before serving. Serve with dollops of whipped cream and more nutmeg, if desired. Store pie in refrigerator. Yield: 1 (9") pie.

**Note**: The chocolate layer will harden as the pie chills in the refrigerator. Use a sharp knife and gentle pressure to slice pie.

*Eggnog Pie*

This dessert's like a "black bottom" eggnog pie.

# Hot Fudge Cheesecake

*This chocoholic's dessert develops a brownielike top as it bakes. Serve leftover Hot Fudge Sauce over ice cream or pound cake or as fondue.*

Prep: 28 min.   Cook: 1hr., 8 min.   Other: 30 min.

| | |
|---|---|
| 1 | cup crushed saltine crackers |
| ½ | cup finely chopped walnuts |
| 6 | tablespoons butter or margarine, melted |
| 3 | tablespoons sugar |
| 6 | (1-ounce) semisweet chocolate squares |
| ¾ | cup butter or margarine |
| 1 | (8-ounce) package cream cheese, softened |
| ¾ | cup sugar |
| 3 | large eggs |

Hot Fudge Sauce
Garnish: walnut halves

Combine first 4 ingredients; stir well. Firmly press onto bottom and 2½" up sides of a lightly greased 7" springform pan. Bake at 350° for 8 minutes. Remove to a wire rack; let cool. Reduce oven temperature to 300°.

Combine chocolate squares and ¾ cup butter in a heavy saucepan. Cook over medium-low heat until mixture is melted and smooth, stirring often. Remove from heat, and let cool.

Hot Fudge Cheesecake

Beat cream cheese at medium speed with an electric mixer until creamy. Add ¾ cup sugar; beat well. Add eggs, 1 at a time, beating after each addition. Stir in cooled chocolate mixture. Pour into prepared crust.

Bake at 300° for 50 minutes to 1 hour or until almost set. Turn oven off. Let cheesecake cool in oven 30 minutes. Remove to a wire rack; let cool to room temperature.

Remove sides of pan. Serve cheesecake with Hot Fudge Sauce. Garnish, if desired. Yield: 8 to 10 servings.

## Hot Fudge Sauce

Prep: 5 min.   Cook: 7 min.

| | |
|---|---|
| 1 | (12-ounce) package semisweet chocolate morsels |
| 1 | cup half-and-half |
| 1 | tablespoon butter or margarine |
| 1 | teaspoon vanilla extract |

Combine chocolate morsels and half-and-half in a heavy saucepan. Cook over medium heat until chocolate melts and mixture is smooth, stirring frequently. Remove from heat; stir in butter and vanilla. Serve warm. Yield: 2 cups.

*make ahead*

## Frozen Pistachio Cheesecake

*No cracks to worry about with this luscious cheesecake; it's frozen, not baked.*

Prep: 30 min.   Cook: 12 min.   Other: 6 hr.

| | |
|---|---|
| 1 | cup pistachio nuts |
| 1 | cup sugar cookie crumbs (16 cookies; we tested with Pepperidge Farm Bordeaux cookies) |
| 3 | tablespoons granulated sugar |
| ⅓ | cup butter or margarine, melted |
| ⅔ | cup whipping cream |
| 12 | ounces white chocolate, finely chopped |
| 4 | (8-ounce) packages cream cheese, softened |
| ½ | cup butter or margarine, softened |
| ⅔ | cup sifted powdered sugar |
| 2 | teaspoons vanilla extract |

Garnish: additional pistachio nuts

Position knife blade in food processor bowl; add 1 cup pistachio nuts. Process until chopped. Add cookie crumbs, 3 tablespoons sugar, and melted butter. Pulse 4 or 5 times or until blended. Press crumb mixture onto bottom and 1½" up

*Frozen Pistachio Cheesecake*

sides of a lightly greased 9" springform pan. Bake crust at 350° for 12 minutes or until lightly browned. Cool completely on a wire rack.

Bring whipping cream to a simmer in a heavy saucepan over medium heat. Remove from heat, and add chopped white chocolate. Let stand 2 to 3 minutes. Stir gently with a rubber spatula until smooth.

Beat cream cheese and softened butter at medium speed with an electric mixer until creamy. Add powdered sugar,

and beat until light and fluffy. Add melted white chocolate mixture and vanilla; beat 3 minutes or until very smooth. Pour batter into prepared crust. Cover and freeze until firm or up to 1 week.

Let stand at room temperature about 30 minutes before serving or until easy to slice. Remove sides of pan. Garnish cheesecake, if desired. Cut frozen cheesecake with a sharp knife, dipping knife in hot water and wiping it dry between each slice. Yield: 10 to 12 servings.

*Double Chocolate Espresso Brownies*

Wow your holiday dinner guests with a
**tower of brownie** cutouts. Drizzle with
fudge sauce, and use tongs for serving.

*make ahead . editor's favorite*

## Double Chocolate Espresso Brownies

*Savor the combination of coffee and chocolate in these luscious brownies.*

Prep: 40 min.   Cook: 50 min.   Other: 2 hr.

1¼ cups all-purpose flour
¼  teaspoon baking soda
⅛  teaspoon baking powder
⅛  teaspoon salt
14  (1-ounce) semisweet chocolate squares, finely chopped
1   cup sugar
½   cup butter or margarine
¼   cup light corn syrup
¼   cup brewed espresso or French roast coffee
3   large eggs
1   tablespoon vanilla extract
1   cup coarsely chopped walnuts
6   ounces premium Swiss dark chocolate or milk chocolate, coarsely chopped

Coat a 13" x 9" pan with cooking spray. Line pan with aluminum foil, allowing ends to hang over short sides of pan. Tuck overlapping ends under rim on short sides. Coat foil with cooking spray; set pan aside.

Combine flour and next 3 ingredients in a small bowl. Place chopped semisweet chocolate in a large bowl; set bowls aside.

Combine sugar and next 3 ingredients in a saucepan. Cook over medium heat, stirring constantly, until sugar and butter melt and mixture comes to a rolling boil. Remove from heat, and pour over chopped chocolate in bowl; let stand 2 minutes (do not stir).

Beat at low speed with an electric mixer until chocolate melts and mixture is smooth. Add eggs, 1 at a time, beating well after each addition. Add flour mixture; beat at medium speed until well blended. Stir in vanilla, walnuts, and dark chocolate.

Spoon batter into prepared pan, spreading evenly.

Bake at 325° for 38 to 40 minutes. Cool completely in pan on a wire rack. Cover and chill at least 2 hours.

Carefully invert brownies from pan, using overlapping foil as handles; remove foil. Invert brownies again onto a cutting board; cut into squares or circles. (We used a 2½" round cutter. There'll be some fudgy scraps left for nibbling or topping with ice cream.) Yield: 4 dozen.

*editor's favorite*

## White Chocolate, Peanut, and Caramel Candy Cookies

*These yummy drop cookies have more than the typical amount of chunks of candy and nuts. For this recipe, chilling the dough twice really helps cookies hold a plump shape during baking.*

Prep: 41 min.   Cook: 11 min. per batch

1   cup butter, softened
1   cup granulated sugar
1   cup firmly packed light brown sugar
2   large eggs
1   teaspoon vanilla extract
2½  cups uncooked regular oats
2   cups all-purpose flour
1   teaspoon baking powder
½   teaspoon baking soda
½   teaspoon salt
3   (1.7-ounce) packages chocolate-covered caramel candies, chilled and chopped (we tested with Rolo)
2   (4-ounce) white chocolate bars, chopped (we tested with Ghirardelli)
1½  cups unsalted peanuts, chopped

Beat butter at medium speed with an electric mixer until creamy; add sugars, beating well. Add eggs and vanilla, beating until blended.

Process oats in a blender or food processor until finely ground. Combine oats, flour, and next 3 ingredients; add to butter mixture, beating well. Stir in chopped candy, white chocolate, and peanuts. Chill dough 1 hour, if desired.

Shape dough into 1½" balls, and place on lightly greased or parchment paper-lined baking sheets. Chill briefly, if desired. Bake at 375° for 10 to 11 minutes or until lightly browned. Cool 1 minute on baking sheets. Remove to wire racks to cool. Yield: 5½ dozen.

*Butter-Nut Truffles*

chute until mixture is smooth, stopping to scrape down sides. Add butter and nut flavoring; process until blended. Transfer mixture to a bowl; stir in chopped candy bars. Cover and chill 30 minutes.

Shape chocolate mixture into 1" balls; roll in finely crushed candy bars. Store truffles in refrigerator up to 1 week. Let stand at room temperature briefly before serving. Yield: about 2½ dozen.

*editor's favorite . make ahead . gift idea*

## Pecan Biscotti

*Cornmeal adds an unusual twist to these crunchy cookies.*

Prep: 23 min.   Cook: 39 min.   Other: 10 min.

1¾ cups all-purpose flour
½ cup yellow cornmeal
1¼ teaspoons baking powder
¼ teaspoon salt
1 cup finely chopped pecans, toasted
2 large eggs, lightly beaten
¾ cup sugar
½ cup vegetable oil
¼ teaspoon almond extract or vanilla extract

Combine first 5 ingredients in a large bowl.

Stir together eggs and remaining 3 ingredients; gradually add to flour mixture, stirring just until dry ingredients are moistened.

Divide dough in half. With lightly floured hands, shape each portion into a 12" x 2" log. Place logs 3" apart on a lightly greased baking sheet.

Bake at 350° for 25 minutes. Cool logs on baking sheet 10 minutes.

Cut each log diagonally into ¾"-thick slices with a serrated knife, using a gentle sawing motion. Return slices, cut side down, to baking sheet.

Bake at 350° for 7 minutes. Turn biscotti over, and bake 7 more minutes. Remove to wire racks to cool completely. Yield: 2½ dozen.

*make ahead . editor's favorite . gift idea*

## Butter-Nut Truffles

*You'll recognize a crispy, chocolaty candy bar in the filling and coating for these bittersweet truffles.*

Prep: 44 min.   Other: 30 min.

5 (2.1-ounce) chocolate-covered crispy peanut-buttery candy bars, frozen (we tested with Butterfinger)
2 (4-ounce) bittersweet chocolate baking bars, broken into pieces (we tested with Ghirardelli)
3 tablespoons whipping cream
3 tablespoons butter or margarine
½ teaspoon butter and nut flavoring

Break 2 candy bars into pieces. Process candy bar pieces in a food processor until finely crushed. Place on a shallow plate; set aside. Chop remaining 3 candy bars; set aside.

Place bittersweet chocolate in food processor bowl, and pulse until finely chopped.

Combine whipping cream and butter in a 1-cup glass measuring cup; microwave on HIGH 1 minute or until butter is melted and cream begins to boil. With processor running, slowly pour hot cream and butter through food

*Apple-Berry Cobbler with*
*Vanilla Bean Hard Sauce*

198

## Apple-Berry Cobbler with Vanilla Bean Hard Sauce

*A combination of apple varieties gives this cobbler depth of flavor.*

Prep: 17 min.   Cook: 50 min.

4   baking apples (about 1¾ pounds), peeled, cored, and sliced (we tested with Braeburn and Granny Smith apples)
2   cups fresh or frozen cranberries, partially thawed
1   cup firmly packed light brown sugar
½   teaspoon ground cinnamon
2   teaspoons cornstarch
¼   cup water
1   cup all-purpose flour
½   cup toasted wheat germ
1   teaspoon baking powder
¼   teaspoon salt
½   cup butter or margarine, softened
½   cup granulated sugar
1½  tablespoons milk
1   large egg
1   teaspoon vanilla extract
Vanilla Bean Hard Sauce

Toss together first 4 ingredients in large bowl. Combine cornstarch and water; stir into apple-cranberry mixture. Spoon apple-cranberry mixture into a greased 11" x 7" baking dish. Cover and set aside.

Combine flour and next 3 ingredients; set aside.

Beat butter at medium speed with an electric mixer until creamy. Gradually add ½ cup sugar, beating well. Add milk, egg, and vanilla, beating well. Stir in flour mixture.

Drop batter by spoonfuls over apple-cranberry mixture. Bake, uncovered, at 350° for 50 minutes or until golden and bubbly. Serve hot with Vanilla Bean Hard Sauce or vanilla ice cream. Yield: 8 servings.

## Vanilla Bean Hard Sauce

Prep: 8 min.

1   vanilla bean, split lengthwise
1   cup butter, softened
2   cups sifted powdered sugar

Scrape seeds from vanilla bean into mixing bowl with butter. Beat butter at medium speed with electric mixer until creamy. Gradually add sugar, beating well. Cover and chill until ready to serve. Soften slightly before serving. Yield: 1⅔ cups.

**Note:** One 6" vanilla bean equals about 1 tablespoon vanilla extract if you want to substitute extract.

Vanilla bean gets star billing in this speckled hard sauce.

*Beef Tenderloin with Shallot Sauce*

## Beef Tenderloin with Shallot Sauce

*Marsala wine and charred shallots impart a rich and smoky essence to this tenderloin's deep brown sauce.*

Prep: 25 min.   Cook: 57 min.

1    pound shallots, peeled and halved lengthwise
2    tablespoons olive oil
¾    teaspoon salt
½    teaspoon pepper
1    tablespoon salt
1½   teaspoons onion powder
1½   teaspoons garlic powder
1½   teaspoons pepper
1½   teaspoons chopped fresh thyme or ½ teaspoon
       dried thyme
1    (8-pound) beef tenderloin, trimmed (see Note)
¼    cup olive oil
3    cups beef broth
1    cup dry Marsala wine
2    tablespoons all-purpose flour
3    tablespoons water
3    tablespoons butter or margarine
¼    teaspoon pepper
Garnish: fresh thyme

Toss shallots and 2 tablespoons oil in a bowl; stir in ¾ teaspoon salt and ½ teaspoon pepper. Set aside.

Stir together 1 tablespoon salt and next 4 ingredients. Rub tenderloin with ¼ cup olive oil; sprinkle seasonings over top and sides of tenderloin, pressing gently with fingers. Place tenderloin in a large lightly greased roasting pan; arrange shallots around tenderloin.

Bake, uncovered, at 500° for 25 minutes. Reduce oven temperature to 375°, and bake 15 to 20 minutes or until a meat thermometer inserted into thickest part of tenderloin registers 145° (medium-rare) or 160° (medium).

Meanwhile, stir together beef broth and Marsala in a large skillet. Bring to a boil; boil 8 minutes or until liquid is reduced to 2 cups.

Remove tenderloin to a serving platter, and cover with aluminum foil; reserve shallots and drippings in pan. Add broth reduction to pan, and place over medium heat on cooktop, stirring to loosen particles from bottom of pan.

Whisk together flour and water until smooth; stir into sauce in roasting pan. Cook over medium heat 3 minutes, or until sauce is slightly thickened, stirring constantly. Add

butter, stirring just until melted. Stir in ¼ teaspoon pepper. Thinly slice tenderloin, and serve with sauce. Garnish, if desired. Yield: 16 servings.

**Note:** Find beef tenderloin sealed in plastic in the meat section of your supermarket. Once you trim the tenderloin you should yield about 6 pounds of meat. To save time, ask your butcher to trim it for you.

## Tawny Baked Ham

*A smoky, sweet aroma will fill your kitchen as this big ham bakes.*

Prep: 15 min.   Cook: 2½ hr.   Other: 10 min.

1    (19-pound) smoked, fully cooked whole ham
35   whole cloves
⅓    cup Dijon mustard
1    cup firmly packed light brown sugar
2    cups apple cider
2    cups pitted whole dates
2    cups dried figs, stems removed
2    cups pitted prunes
2    cups tawny port wine
Garnishes: kumquats, dried figs, apples

Remove and discard skin from ham. Make ⅛"-deep cuts in fat on ham in a diamond design. Using a metal skewer, make a hole in center of each diamond. Insert a clove into each hole. Brush mustard over top and sides of ham. Coat ham with brown sugar, pressing into mustard, if necessary.

Place ham, fat side up, in a lightly greased large shallow roasting pan. Insert a meat thermometer, making sure it does not touch fat or bone. Pour apple cider into pan.

Bake, uncovered, at 350° for 2 hours, basting often with apple cider.

Combine dates and next 3 ingredients; pour into pan with ham. Bake 30 minutes or until meat thermometer registers 140°, basting often with mixture in pan; cover ham with aluminum foil, if necessary, to prevent burning.

Transfer ham to a serving platter; let stand 10 minutes before slicing. Remove fruit from pan, using a slotted spoon.

Pour pan drippings into a large saucepan. Strain fat, if desired. Cook over medium-high heat 5 minutes or until reduced by half. Stir in reserved fruit. Serve sauce with ham. Garnish, if desired. Yield: 35 servings.

## Seasoned Roast Turkey

*Nine spices season this bird that yields drippings for some dynamite gravy.*

Prep: 18 min.   Cook: 3½ hr.   Other: 15 min.

1   (12- to 14-pound) fresh or frozen turkey, thawed
1   tablespoon salt
2   teaspoons seasoned salt
1   teaspoon ground black pepper
1   teaspoon poultry seasoning
1   teaspoon garlic powder
1   teaspoon paprika
1   teaspoon ground red pepper
1   teaspoon dried basil
½   teaspoon ground ginger
2   tablespoons butter or margarine, softened
1   cup water
Giblet Gravy
Garnishes: red grapes, Seckel pears

Remove giblets and neck from turkey; reserve for making Giblet Gravy, if desired. Rinse turkey with cold water; pat dry. Place turkey, breast side up, in a lightly greased broiler pan or roasting pan.

Combine salt and next 8 ingredients. Using fingers, carefully loosen skin from turkey at neck area, working down to breast and thigh area. Rub about one-third of seasonings under skin. Rub skin with softened butter; rub with remaining seasonings. Tie legs together with heavy string, or tuck under flap of skin. Lift wing tips up and over back; tuck under turkey.

Add water to pan. Cover turkey with aluminum foil. Bake at 325° for 3 to 3½ hours or until a meat thermometer inserted into meaty part of thigh registers 180°, uncovering turkey after 2 hours. Transfer turkey to a serving platter, reserving pan drippings for gravy. Let turkey stand 15 minutes before carving. Garnish, if desired. Serve with Giblet Gravy. Yield: 12 to 14 servings.

**Note:** Remember to allow about 3 days for a 12- to 14-pound frozen turkey to thaw in the refrigerator. And be sure to hunt down your carving set well before Christmas day. Sharpen carving knife, if needed.

## Giblet Gravy

*A long-simmering broth and pan drippings contribute rich flavor to this abundant gravy that's not overly thick.*

Prep: 5 min.   Cook: 2 hr., 10 min.

Neck and giblets reserved from turkey
4   cups water
1   celery rib with leaves, cut into pieces
1   medium onion, quartered
½   cup all-purpose flour
½   cup water
½   teaspoon salt
1   teaspoon pepper

Combine first 4 ingredients in a large saucepan. Bring to a boil; cover, reduce heat, and simmer 2 hours, removing liver after 20 minutes to prevent overcooking. Remove from heat. Pour broth through a wire-mesh strainer into a bowl. Remove neck meat from bone; chop and set aside. Chop remaining giblets, and set aside.

Stir 3½ cups broth into reserved turkey drippings in pan that turkey roasted in, or in a large saucepan. Bring to a boil. Combine flour and ½ cup water, stirring until smooth; gradually whisk into boiling broth. Add salt and pepper. Reduce heat to medium, and cook, whisking constantly, 5 minutes or until thickened. Stir in chopped neck meat and giblets; cook until thoroughly heated. Yield: 6 cups.

Carving the holiday bird is a rite of passage.

## Leslie's Favorite Chicken-and-Wild Rice Casserole

*Southern Living reader Leslie Flemister declares this dish perfect for a big family get-together. Make and freeze the casserole ahead, or make two small casseroles.*

Prep: 57 min.   Cook: 50 min.

2   (6.2-ounce) packages fast-cooking long-grain and wild rice mix
¼   cup butter or margarine
4   celery ribs, chopped
2   medium onions, chopped
2   (8-ounce) cans sliced water chestnuts, drained
5   cups chopped cooked chicken
4   cups (1 pound) shredded Cheddar cheese, divided
2   (10¾-ounce) cans cream of mushroom soup, undiluted
1   (16-ounce) container sour cream
1   cup milk
½   teaspoon salt
½   teaspoon pepper
2   cups soft breadcrumbs (homemade)
1   (2.25-ounce) package sliced almonds, toasted

Prepare rice mixes according to package directions.

Meanwhile, melt butter in a large skillet over medium heat; add celery and onion. Sauté 10 minutes or until tender.

Combine water chestnuts, cooked rice, celery and onion, chicken, 3 cups cheese, and next 5 ingredients in a very large bowl.

Spoon mixture into a lightly greased 15" x 10" baking dish or a 4-quart baking dish. Top casserole with breadcrumbs. Bake, uncovered, at 350° for 35 minutes. Sprinkle with remaining 1 cup cheese and almonds; bake 5 more minutes. Yield: 10 to 12 servings.

**Note:** You can divide this casserole evenly between 2 (11" x 7") baking dishes. Bake as directed above, or freeze casserole up to 1 month. Remove from freezer, and let stand at room temperature 1 hour. Bake, covered, at 350° for 30 minutes. Uncover casserole, and bake 55 more minutes. Sprinkle with remaining 1 cup cheese and almonds; bake 5 more minutes.

## Beet Salad with Curried Walnuts

*Roasted beets are the heart of this pretty salad, and curried nuts make a great topping. Prepare the walnuts ahead, and store them in an airtight container.*

Prep: 22 min.   Cook: 1 hr., 25 min.   Other: 1 hr.

1¼   pounds fresh beets (about 4 medium or 2 large)
1   tablespoon olive oil
2   shallots, minced
¼   cup mirin (rice wine)
2   tablespoons chopped fresh mint
3   tablespoons fresh lemon juice
½   teaspoon salt
1   tablespoon butter or margarine
1   tablespoon sugar
1   tablespoon water
1   teaspoon curry powder
¼   teaspoon salt
1   cup walnut halves
3   cups arugula, watercress, or other greens
1   tablespoon olive oil

Trim beets, leaving roots and 1" stems. Scrub beets with a vegetable brush. Drizzle beets with 1 tablespoon olive oil. Place beets in a small roasting pan or cast-iron skillet.

Roast at 425° for 1 hour and 15 to 25 minutes or until tender. Cool beets slightly; trim ends, and rub off skins. Cut beets into 1" chunks.

Combine shallot and next 4 ingredients in a large bowl; add beets, and toss well. Cover and chill 1 hour.

Melt butter in a skillet over medium heat. Add sugar and next 3 ingredients, stirring well to dissolve sugar. Add walnuts, stirring well to coat. Remove from heat.

Spread walnuts in a single layer on a lightly greased jelly-roll pan. Bake at 325° for 15 minutes, stirring twice. Toss well to coat. Cool completely.

Toss arugula and 1 tablespoon olive oil. Divide arugula evenly among 6 salad plates; top evenly with beet salad and curried walnuts. Yield: 6 servings.

**Fix it Faster:** Forego the roasted beets and use canned or jarred beets.

Sweet Potato-Peanut Soup with Ham Croutons

Process potato mixture, in batches, in a food processor or blender until smooth. Return potato mixture to Dutch oven; stir in peanut butter. Cook over medium-low heat until soup is smooth, stirring often. Stir in whipping cream, salt, and pepper; cook until thoroughly heated.

To serve, ladle soup into individual bowls. Top each serving with ham. Garnish, if desired. Yield: 10 cups.

*editor's favorite • make ahead*

## Roasted Sweet Potato Salad

Prep: 18 min.   Cook: 45 min.

4    large sweet potatoes, peeled and cubed
2    tablespoons olive oil, divided
¼    cup honey
3    tablespoons white wine vinegar
2    tablespoons chopped fresh rosemary
½    teaspoon salt
½    teaspoon freshly ground pepper
2    garlic cloves, minced
Garnish: fresh rosemary

Coat a large roasting pan with cooking spray; toss together sweet potato and 1 tablespoon oil in pan.

Bake, uncovered, at 450° for 40 to 45 minutes or until sweet potato is tender and roasted, stirring after 30 minutes.

Whisk together remaining 1 tablespoon oil, honey, and next 5 ingredients in a serving bowl. Add warm potato, and toss gently. Cool. Garnish, if desired. Yield: 6 to 8 servings.

*editor's favorite*

## Sweet Potato-Peanut Soup with Ham Croutons

*Peanut flavor in this thick, rich appetizer soup comes from creamy peanut butter. The crisp ham croutons are addictive.*

Prep: 23 min.   Cook: 45 min.

¼    cup butter or margarine
1    medium onion, chopped
¾    cup chopped celery
2    garlic cloves, chopped
6    cups chicken broth
3    pounds sweet potatoes, peeled and coarsely chopped
1    tablespoon chopped fresh rosemary
2    cups cubed cooked ham
⅔    cup creamy peanut butter
1    cup whipping cream
1    teaspoon salt
¼    teaspoon freshly ground pepper
Garnish: fresh rosemary sprigs

Melt butter in a Dutch oven over medium heat; add onion, celery, and garlic, and sauté 10 minutes or until tender. Add broth, potato, and chopped rosemary. Bring to a boil; cover, reduce heat, and simmer 25 minutes or until potato is very tender.

Meanwhile, heat a large nonstick skillet over medium-high heat. Add ham, and cook until browned and crisp on all sides. Remove from heat; set aside.

Roasted Sweet Potato Salad

Grits Dressing

Spoon grits into a greased 13" x 9" baking dish. Cover and chill until firm. Unmold onto a large cutting board, sliding knife or spatula under grits to loosen them from dish. Cut grits into ¾" cubes. Place in a single layer on a large greased rimmed baking sheet or jellyroll pan.

Bake at 450° for 20 minutes; turn grits, and bake 10 to 12 more minutes or until crisp and browned.

Meanwhile, cook sausage in a large skillet, stirring until it crumbles and is no longer pink; drain.

Melt butter in a large skillet over medium heat; add celery, garlic, and onion. Sauté 5 minutes or until tender. Stir together onion mixture, sausage, and grits croutons, tossing gently. Drizzle egg over mixture; add parsley, stirring gently. Spoon dressing loosely into a greased 11" x 7" baking dish.

Bake, uncovered, at 350° for 35 to 45 minutes or until browned. Yield: 8 servings.

*editor's favorite*

## Green Peas and Baby Limas with Pine Nuts

*Fresh rosemary and pine nuts sautéed in butter give these green veggies great flavor.*

Prep: 9 min.    Cook: 28 min.

1   (14-ounce) can chicken broth
1   (10-ounce) package frozen baby lima beans
4½  cups frozen petite green peas (1½ [16-ounce] packages)
½   teaspoon sugar
¾   cup pine nuts
2   tablespoons butter or margarine, melted
3   green onions, chopped
1   tablespoon chopped fresh rosemary
½   teaspoon salt
¼   teaspoon pepper
3   tablespoons butter or margarine

Bring broth to a boil in a large saucepan; add lima beans. Return to a boil; cover, reduce heat, and simmer 15 minutes or until tender. Stir in peas and ½ teaspoon sugar; cook 2 minutes. Drain.

Sauté pine nuts in 2 tablespoons melted butter in a large skillet over medium heat 2 to 3 minutes or until golden. Add pine nuts to peas and beans; stir in green onions and next 3 ingredients. Cook 1 minute or until thoroughly heated. Stir in 3 tablespoons butter until melted. Yield: 12 servings.

*editor's favorite • make ahead*

## Grits Dressing

*This unique Southern dressing sports crusty grits croutons and spicy sausage. Serve it for Sunday brunch or Christmas dinner. Make the croutons and brown the sausage a day in advance.*

Prep: 20 min.   Cook: 1 hr., 20 min.   Other: 20 min.

3   (10½-ounce) cans condensed chicken broth, undiluted
1¼  cups uncooked quick-cooking grits
1   cup freshly grated Parmesan cheese
1   pound ground hot pork sausage
⅓   cup butter or margarine
5   celery ribs with leaves, finely chopped
4   garlic cloves, minced (about 1 tablespoon)
1   large onion, chopped
1   large egg, lightly beaten
½   cup chopped fresh flat-leaf parsley

Bring broth to a boil in a large saucepan. Stir in grits, and return to a boil. Cover, reduce heat, and simmer 7 minutes or until grits are thickened, stirring twice. Stir in cheese. Remove from heat.

# Appetizers with Appeal

*Each of these hors d'oeuvres is either
make ahead or quick & easy—or both.*

*Asian Curry Dip*

## Asian Curry Dip

*This spicy dip is great served with store-bought sweet potato chips, raw vegetables such as sugar snap peas, or boiled shrimp.*

Prep: 6 min.   Other: 30 min.

½   cup sour cream
2   tablespoons seasoned rice vinegar
1   tablespoon soy sauce
1   tablespoon honey
1   teaspoon curry powder
1   teaspoon grated fresh ginger
1   teaspoon dark sesame oil
¼   teaspoon ground red pepper

Whisk together all ingredients in a small bowl. Cover and chill at least 30 minutes. Yield: ¾ cup.

**Note:** We tested with Terra exotic vegetable chips as dippers.

## Smoked Salmon Spread

*Serve this creamy spread with bagel chips or endive leaves.*

Prep: 15 min.   Other: 1 hr.

2   (8-ounce) packages cream cheese, softened
2   (4-ounce) packages smoked salmon, coarsely chopped
⅔   cup chopped red onion
2   tablespoons chopped fresh dill or 2 teaspoons dried dill
1½ to 2 teaspoons freshly ground pepper
½   teaspoon grated lemon rind
1   tablespoon caper juice (from a jar of capers) or fresh lemon juice
Garnish: finely chopped red onion
Capers

Process cream cheese and salmon in a food processor until smooth, stopping to scrape down sides. Add ⅔ cup red onion and next 4 ingredients; process just until combined, stopping to scrape down sides. Transfer spread to a bowl. Cover and chill at least 1 hour. Garnish, if desired. Serve capers as an accompaniment. Yield: 3⅓ cups.

## Reuben Cheese Ball

*This cheese ball combines the flavors of a Reuben sandwich into the perfect party appetizer. Make the cheese mixture ahead, and roll in breadcrumbs just before serving. Spread leftovers on a sandwich.*

Prep: 45 min.   Cook: 11 min.   Other: 1 hr.

1   (8-ounce) package cream cheese, softened
⅓   cup sour cream
2   cups (8 ounces) shredded Swiss cheese
1   cup (4 ounces) shredded extra-sharp Cheddar cheese (do not use preshredded)
1   cup chopped deli corned beef (6 ounces sliced)
¼   cup chopped sauerkraut, drained and squeezed dry
1   tablespoon spicy brown mustard
1   teaspoon caraway seeds, crushed
2   (1-pound) loaves party pumpernickel or rye bread
1   teaspoon butter or margarine, melted
¼   cup chopped fresh Italian parsley

Combine cream cheese and sour cream in a large bowl; beat at medium speed with an electric mixer until smooth. Add Swiss cheese and next 5 ingredients; beat at low speed until blended. Cover and chill 1 hour.

Process enough bread slices (about 3 or 4) to make ½ cup crumbs. Combine crumbs and melted butter; spread crumbs on a jelly-roll pan. Bake at 350° for 5 to 6 minutes or until toasted. Cool completely. Combine toasted breadcrumbs and chopped parsley.

Shape chilled cheese mixture into a ball; roll in breadcrumbs and parsley. Cover cheese ball, and chill briefly until ready to serve.

Arrange remaining bread slices on a baking sheet; bake at 350° for 5 minutes or until toasted. Serve with cheese ball. Yield: 20 servings.

## Marinated Goat Cheese and Pine Nuts

*This colorful make-ahead marinated cheese is ideal for entertaining.*

Prep: 13 min.   Other: 3 hr., 30 min.

1   (8-ounce) jar dried tomatoes in oil with herbs
Olive oil
2   garlic cloves, minced
2   tablespoons chopped fresh rosemary or
    2 tablespoons dried rosemary
1   teaspoon grated lemon rind
½   teaspoon dried crushed red pepper
½   teaspoon freshly ground black pepper
3   (3-ounce) packages goat cheese
¼   cup pine nuts, toasted

Drain tomatoes, reserving oil. Add enough olive oil to measure ¾ cup oil. Chop enough tomatoes to yield ½ cup; reserve remaining tomatoes for other uses.

Combine oil, tomatoes, garlic, and next 4 ingredients in a small bowl.

Using a sharp knife, carefully slice goat cheese in ¼"-thick slices. Place cheese in an 11" x 7" dish; pour marinade over cheese. Cover and chill several hours. Place marinated cheese on a serving platter; pour marinade over cheese, and sprinkle with pine nuts. Serve with crackers. Yield: 8 servings.

## Sugar and Spice Pecans

*Package these coated pecans in little gift bags, or set them out as hors d'oeuvres at a holiday gathering.*

Prep: 5 min.   Cook: 45 min.

1   cup sugar
2   teaspoons pumpkin pie spice
2   teaspoons grated orange rind
¼   teaspoon salt
2   egg whites
¼   cup butter, melted
4   cups pecan halves

Stir together first 4 ingredients.

Beat egg whites at high speed with an electric mixer until foamy. Gradually add sugar mixture, beating at high

*Sugar and Spice Pecans*

speed until soft peaks form. Fold in melted butter and pecan halves. Spread coated nuts in a single layer on a large jelly-roll pan lined with nonstick aluminum foil or parchment paper.

Bake at 250° for 45 minutes or until nuts are toasted, stirring every 15 minutes. Remove from oven; let cool completely on pan. Remove from pan. Store in an airtight container up to 2 weeks. Yield: 4 cups.

## Red Pepper-Ham Roll-Ups

*Get a jump on your holiday party food; make and freeze these rolls up to 1 month ahead. Slice frozen roll-ups, and let them thaw before serving.*

Prep: 20 min.   Other: 20 min.

1   (8-ounce) package cream cheese, softened
1   (3-ounce) package cream cheese, softened
2   garlic cloves, finely chopped
⅓   cup finely chopped walnuts, toasted
¼   cup pitted kalamata or pimiento-stuffed olives, chopped
¼   cup roasted red bell peppers from a jar, patted dry and chopped
¼   teaspoon pepper
8   (⅛"-thick) slices premium deli ham (we tested with Boar's Head Black Forest Ham)
54  pitted kalamata olives

Beat cream cheese at medium speed with an electric mixer until creamy; stir in garlic and next 4 ingredients.

Spread about 2 tablespoons cream cheese mixture over each ham slice. Roll up, jelly-roll fashion, starting with the long side. Place roll-ups, seam side down, on a baking sheet. Fill ends of rolls with remaining cream cheese mixture. Cover and freeze roll-ups 20 minutes.

Meanwhile, place olives on small wooden picks.

Using a sharp knife, slice each roll-up into 1" pieces; secure each with 1 olive pick. Cover and chill until ready to serve. Yield: about 4½ dozen.

*Pizza Bread*

## Pizza Bread

*Add your favorite toppings to these kid-friendly pizzas. We liked using both green and black olives.*

Prep: 7 min.   Cook: 15 min.

1   (16-ounce) package twin French bread loaves (we tested with Pepperidge Farm)
1   (8-ounce) package cream cheese, softened
2   tablespoons mayonnaise
1   teaspoon dried Italian seasoning
1   (3.5-ounce) package pepperoni slices, chopped (we tested with Hormel)
1   (2¼-ounce) can sliced ripe olives or ½ cup pimiento-stuffed olives, sliced, or both
1   cup (4 ounces) shredded mozzarella cheese

Slice bread loaves in half horizontally.

Combine cream cheese, mayonnaise, and Italian seasoning in a small bowl; stir well. Spread evenly over cut sides of bread; sprinkle evenly with pepperoni and olives. Top with cheese. Place on a baking sheet. Bake at 375° for 12 to 15 minutes or until lightly browned. Cut each loaf half into 12 slices. Yield: 4 dozen appetizers.

*Red Pepper-Ham Roll-Ups*

# Smoked Sausage Bundles

Prep: 15 min.   Cook: 19 min.

1   (16-ounce) package fully cooked smoked sausage
2   (17.3-ounce) packages frozen puff pastry sheets, thawed
½   cup honey mustard dressing (we tested with Naturally Fresh)
1   large egg, lightly beaten
1   tablespoon water
Additional honey mustard dressing

Slice sausage into 36 slices; set aside.

Cut pastry sheets into 36 (3") squares; spread center of each square with ½ teaspoon honey mustard dressing. Place 1 piece sausage on dressing. Bring edges of pastry together; press to seal. Place bundles on lightly greased baking sheets. Whisk together egg and water; brush over bundles.

Bake at 400° for 19 minutes or until golden. Remove from baking sheet to a serving platter. Serve with additional dressing, if desired. Yield: 3 dozen.

# Cheese-Jalapeño Jelly Thumbprints

*Adults will love this savory twist on the traditional thumbprint cookie.*

Prep: 39 min.   Cook: 14 min.   Other: 1 hr., 5 min.

1   (8-ounce) block sharp white Cheddar cheese, shredded
⅓   cup butter, softened
⅓   cup freshly grated Parmesan cheese
1   egg yolk
1¼  cups all-purpose flour
¼   teaspoon ground red pepper
¼   teaspoon salt
1   cup toasted pecan halves, finely ground
⅓   cup jalapeño pepper jelly

Process first 4 ingredients in a food processor until blended. Add flour, ground red pepper, and salt; process until dough forms a ball, stopping often to scrape down sides. Shape dough into a disc; cover and chill 1 hour.

Let dough stand at room temperature 5 minutes. Shape dough into 1" balls; roll in ground pecans.

Place balls 1" apart on ungreased baking sheets. Press thumb in center of each ball to make an indention.

Bake at 400° for 14 minutes or until browned. Immediately fill each center with a heaping ¼ teaspoon jelly, pressing gently into cookie with back of spoon. Remove from pans to wire racks; cool completely. Store in an airtight container between layers of wax paper up to 2 days. Yield: 3 dozen.

# Jalapeño-Sausage Cheese Squares

*These spicy bites are great for a brunch buffet.*

Prep: 8 min.   Cook: 42 min.   Other: 10 min.

1   pound hot or mild ground pork sausage
1   (12-ounce) jar pickled jalapeño slices, drained and patted dry
1½  (8-ounce) blocks Cheddar and Monterey Jack cheese, shredded
6   large eggs, lightly beaten
1   cup milk
1   teaspoon garlic powder
¼   teaspoon pepper

Cook sausage in a large skillet over medium-high heat, stirring until sausage crumbles and is no longer pink. Drain.

Place jalapeño slices in a lightly greased 13" x 9" baking dish. Top with sausage; sprinkle with cheese.

Whisk together eggs and next 3 ingredients. Pour over cheese.

Bake at 350° for 35 minutes or until set. Let stand 10 minutes. Cut into bite-size squares. Serve warm. Yield: about 4 dozen.

**Note:** To make this recipe ahead, bake as directed; let cool, cover, and chill up to 1 day. Reheat at 350° for 15 minutes; let stand briefly, and then cut into squares just before serving.

*Bacon-Wrapped Shrimp and Snow Peas*

*quick & easy*

# Bacon-Wrapped Shrimp and Snow Peas

*Leave the tails on the shrimp if you're entertaining.*

Prep: 18 min.   Cook: 12 min.   Other: 5 min.

1   tablespoon grated lime rind
2   tablespoons fresh lime juice
1   tablespoon dark sesame oil
1   teaspoon salt
½   to 1 teaspoon pepper
2   teaspoons hot sauce
12  jumbo shrimp, peeled (about ¾ pound)
12  fresh snow peas
12  fully cooked bacon slices (we tested with Armour Ready Crisp Bacon)

Toss together first 7 ingredients in a large bowl until shrimp are coated; let stand 5 minutes.

Trim ends of snow peas. Wrap each slice of bacon around 1 shrimp and 1 snow pea; secure with a wooden pick. Place shrimp on a lightly greased rack of a broiler pan. Repeat procedure with remaining shrimp, snow peas, and bacon.

Broil 3" from heat 12 minutes or until shrimp turn pink, turning after 6 minutes. Arrange appetizers on a serving platter. Serve hot. Yield: 6 appetizer servings.

**Note:** Use round rather than flat wooden picks; they're less likely to burn. Our secret to plump, pretty snow peas after baking is to first soak snow peas in a bowl of cold water 1 hour; then drain before skewering.

# For the Love of *Eggnog*

*The velvety smooth holiday drink becomes
a key ingredient in these recipes.*

*Hazelnut-Eggnog
Punch*

*editor's favorite*

# Hazelnut-Eggnog Punch

*Serve this as a luscious dessert drink.*

Prep: 7 min.   Other: 1 hr., 15 min.

2    cups milk
1    vanilla bean, split lengthwise
1    (3") cinnamon stick
6    cups refrigerated or canned eggnog
1½  cups Frangelico or other hazelnut liqueur
1    cup whipping cream, whipped
1    quart vanilla ice cream, softened
Grated nutmeg (optional)

Combine first 3 ingredients in a small saucepan; place over medium heat, and cook until hot (do not boil), stirring often. Remove from heat. Cover and let stand 30 minutes. Scrape vanilla bean seeds into milk mixture. Cover and chill. Discard vanilla bean and cinnamon stick.

Combine chilled milk mixture, eggnog, and Frangelico in a punch bowl; fold in whipped cream. Scoop ice cream into punch; stir gently. Sprinkle lightly with nutmeg, if desired. Yield: 15 cups.

*make ahead*

# Eggnog Panna Cotta

*Panna cotta is a light, silky smooth Italian custard.*
*This version gets a dark caramel glaze.*

Prep: 6 min.   Cook: 12 min.   Other: 8 hr.

3    cups refrigerated or canned eggnog
¼    teaspoon freshly grated nutmeg
1    envelope unflavored gelatin
¼    cup cold water
1    teaspoon clear vanilla extract
½    cup unsalted butter
½    cup firmly packed dark brown sugar
⅛    teaspoon salt
¼    cup dark rum

Coat 6 (4-ounce) ramekins or 6-ounce custard cups with vegetable cooking spray. Set aside.

Combine eggnog and nutmeg in a medium saucepan; bring to a simmer over medium heat, stirring often. Meanwhile, sprinkle gelatin over cold water in a large bowl; let stand 1 minute. Remove eggnog from heat; stir in vanilla.

## our test kitchens' eggnog tips

*After testing dozens of holiday recipes using canned and refrigerated eggnog, our staff decided we had definite opinions about the creamy drink as an ingredient. Here's our best advice this holiday season.*

**Freezing eggnog works like a charm.** Buy eggnog after Christmas when store owners are ready to restock. For eggnog that comes in a carton, freeze it in its original carton up to 1 year. When ready to use, thaw frozen eggnog in the refrigerator overnight, and shake it well before opening. Keep canned, unopened eggnog in a cool dark spot in the pantry up to 18 months.

**Eggnog as an ingredient gives great flavor to desserts.** In testing, we found that store-bought eggnog's slight cinnamon flavor and creamy texture add depth to a variety of desserts, especially ice cream. We don't recommend substituting low-fat refrigerated eggnog in any of these recipes.

**Refrigerated eggnog tastes best.** We prefer the refrigerated eggnog that comes in a carton versus canned eggnog (although canned tends to be more readily available). The refrigerated version has a richer consistency and more flecks of spice. We suggest using the refrigerated eggnog for many of the following recipes, but they'll work just fine if canned eggnog is what's available.

**Rich memories can linger.** Follow our freezing advice above to enjoy these eggnog recipes year-round and to keep the thoughts and tastes of Christmas alive throughout the year.

Gradually whisk hot eggnog mixture into softened gelatin, stirring until gelatin dissolves. Pour ½ cup custard mixture into each ramekin. Cover and chill 8 hours.

Melt butter in a small heavy saucepan over medium heat. Gradually add sugar and salt; cook 8 minutes or until sugar dissolves and mixture is smooth, whisking constantly. Remove from heat; whisk in rum. Cover and chill.

To serve, gently invert each panna cotta onto a dessert plate. Drizzle each dessert plate with chilled rum sauce. Serve immediately. Yield: 6 servings.

*Eggnog Fudge*

make ahead . gift idea

# Eggnog Fudge

*Candied cherries and toasted nuts flavor this creamy fudge.*

Prep: 13 min.   Cook: 19 min.   Other: 18 min.

2   cups sugar
1   cup refrigerated eggnog
2   tablespoons butter
2   tablespoons light corn syrup
¼   cup chopped pecans, toasted
¼   cup slivered almonds, toasted and chopped
½   cup chopped red candied cherries
1   teaspoon vanilla extract

Line an 8" x 4" loafpan with aluminum foil; butter foil, and set aside.

Combine first 4 ingredients in a 4-quart heavy saucepan. Cook over medium heat, stirring constantly, until mixture comes to a boil. Wash down crystals from sides of pan, using a pastry brush dipped in hot water. Insert a candy thermometer into eggnog mixture. Cook, stirring occasionally, until thermometer registers 238°. Remove from heat and cool, undisturbed, until temperature drops to 190° (15 to 18 minutes).

Stir in pecans and remaining 3 ingredients; beat with a wooden spoon until fudge thickens and just begins to lose its gloss (5 to 8 minutes). Pour candy into prepared pan. Cool completely; cut into squares. Yield: about 1½ pounds.

editor's favorite . make ahead

# Creamy Eggnog Ice Cream

Prep: 10 min.   Cook: 25 min.   Other: 2 hr., 50 min.

2     cups milk
1     vanilla bean, split lengthwise
8     egg yolks
1     cup sugar
1½   teaspoons ground cinnamon
½     teaspoon ground nutmeg
½     teaspoon salt
3     cups whipping cream
1     cup refrigerated eggnog

Cook milk in a heavy saucepan over medium heat, stirring often, just until bubbles appear; remove from heat. Add vanilla bean; cover and let stand 20 minutes. Remove vanilla bean from milk; using the tip of a small sharp knife, scrape vanilla bean seeds into milk. Discard vanilla bean pod.

Whisk together egg yolks and next 4 ingredients in a large bowl until thickened. Gradually whisk warm vanilla milk into yolk mixture; return to saucepan.

Cook over low heat, whisking constantly, 20 minutes or until a thermometer registers 160° and custard coats a spoon. Remove from heat; pour through a wire-mesh strainer into a bowl. Cool at room temperature about 30 minutes, stirring occasionally. Stir in whipping cream and eggnog; cover and chill 1 hour.

Pour custard mixture into freezer container of a 1-gallon hand-turned or electric freezer. Freeze according to manufacturer's instructions. Pack freezer with additional ice and rock salt; let stand 1 hour before serving. Yield: about 2 quarts.

*Creamy Eggnog Ice Cream*

# Belgian Waffles with Eggnog Butter and Orange Syrup

*Make these waffles ahead, and freeze them. Reheat in a toaster to recrisp them.*

Prep: 8 min.   Cook: 52 min.   Other: 8 hr.

*Belgian Waffles with Eggnog Butter and Orange Syrup*

2⅔ cups all-purpose flour
2    tablespoons sugar
1    teaspoon salt
1    (¼-ounce) envelope active dry yeast
1¾ cups milk
¼    cup water
¼    cup butter or margarine, softened
3    large eggs
Eggnog Butter
Orange Syrup

Stir together first 4 ingredients in a large bowl; set aside.

Combine milk, water, and butter in a 4-cup glass measuring cup; microwave on HIGH 1½ minutes or until mixture reaches 120° to 130°.

Add milk mixture to dry ingredients alternately with eggs, beating at medium speed with an electric mixer just until dry ingredients are blended. Cover and chill batter 8 hours.

Pour batter, 1 cup at a time, into a preheated, oiled waffle iron; cook until golden. Serve warm with Eggnog Butter and Orange Syrup. Yield: 16 (4") waffles.

## Eggnog Butter

*This flavored butter can be made ahead. Soften butter at room temperature before serving.*

Prep: 5 min.

1    cup butter, softened
½    cup sifted powdered sugar
½    teaspoon ground nutmeg
1    teaspoon rum extract
½    teaspoon vanilla extract

Beat butter at high speed with an electric mixer until creamy. Gradually add powdered sugar, beating well. Stir in nutmeg and extracts. Cover and chill. Yield: 1¼ cups.

## Orange Syrup

*Syrup can be made ahead and reheated in the microwave before serving.*

Prep: 1 min.   Cook: 5 min.

1    cup pure maple syrup
½    cup orange marmalade

Combine syrup and marmalade in a small saucepan over medium heat. Cook until mixture comes to a simmer and marmalade melts, about 5 minutes. Yield: 1½ cups.

**Note:** We tested with a Belgian Waffle iron. For each batch, we used 1 cup batter and cooked 4 (4") waffles.

**Fix it Faster:** Buy frozen waffles, and top them with the Eggnog Butter and Orange Syrup.

# Bread Pudding with White Chocolate-Brandied Eggnog Sauce

*Our staff declared this one of the best bread puddings around, mainly because of the yummy sauce.*

Prep: 16 min.   Cook: 1 hr., 5 min.   Other: 1 hr., 5 min.

1½ (1-pound) loaves cinnamon-raisin bread, cubed
½ cup chopped pecans, toasted
4 large eggs, lightly beaten
2 cups milk
2 cups whipping cream
½ cup granulated sugar
½ cup firmly packed light brown sugar
3 tablespoons butter or margarine, melted
1 teaspoon ground cinnamon
½ teaspoon ground nutmeg
1 teaspoon vanilla extract
White Chocolate-Brandied Eggnog Sauce

Arrange bread cubes in a lightly greased 13" x 9" baking dish; sprinkle pecans over bread cubes.

Whisk together eggs and next 8 ingredients. Pour egg mixture over bread cubes, pressing down cubes gently to absorb liquid. Cover and chill 1 hour.

Bake at 350° for 1 hour and 5 minutes or until a knife inserted in center comes out clean, shielding with aluminum foil after 30 minutes to prevent excessive browning. Let stand 5 minutes before serving. Serve warm with warm White Chocolate-Brandied Eggnog Sauce. Yield: 8 to 10 servings.

## White Chocolate-Brandied Eggnog Sauce

Prep: 2 min.   Cook: 8 min.

½ cup sugar
½ cup butter
½ cup refrigerated eggnog
½ cup whipping cream
1½ teaspoons cornstarch
¼ cup water
1 (4-ounce) white chocolate baking bar, chopped (we tested with Ghirardelli)
2 tablespoons brandy (optional)

Combine first 4 ingredients in a heavy saucepan; cook over low heat 5 minutes or until sugar dissolves and butter melts, stirring occasionally.

Combine cornstarch and water; stir into eggnog mixture. Bring to a boil; boil 1 minute, stirring constantly. Remove from heat. Add white chocolate, stirring until chocolate melts. Stir in brandy, if desired. Serve warm. Yield: 2¾ cups.

# Spiced Eggnog Pound Cake

*Cake flour gives this cake its light texture. For a splurge, serve cake with Creamy Eggnog Ice Cream (recipe on page 290).*

Prep: 25 min.   Cook: 55 min.   Other: 15 min.

1 cup butter, softened
3 cups granulated sugar
6 large eggs
3 cups sifted cake flour
¾ teaspoon baking powder
½ teaspoon salt
1 cup refrigerated or canned eggnog
2 teaspoons vanilla extract
2 tablespoons brandy (optional)
1 teaspoon ground cinnamon
¾ teaspoon freshly grated nutmeg
½ teaspoon ground allspice
¼ teaspoon ground cloves
Powdered sugar
1 cup sifted powdered sugar
2 tablespoons plus 1 teaspoon whipping cream

Generously grease and flour a 12-cup Bundt pan; set aside.

Beat butter at medium speed with an electric mixer about 2 minutes or until creamy. Gradually add granulated sugar, beating 5 to 7 minutes. Add eggs, 1 at a time, beating just until yellow disappears.

Combine flour, baking powder, and salt. Add to butter mixture alternately with 1 cup eggnog, beginning and ending with flour mixture. Beat at low speed just until blended after each addition. Stir in vanilla and, if desired, brandy.

Pour half of batter into prepared pan. Stir cinnamon and next 3 ingredients into remaining batter. Spoon spice batter over plain batter. Swirl batters together, using a knife.

Bake at 350° for 50 to 55 minutes or until a long wooden pick inserted in center comes out clean. Cool in pan on a wire rack 15 minutes. Remove from pan; cool on wire rack.

Place cake on a cake plate; dust with powdered sugar.

Combine 1 cup powdered sugar and whipping cream, stirring until smooth. Drizzle glaze over cake. Yield: 16 servings.

*Spiced Eggnog Pound Cake*

# Frozen White Chocolate Terrine with a Pistachio Crust

*Make this festive frozen dessert in a loafpan or individual muffin cups.*

Prep: 17 min.   Cook: 10 min.   Other: 8 hr., 10 min.

1    cup shelled pistachio nuts
¼    cup graham cracker crumbs
2    tablespoons butter or margarine, melted
1    tablespoon sugar
9    ounces white chocolate, chopped
1    cup refrigerated or canned eggnog
1    teaspoon clear vanilla extract
1½   teaspoons rum extract
1    cup whipping cream

Line an 8½" x 4½" loafpan with a smooth piece of foil; butter bottom of foil-lined pan.

Process first 4 ingredients in a food processor until blended; press crumb crust into bottom of prepared pan. Bake at 350° for 7 minutes. Cool completely on a wire rack.

Place chopped white chocolate in a metal bowl.

Bring eggnog to a simmer in a small saucepan over medium heat. Pour hot eggnog over chopped white chocolate, stirring gently until blended and smooth. Stir in extracts. Chill white chocolate mixture over a large bowl of ice water 10 minutes or until slightly chilled, stirring occasionally.

Beat whipping cream at high speed with an electric mixer until stiff peaks form. Gradually fold whipped cream into chilled white chocolate mixture; pour over crust in pan. Cover and freeze 8 hours or until firm.

To serve, invert frozen terrine onto a cutting board; carefully remove foil. Cut terrine into 1"-thick slices. Serve immediately. Yield: 8 servings.

**Mini White Chocolate Terrines:** Cut crust ingredients in half. Place foil baking cups in muffin pans; butter baking cups. Press 1 tablespoon pistachio crust mixture into bottom of each cup. Bake at 350° for 5 minutes. Cool completely. Fill each cup with ⅓ cup white chocolate filling. Cover and freeze as directed above. To serve, carefully remove foil lining from each terrine, and invert onto serving plates. Serve immediately. Yield: 1 dozen.

# Toasted Coconut-Eggnog Cheesecake

*Any type of rum can be substituted for dark rum in this recipe.*

Prep: 21 min.   Cook: 1 hr., 14 min.   Other: 8 hr.

1¼   cups sweetened flaked coconut
12   vanilla cream sandwich cookies, broken into pieces
     (we tested with Vienna Fingers)
½    cup chopped pecans, toasted
¼    cup butter or margarine, melted
4    (8-ounce) packages cream cheese, softened
1    cup sugar
½    cup refrigerated eggnog
1    tablespoon cornstarch
1    teaspoon ground cinnamon
¼    teaspoon ground nutmeg
2    tablespoons dark rum
4    large eggs
1    teaspoon vanilla extract
Garnishes: sweetened whipped cream, ground cinnamon

Bake 1¼ cups coconut in a shallow pan at 350°, stirring occasionally, 8 to 9 minutes or until toasted. Reserve ¼ cup for garnish.

Process cookies and pecans in a food processor until cookies are finely crushed. Add butter; pulse until crumbs are moistened. Add 1 cup toasted coconut; pulse just until combined. Press crumb mixture into bottom and 1" up sides of a 9" springform pan.

Bake at 350° for 10 minutes; let cool. Reduce oven temperature to 325°.

Meanwhile, beat cream cheese at medium speed with an electric mixer until creamy; gradually add sugar, beating well. Add eggnog and next 4 ingredients, beating just until combined. Add eggs, 1 at a time, beating just until yellow disappears. Stir in vanilla. (Do not overbeat.) Pour batter into baked crust.

Bake at 325° for 55 minutes or until set. Remove from oven, and immediately run a knife around edge of pan, releasing sides.

Cool completely in pan on a wire rack. Cover and chill 8 hours. Garnish, if desired. Sprinkle with reserved ¼ cup toasted coconut. Yield: 10 to 12 servings.

*Toasted Coconut-Eggnog Cheesecake*

## Eggnog Soufflés with Rum Crème Anglaise

*These soufflés can be frozen ahead and then placed in the oven during dinner. Rum Crème Anglaise is also good served with fruit or waffles.*

Prep: 19 min.   Cook: 43 min.   Other: 20 min.

1   tablespoon butter, softened
2   tablespoons granulated sugar
6   tablespoons butter
3   tablespoons all-purpose flour
½   teaspoon freshly grated nutmeg
¼   teaspoon ground cardamom
¾   cup half-and-half
½   cup granulated sugar
5   large eggs, separated
1   tablespoon vanilla extract
⅛   teaspoon salt
¼   teaspoon cream of tartar
Sifted powdered sugar
Rum Crème Anglaise

Butter bottom and sides of 6 (6-ounce) ramekins; sprinkle with 2 tablespoons sugar. Set aside.

Melt 6 tablespoons butter in a heavy saucepan over medium heat. Add flour, nutmeg, and cardamom, stirring until smooth. Cook 2 minutes, stirring constantly. Whisk in half-and-half and ½ cup granulated sugar; cook over medium heat 6 to 8 minutes, stirring constantly, until thickened. Remove from heat, and set aside.

Beat egg yolks at high speed with an electric mixer until thick and pale. Gradually stir about half of hot mixture into egg yolks. Add egg yolk mixture back to pan; cook over medium heat 2 minutes, stirring constantly, until thickened. Remove from heat; stir in vanilla. Set aside to cool 10 to 20 minutes.

Beat egg whites and salt in a large bowl at high speed until foamy. Add cream of tartar, beating until soft peaks form. Gradually fold beaten egg whites into custard mixture. Spoon into prepared ramekins, and place on a baking sheet. (Or cover and freeze soufflés up to 2 weeks.)

Bake at 350° for 30 minutes or until puffed and set. Sprinkle with powdered sugar; serve immediately with Rum Crème Anglaise. Yield: 6 servings.

**Note:** If freezing soufflés, let stand at room temperature 30 minutes before baking.

## Rum Crème Anglaise

Prep: 5 min.   Cook: 30 min.

2   cups half-and-half
½   vanilla bean, split lengthwise
5   egg yolks
½   cup sugar
2   tablespoons rum or spiced rum

Place half-and-half and vanilla bean in a heavy saucepan; bring just to a boil. Remove from heat; with the tip of a small sharp knife, scrape vanilla bean seeds into half-and-half, and discard pod.

Combine egg yolks and sugar in a large bowl; gradually whisk in hot half-and-half. Add yolk mixture back to pan, and cook, stirring constantly, until custard thickens and coats a spoon. Do not boil. Pour custard through a wire-mesh strainer into a bowl, and cool. Stir in rum. Cover and chill. Yield: 2 cups.

*Eggnog Soufflés with Rum Crème Anglaise*

*Cheesecake Swirl Bars*

## Cheesecake Swirl Bars

*Cheesecake brownies get a splash of rum flavor. Cut them into large bars for a special occasion splurge.*

Prep: 26 min.   Cook: 41 min.   Other: 1 hr.

55   vanilla wafers, crushed (2 cups)
6   tablespoons butter or margarine, melted
½   cup finely chopped pecans, toasted
2   (8-ounce) packages cream cheese, softened
½   cup sugar
1½   teaspoons rum extract
2   large eggs
¼   cup refrigerated eggnog
½   cup white chocolate morsels, melted
½   cup double chocolate morsels, melted (we tested with Ghirardelli), or regular semisweet morsels

Combine first 3 ingredients in a large bowl, stirring until blended. Press crumb mixture into bottom of a lightly greased 8" or 9" square pan. Bake at 350° for 8 minutes. Cool.

Beat cream cheese, sugar, and rum extract at medium speed with an electric mixer just until smooth. Add eggs, 1 at a time, beating just until blended. Pour 1½ cups cream cheese batter evenly over baked crust.

Stir eggnog into remaining batter. Divide batter in half; stir melted white chocolate into 1 portion. Spoon evenly over cream cheese batter. Stir melted semisweet chocolate into remaining batter. Drop spoonfuls of chocolate batter evenly over white chocolate layer; gently swirl batters with a knife.

Bake at 350° for 30 to 33 minutes or until almost set. Cool completely on a wire rack. Cover and chill at least 1 hour before serving. Cut into bars. Yield: 1 dozen.

*Croquembouche Christmas Tree*

Croquembouche (kroh-kuhm-BOOSH) is French for "crunch in the mouth." We've simplified this classic cream puff tree by using melted white chocolate as the "glue."

*make ahead . editor's favorite*

## Croquembouche Christmas Tree

*This is the ultimate grand dessert. Don't be intimidated by the length of the recipe; almost everything can be made in advance and assembled a few hours before serving.*

Prep: 1 hr., 6 min.  Cook: 41 min.  Other: 2 hr., 35 min.

Eggnog Pastry Cream
1½ cups water
¾ cup butter
1½ cups all-purpose flour
¼ teaspoon salt
6 large eggs
1 (9" or 12") white plastic craft foam cone
6 (4-ounce) packages white chocolate baking bars, coarsely chopped (we tested with Ghirardelli)
1 tablespoon plus 1 teaspoon shortening
Garnishes: silver and white edible glitter

Prepare Eggnog Pastry Cream; cover and chill.

Combine water and butter in a heavy saucepan; bring to a boil over medium-high heat. Add flour and salt all at once, stirring vigorously with a wooden spoon until mixture leaves sides of pan and forms a smooth ball. Remove from heat, and cool 5 minutes.

Add eggs, 1 at a time, beating well with a wooden spoon after each addition; then beat until dough is smooth.

Drop cream puff paste by rounded teaspoonfuls 2" apart onto ungreased baking sheets; then quickly smooth tops with the back of a spoon or wet fingers to round puffs.

Bake at 425° for 10 minutes. Reduce oven temperature to 400°, and switch positions of baking sheets. Bake 18 to 20 more minutes or until puffed and golden, switching position of baking sheets again halfway through baking. Turn off oven; let puffs stand in oven to dry 15 minutes. Remove puffs to wire racks to cool completely.

Pipe Eggnog Pastry Cream through side of each cream puff, using a pastry bag fitted with a long, narrow round tip. (We tested with a #10 round tip.)

Wrap cone with white parchment paper; secure paper onto cone with straight pins. Otherwise wrap cone in plastic wrap. Place cone on a large serving platter.

Melt chopped white chocolate bars and shortening in a heavy saucepan over low heat, stirring until smooth. Remove from heat.

Working with tongs, dip bottom of each cream puff, 1 at a time, into melted white chocolate. Starting at the base,

position enough cream puffs, side by side, on platter surrounding cone to form a ring. Add a second layer of cream puffs outside the first ring of puffs. Begin stacking rings of cream puffs, reducing the number on each layer so that it forms a pyramid (and hugs the cone). Reheat white chocolate over low heat, if necessary.

Drizzle any remaining white chocolate over finished tree. Sprinkle with edible glitter, if desired. Chill up to 2 hours before serving to set chocolate. Serve with small tongs. Yield: 85 cream puffs.

**Note:** The puffs can be baked a week in advance and frozen. To freeze, cool puffs completely on wire racks. Place in large zip-top freezer bags; seal tightly. Place bags in freezer. To recrisp puffs, thaw at room temperature. Place puffs on ungreased baking sheets. Bake at 400° for 5 minutes; cool completely before filling with Eggnog Pastry Cream.

**Fix it Faster:** If you don't have time to build this tree, just pile some puffs on individual dessert plates.

## Eggnog Pastry Cream

Prep: 4 min.  Cook: 42 min.  Other: 8 hr.

¾ cup all-purpose flour
3 cups refrigerated eggnog
7 egg yolks
1½ tablespoons butter, softened
1½ teaspoons rum extract
1½ teaspoons vanilla extract

Place flour in a heavy saucepan; gradually whisk in eggnog until blended and smooth. Add egg yolks, 1 at a time, whisking until just combined after each addition.

Cook over medium-low heat, stirring constantly, until thickened (about 42 minutes). Remove from heat; stir in butter and extracts. Transfer pastry cream to a bowl. Cover surface with plastic wrap; chill 8 hours or overnight. (Pastry cream will be very thick.) Yield: 3½ cups.

**Edible Tree Tips:** Allow 45 minutes to build this edible tree and then at least 30 minutes in the refrigerator for it to firm up or 1 hour at room temperature before serving. If you chill it, you may need to temporarily remove a refrigerator shelf in order for the tree to fit.

# Seasonal Pantry *Favorites*

Cranberries, vanilla, and coconut—3 holiday
pantry staples—are highlighted in these recipes.

*gift idea • make ahead*

## Chocolate-Almond-Coconut Macaroons

*These cookies are even scrumptious unadorned. (pictured at left)*

Prep: 18 min.   Cook: 22 min.

1   (14-ounce) package sweetened flaked coconut
¾   cup sweetened condensed milk
½   (7-ounce) package almond paste, grated (we tested with Odense)
2   tablespoons all-purpose flour
½   teaspoon vanilla extract
½   teaspoon almond extract
½   teaspoon grated orange rind
¼   teaspoon salt
¼   cup semisweet chocolate mini-morsels
1   egg white
½   cup semisweet chocolate morsels (optional)
1   tablespoon shortening (optional)
¼   cup sliced almonds, toasted (optional)

Combine coconut and sweetened condensed milk in a large bowl. Add almond paste and next 5 ingredients. Stir in mini morsels.

Beat egg white at high speed with an electric mixer until still peaks form; fold into coconut mixture.

Drop by heaping tablespoonfuls onto parchment paper-lined baking sheets.

Bake at 325° for 20 to 21 minutes or until edges are golden and tops are lightly browned. Cool completely on baking sheets.

If desired, microwave chocolate morsels and shortening in a 1-cup glass measuring cup on HIGH 1 minute or until melted, stirring once.

Pour melted chocolate into a small zip-top freezer bag. Snip a small hole in 1 corner of bag; drizzle chocolate over macaroons, and sprinkle with toasted almonds, if desired. Let stand until chocolate is firm. Yield: 2 dozen.

*make ahead*

## Coconut-Cranberry Trifle

*Convenience products simplify this holiday trifle. The hard part is waiting four hours for it to chill.*

Prep: 23 min.   Cook: 5 min.   Other: 4 hr., 45 min.

1   (16-ounce) can whole-berry cranberry sauce
1   (12-ounce) jar red currant jelly (we tested with Crosse & Blackwell)
2   tablespoons grated orange rind (rind of 2 oranges)
1   tablespoon cornstarch
3   (3.4-ounce) packages coconut cream or vanilla instant pudding mix
4   cups milk
1   (16-ounce) frozen pound cake, thawed, cut into 1" cubes, and divided
6   tablespoons Grand Marnier, divided
1½   cups sweetened flaked coconut, toasted and divided
2   cups frozen whipped topping, thawed

Combine first 4 ingredients in a medium saucepan. Bring to a boil over medium heat; cook 1 minute or until thickened and bubbly. Chill 15 minutes or until completely cooled, stirring occasionally.

Combine pudding mix and milk in a large bowl; whisk 2 minutes or until thickened.

Place one-third of pound cake cubes in a 3-quart trifle bowl; drizzle with 2 tablespoons liqueur. Top with one-third of cranberry-orange sauce and one-third of pudding. Sprinkle with ½ cup coconut.

Repeat layers twice using remaining cake cubes, orange liqueur, cranberry-orange sauce, pudding, and coconut, reserving last ½ cup coconut for garnish.

Spread whipped topping over trifle. Sprinkle with reserved coconut. Cover and chill at least 4 hours. Yield: 12 servings.

# Coconut-Chocolate Pastries

*These candy-filled pillows make a nice gift from the kitchen along with a bag of gourmet coffee.*

Prep: 35 min.   Cook: 12 min. per batch   Other: 5 min.

½  (8-ounce) package cream cheese, softened
½  cup powdered sugar
1   teaspoon vanilla extract
1   cup sweetened flaked coconut
1   (17.3-ounce) package frozen puff pastry sheets, thawed
5   (1.55-ounce) milk chocolate candy bars, broken into sections
1   large egg
1   tablespoon water
Powdered sugar

Beat cream cheese at medium speed with an electric mixer in a medium-sized bowl until creamy. Add ½ cup powdered sugar and vanilla; beat until smooth. Stir in coconut.

Roll 1 sheet puff pastry into a 12" x 12" rectangle. (Pastry will be thin.) Cut into 9 (4") squares. Stack 2 chocolate sections, just off center, on each square; top chocolate with 1 heaping teaspoon coconut mixture.

Whisk together egg and water in a small bowl. Lightly brush edges of squares with egg mixture; fold into triangles. Seal edges with a fork. Place pastries on parchment paper-lined baking sheets.

Repeat procedure with remaining sheet of pastry, chocolate (reserve extra chocolate sections for another use), and coconut mixture. Brush remaining egg wash over tops of pastries.

Bake at 400° for 12 minutes or until golden. Cool on baking sheets 5 minutes; transfer to wire racks to cool completely. Sift powdered sugar over pastries. Yield: 1½ dozen.

Toasted Coconut-Chocolate Chunk Pecan Pie

# Toasted Coconut-Chocolate Chunk Pecan Pie

*A long, slow bake time yields deep-dish chocolate paradise.*

Prep: 7 min.   Cook: 1 hr., 15 min.

1   (15-ounce) package refrigerated piecrusts
⅓  cup butter or margarine, melted
1   cup sugar
1   cup light corn syrup
4   large eggs, lightly beaten
1   teaspoon vanilla extract
¼  teaspoon salt
1½ cups pecan halves
1   cup sweetened flaked coconut, toasted
¾  cup semisweet chocolate chunks or morsels

Unroll 1 piecrust, and place on a lightly floured surface; lightly brush top of crust with water. Unroll remaining crust, and place over bottom crust; gently roll into a 10" circle. Fit into a 9" deep-dish pieplate; fold edges under, and crimp.

Stir together butter and next 5 ingredients in a large bowl; stir well. Stir in pecans and remaining ingredients. Pour filling into piecrust.

Bake at 325° for 1 hour and 15 minutes or until set, shielding crust after 45 minutes with aluminum foil, if necessary. Cool completely on a wire rack. Yield: 8 to 10 servings.

Coconut-Chocolate Pastries

## White Chocolate-Dipped Oatmeal-Cranberry Cookies

Prep: 46 min.   Cook: 11 min. per batch

1    cup butter or margarine, softened
1    cup firmly packed light brown sugar
½   cup granulated sugar
1    large egg
1    tablespoon vanilla extract
2    cups all-purpose flour
1    teaspoon baking soda
½   teaspoon baking powder
½   teaspoon salt
2    cups sweetened dried cranberries (we tested with Craisins)
1½  cups pecan pieces, toasted
1¼  cups uncooked quick-cooking oats
3    (4-ounce) white chocolate baking bars, coarsely chopped (we tested with Ghirardelli)
3    tablespoons shortening

Beat butter at medium speed with an electric mixer until creamy; gradually add sugars, beating well. Add egg and vanilla, beating until blended.

Combine flour and next 3 ingredients; gradually add to butter mixture, beating until blended. Stir in cranberries, pecans, and oats.

Drop dough by heaping tablespoonfuls 2" apart onto lightly greased baking sheets.

Bake at 375° for 9 to 11 minutes or until lightly browned. Cool on baking sheets 2 minutes. Transfer to wire racks to cool completely.

Microwave white chocolate and shortening in a medium-size microwave-safe bowl on HIGH 1 minute or until chocolate melts, stirring once. Dip half of each cookie into melted chocolate, letting excess drip back into bowl. Place dipped cookies on wax paper; let stand until firm. Yield: about 4 dozen.

## Dipping these chunky cookies into white chocolate adds a special holiday touch, but they're great plain, too.

**White Chocolate-Dipped Oatmeal-Cranberry Cookies**

# Cranberry-Couscous Salad

*Pair this cinnamon-scented side with grilled chicken or lamb.*

Prep: 10 min.   Cook: 4 min.   Other: 5 min.

1½  cups chicken broth
½   cup dried cranberries
1    teaspoon ground cinnamon
¼   teaspoon ground cumin
1    cup uncooked couscous
⅓   cup vegetable or canola oil
2    tablespoons rice vinegar
½   cup sliced almonds, toasted
⅓   cup chopped green onions
2    tablespoons chopped fresh mint or parsley
Red leaf lettuce leaves

Combine first 4 ingredients in a medium saucepan; bring to a boil. Remove from heat, and stir in couscous. Cover and let stand 5 minutes. Fluff with a fork; let cool, uncovered.

Whisk oil and vinegar; pour vinaigrette over couscous. Add almonds, green onions, and mint; toss well. Serve at room temperature or chilled over red leaf lettuce. Yield: 6 servings.

# Holiday Granola Bars

Prep: 20 min.   Cook: 40 min.

¼   cup butter or margarine, softened
½   cup firmly packed light brown sugar
1    large egg, lightly beaten
½   cup honey
½   cup vanilla yogurt
1    teaspoon vanilla extract
1    cup all-purpose flour
1    teaspoon ground cinnamon
½   teaspoon baking powder
¼   teaspoon salt
1½  cups uncooked quick-cooking oats
1¼  cups crisp rice cereal
1    cup dried cranberries
½   cup sliced almonds
½   cup chopped pecans
½   cup sunflower seed kernels
2    tablespoons sesame seeds

Beat butter at medium speed with an electric mixer until creamy. Gradually add sugar, beating until light and fluffy. Add egg, beating well. Stir in honey, yogurt, and vanilla.

Combine flour and next 3 ingredients in a large bowl. Stir in oats and remaining ingredients; add to butter mixture, stirring well. Press mixture into a foil-lined 13" x 9" pan coated with cooking spray.

Bake at 350° for 35 to 40 minutes or until lightly browned. Cut into bars while warm. Cool completely in pan on a wire rack. Store in an airtight container up to 5 days. Yield: 2 dozen.

Note: Always taste nuts and sunflower seeds before using in a recipe. If not stored properly, they become rancid quickly.

# Brown Sugar-Pecan Cupcakes

*Satisfy your sweet tooth with the delicate crunch of brown sugar and pecans that top these little cakes.*

Prep: 32 min.   Cook: 22 min.

¾   cup chopped pecans
¼   cup butter or margarine, softened
¼   cup shortening
1    cup granulated sugar, divided
3    large eggs, separated
2    teaspoons vanilla bean paste
1    cup all-purpose flour
½   teaspoon baking soda
½   cup buttermilk
¼   cup firmly packed light brown sugar
Browned Butter Frosting

Bake pecans in a shallow pan at 350°, stirring occasionally, 8 minutes or until toasted. Cool completely. Process ¼ cup pecans in a food processor until finely chopped. Set aside.

Beat butter and shortening at medium speed with an electric mixer until fluffy; gradually add ¾ cup granulated sugar, beating well. Add egg yolks, 1 at a time, beating until blended after each addition. Stir in vanilla bean paste.

Combine flour and baking soda; add to butter mixture alternately with buttermilk, beginning and ending with flour. Beat at low speed until blended after each addition.

Beat egg whites at medium speed until soft peaks form; add remaining ¼ cup granulated sugar, 1 tablespoon at a time, beating until stiff peaks form. Fold one-third of egg whites into batter; fold in remaining egg whites and ½ cup toasted pecans. Spoon batter into paper-lined muffin cups, filling two-thirds full.

Bake at 350° for 22 minutes or until a wooden pick inserted in center comes out clean. Cool in pans 5 minutes on a wire rack. Remove from pans, and cool completely.

Combine reserved ¼ cup finely chopped pecans and brown sugar in a small bowl. Spread a generous 2 tablespoons Browned Butter Frosting onto each cupcake. Sprinkle tops of cupcakes with pecan-sugar mixture. Yield: 18 cupcakes.

## Browned Butter Frosting

*There's no substitute for butter in this recipe. Only browned butter achieves the nutty flavor that makes this unique frosting so good.*

Prep: **8 min.**   Cook: **4 min.**   Other: **20** min.

¼   cup butter
1   (8-ounce) package cream cheese, softened
1   (16-ounce) package powdered sugar
1½ teaspoons vanilla bean paste

Cook butter in a small heavy saucepan over medium heat, stirring constantly, 3 to 4 minutes or until browned. Transfer to a large mixing bowl, and chill 20 minutes.

Add cream cheese to browned butter; beat at medium speed until smooth. Gradually add powdered sugar, beating until light and fluffy. Stir in vanilla bean paste. Yield: 2¾ cups.

## the essence of vanilla

We recommend using vanilla bean paste in these cupcakes. It has a speckled, syrupy consistency. Find it at Williams-Sonoma or other cook stores. If you want to substitute, the conversions are: 1 tablespoon vanilla bean paste= 1 tablespoon vanilla extract=1 whole vanilla bean.

**Brown Sugar-Pecan Cupcakes**

# Twice as Nice

Holiday recipes serve double duty in this chapter.
Each recipe is a delicious idea on its own, but look for another
suggested way to enjoy it in secondary recipes.

## Brown Sugar Cake with Peanut Buttercream and Brittle Topping

*(pictured at left)*

Prep: 42 min.   Cook: 25 min.   Other: 10 min.

Old-Fashioned Peanut Brittle (recipe at right)
1½ cups butter, softened
2 cups firmly packed light brown sugar
6 large eggs
3 cups sifted cake flour
1 teaspoon baking powder
1 cup milk
2 teaspoons vanilla extract
Peanut Buttercream
½ cup semisweet chocolate morsels
2 tablespoons milk
1 tablespoon butter

Prepare Old-Fashioned Peanut Brittle.

Beat 1½ cups butter at medium speed with an electric mixer until creamy. Gradually add sugar, beating 7 minutes or until fluffy. Add eggs, 1 at a time, beating just until yellow disappears.

Combine flour and baking powder. Combine milk and vanilla. Gradually add alternately to butter mixture, beginning and ending with flour mixture. Beat at low speed just until blended after each addition. Spread batter into 2 greased and floured 9" cakepans.

Bake at 350° for 24 to 25 minutes or until a wooden pick inserted in center comes out clean. Cool in pans on wire racks 10 minutes. Remove from pans; cool on wire racks.

Break one-fourth of Old-Fashioned Peanut Brittle into 1½" to 2" pieces. Place an additional one-fourth of brittle in a large zip-top freezer bag; crush into coarse crumbs using a mallet or rolling pin. Reserve remaining brittle for another use.

Spread Peanut Buttercream between layers and on top and sides of cake. Press coarsely crushed brittle onto sides of cake.

Place chocolate morsels, milk, and 1 tablespoon butter in a small glass bowl. Microwave on HIGH 1 minute. Stir until smooth. Dip ends of peanut brittle pieces in chocolate ganache; place on wax paper to harden. Drizzle remaining ganache over cake. Arrange dipped brittle on top of cake. Yield: 1 (2-layer) cake.

**Make-Ahead Note:** Prepare the peanut brittle and cake layers a day ahead, or make the entire cake a day ahead. Either way, add chocolate-dipped brittle just before serving.

## Peanut Buttercream

Prep: 6 min.

9 tablespoons butter, softened
¼ cup creamy peanut butter
½ cup milk
1½ teaspoons vanilla extract
5½ cups powdered sugar

Beat butter and peanut butter in a large bowl at medium speed with an electric mixer until blended. Combine milk and vanilla. Gradually add sugar and vanilla milk, 1 tablespoon at a time, beating until spreading consistency. Yield: 4 cups.

## Old-Fashioned Peanut Brittle

*We've perfected this classic candy with easy microwave directions. Follow the cook times closely based on the wattage of your microwave. Munch on half of the brittle, and use the rest in Brown Sugar Cake with Peanut Buttercream and Brittle Topping (recipe at left).*

Prep: 7 min.   Cook: 9 min.

1 cup sugar
½ cup light corn syrup
⅛ teaspoon salt
1½ cups shelled raw peanuts
1 tablespoon butter
1 teaspoon vanilla extract
1 teaspoon baking soda

Microwave first 3 ingredients in a 2-quart glass bowl on HIGH 5 minutes, using an 1100-watt microwave oven. (Microwave 1 more minute if using a 700-watt microwave.) Stir in peanuts. Microwave 3 more minutes in an 1100-watt oven (add 1 more minute in 700-watt oven). Stir in butter and vanilla. Microwave 45 seconds in an 1100-watt oven (add 1 more minute in 700-watt oven) or until candy is the color of peanut butter. Stir in baking soda (mixture will bubble). Working quickly, spread hot candy in a thin layer onto a lightly greased baking sheet using two metal forks. Cool completely. Break candy into pieces. Yield: 1 pound.

# Cranberry Liqueur

*This makes an impressive gift any time of the year. Mix it with Champagne for an unexpected holiday treat, or make our Holiday Martinis (recipe follows).*

Prep: 10 min.   Cook: 5 min.   Other: 1 month

2¼ cups sugar
1   cup water
1   orange
1   pound fresh cranberries (4 cups)
4   cups vodka

Combine sugar and water in a medium saucepan; cook, stirring constantly, over medium heat 5 minutes or until sugar dissolves. Remove from heat, and cool completely.

Meanwhile, remove rind from orange with a vegetable peeler, being careful not to get the bitter white pith. Cut rind into strips, and set aside.

Process cranberries in a food processor 2 minutes or until very finely chopped. Combine sugar solution, orange rind, and cranberries in a 1-gallon jar; stir in vodka. Cover with lid, and store in a cool, dark place for 1 month.

Line a wire-mesh strainer with 2 layers of cheesecloth; strain liqueur through cheesecloth into a bowl. Discard solids. Carefully pour liqueur into clean bottles or jars. Yield: 5 cups.

**Note:** Cranberry Liqueur can be stored in a cool, dark place for up to a year.

# Holiday Martinis

*Homemade Cranberry Liqueur replaces vodka in this pretty variation of a Cosmopolitan cocktail.*

Prep: 3 min.

⅓   cup cranberry juice cocktail
¼   cup Cranberry Liqueur (recipe above)
¼   cup Grand Marnier or Cointreau
1   tablespoon fresh lime juice
Garnish: twist of lime

Combine first 4 ingredients in a martini shaker; add ice cubes to fill container. Cover with lid, and shake 30 seconds or until thoroughly chilled. Remove lid, and strain into a martini glass. Serve immediately. Garnish, if desired. Yield: 1 serving.

# Sweet Potato-Butter Pecan Biscuits

*These biscuits are great served alone, with ham, or as the base for the Winter Shortcakes (at right). We don't recommend substituting canned sweet potatoes in this recipe.*

Prep: 17 min.   Cook: 1 hr., 21 min.

1   small sweet potato (about 8 ounces)
1   tablespoon butter or margarine
½   cup chopped pecans
2¼ cups all-purpose flour
1   tablespoon baking powder
½   teaspoon salt
½   cup cold butter, cut into pieces
½   cup sour cream
2   tablespoons light brown sugar
2   tablespoons maple syrup
2   tablespoons butter, melted

Scrub sweet potato; wrap in aluminum foil. Bake at 350° for 45 minutes to 1 hour. Cool completely. Scoop out pulp, and mash to equal ¾ cup. Set aside.

Melt 1 tablespoon butter in a small skillet over medium heat. Add pecans; cook, stirring constantly, 6 minutes or until toasted. Remove from heat; cool completely.

Combine flour, baking powder, and salt in a large bowl. Cut ½ cup butter into flour mixture with a pastry blender until crumbly; stir in pecans. Combine ¾ cup mashed sweet potato, sour cream, brown sugar, and maple syrup; add to flour mixture, stirring just until dry ingredients are moistened.

Turn dough out onto a heavily floured surface; knead 6 to 8 times, and pat into a 7" square (¾" thick). Cut dough into 9 squares; place squares 2" apart on a lightly greased baking sheet.

Bake at 425° for 15 minutes or until lightly browned. Brush with melted butter. Serve warm. Yield: 9 servings.

**Fix it Faster:** Pierce sweet potato skin with a knife, and microwave potato on HIGH 3 to 5 minutes; let stand 5 minutes after cooking. Bake or microwave sweet potato up to a day ahead, and mash. Chill overnight.

**Winter Shortcakes**

*editor's favorite*

# Winter Shortcakes

Prep: 14 min.   Cook: 21 min.

1    cup whipping cream
2    tablespoons powdered sugar
¼    teaspoon ground cinnamon
¼    cup butter
6    medium Granny Smith apples, peeled, cored, and
      sliced (about 7 cups)
1    cup sugar
½    cup chopped dates
1    teaspoon ground cinnamon
¼    teaspoon ground nutmeg
¼    teaspoon salt
Sweet Potato-Butter Pecan Biscuits (recipe at left)

Shortcake's not just meant for berries. This one sports a spiced apple filling piled onto a sweet potato biscuit.

Beat first 3 ingredients in a medium bowl at high speed with an electric mixer until soft peaks form. Cover and chill.

Melt butter in a large nonstick skillet over medium heat. Add apples and next 5 ingredients; cook over medium heat 20 minutes or until apples are tender, stirring often. Cool.

Split biscuits in half. Place biscuit bottoms on individual serving plates. Spoon ⅓ cup apple mixture evenly over each biscuit bottom. Place top half of each biscuit over filling. Spoon ⅓ cup apple mixture over biscuit top. Dollop with cinnamon whipped cream. Yield: 9 servings.

233

## Gingerbread Biscotti

*Bag these cookies for the ideal gift, but save enough to make the crust for Lemon Cheesecake (below).*

**Prep: 18 min.   Cook: 48 min.   Other: 15 min.**

½   cup butter, softened
½   cup firmly packed light brown sugar
½   cup sugar
2   large eggs
¼   cup molasses
2½ cups all-purpose flour
1   teaspoon baking powder
1   teaspoon baking soda
1½ teaspoons ground ginger
1   teaspoon ground cinnamon
½   teaspoon ground nutmeg
¼   teaspoon ground cloves
¼   teaspoon salt
½   cup sliced almonds

Beat butter and sugars in a large bowl at medium speed with an electric mixer until light and fluffy. Add eggs, beating well; beat in molasses.

Combine flour and next 7 ingredients; add to butter mixture, beating at low speed until blended. Stir in almonds.

Divide dough in half; using floured hands, shape each portion into a 9" x 2" log on a lightly greased baking sheet.

Bake at 350° for 28 minutes or until firm. Cool on baking sheet 5 minutes. Remove to a wire rack to cool 10 minutes. Reduce oven temperature to 300°.

Cut each log diagonally into ¾"-thick slices with a serrated knife, using a gentle sawing motion. Place slices on ungreased baking sheets. Bake 8 to 10 minutes; turn cookies over, and bake 8 to 10 more minutes. Cool completely on wire racks. Yield: about 2 dozen.

## Lemon Cheesecake

**Prep: 27 min.   Cook: 1 hr.   Other: 9 hr.**

2   cups finely crushed Gingerbread Biscotti (recipe above)
¼   cup butter, melted
4   (8-ounce) packages cream cheese, softened
1½ cups sugar
1   (8-ounce) container sour cream
1   tablespoon cornstarch
4   large eggs
1   tablespoon grated lemon rind
⅓   cup fresh lemon juice
1   teaspoon vanilla extract

**Gingerbread Biscotti**

# These crisp Italian cookies have a subtle ginger flavor; they're put to perfect use as a cheesecake crust.

Stir together crushed biscotti and butter in a bowl. Press cookie crumb mixture into bottom and 1" up sides of an ungreased 9" springform pan.

Bake at 325° for 10 minutes; let cool.

Meanwhile, beat cream cheese at medium speed with an electric mixer until creamy; gradually add sugar, beating well. Add sour cream and cornstarch, beating just until combined. Add eggs, 1 at a time, beating just until yellow disappears. Stir in lemon rind and remaining ingredients. (Do not overbeat.) Pour batter into baked crust.

Bake at 325° for 50 minutes or until set. Turn off oven. Immediately run a knife around edge of pan, releasing sides. Close oven door, and let cheesecake stand in oven 1 hour.

Remove from oven; cool completely in pan on a wire rack. Cover and chill 8 hours. Yield: 12 servings.

*editor's favorite • gift idea*

## Homemade Caramel Sauce

*Drizzle this golden sauce over Mile-High Turtle Ice Cream Pie (below), or serve as a topping for pound cake or ice cream.*

Prep: 2 min.   Cook: 12 min.

1¼ cups sugar
⅓  cup water
¾  cup whipping cream
⅓  cup butter, cut into pieces
½  teaspoon vanilla extract

Combine sugar and water in a large heavy saucepan; cook over medium-low heat, stirring often, until sugar dissolves. Increase heat to medium-high, and boil gently, without stirring, until syrup turns a deep amber color, occasionally brushing down sides of pan with a wet pastry brush and swirling pan (about 8 minutes). (Swirling the pan, instead of stirring, promotes more even cooking.) Gradually add cream (sauce will bubble vigorously). Add butter; stir gently until smooth. Remove from heat, and stir in vanilla. Yield: 1¾ cups.

Homemade Caramel Sauce

*editor's favorite • make ahead*

## Mile-High Turtle Ice Cream Pie

Prep: 25 min.   Cook: 10 min.   Other: 6 hr., 30 min.

2    cups chocolate cookie crumbs (about 40 cookies)
¼   cup butter or margarine, melted and cooled
2    pints dulce de leche ice cream, softened and divided (we tested with Häagen-Dazs)
1    cup Homemade Caramel Sauce, divided (recipe above)
1½  cups chopped pecans, toasted and divided
1    pint chocolate ice cream, softened
1    (7-ounce) can sweetened whipped cream (we tested with Reddi-wip®)
¾   cup Homemade Caramel Sauce

Combine crumbs and melted butter in a small mixing bowl; stir well. Press crumbs in bottom of a 9" springform pan. Bake at 325° for 10 minutes. Cool completely.

Spoon 1 pint dulce de leche ice cream into cooled crust, and spread evenly; drizzle ⅓ cup Homemade Caramel Sauce over ice cream, and sprinkle with ¾ cup chopped pecans. Freeze 15 minutes or until ice cream is almost firm. Repeat procedure with chocolate ice cream, ⅓ cup Caramel Sauce, and remaining pecans; freeze until almost firm. Top with remaining dulce de leche ice cream and ⅓ cup Caramel Sauce. Cover and freeze 6 hours or up to 2 weeks in advance.

Mile-High Turtle Ice Cream Pie

Before serving, remove sides and bottom of pan; transfer pie to a serving platter. Top with sweetened whipped cream. Place ¾ cup Homemade Caramel Sauce in a microwave-safe bowl. Microwave at HIGH 1 minute or until warm. Drizzle 1 tablespoon sauce over each serving. Yield: 12 servings.

# Carnitas

*Carnitas is a Mexican version of barbecue braised on the stovetop. Slowly simmered in broth or water, the meat becomes deliciously tender; then it's browned for a crisp exterior. Serve it plain or as tacos (see recipe at right). Using a slow cooker delivers authentic results without watching the pot.*

Prep: 16 min.   Cook: 6 hr.

| | |
|---|---|
| 2 | tablespoons tomato paste |
| 2 | tablespoons adobo sauce* |
| 3 | tablespoons chopped garlic |
| 1 | tablespoon chili powder |
| 1 | teaspoon salt |
| 1 | teaspoon pepper |
| 3 | pounds boneless Boston butt pork roast, cut into 2" pieces |
| 1 | cup beer or chicken broth |

Combine first 6 ingredients in a 5-quart slow cooker; stir in pieces of roast. Microwave beer in a 2-cup glass measuring cup on HIGH 2 minutes or until very hot. Pour beer over meat in slow cooker; do not stir. Cover and cook on HIGH for 6 hours or until very tender.

Shred meat using 2 forks. Serve hot or see notes below. Yield: 6 cups shredded meat.

* We used adobo sauce from canned chipotle chiles in adobo sauce.

**Make-Ahead Note:** Transfer meat mixture and juices to a 13" x 9" baking dish; cover and chill overnight. To reheat, crumble meat mixture into a large skillet, and cook over medium-high heat 15 minutes or until browned and hot.

**Microwave Option:** Traditionally, Carnitas are browned in their own drippings until they are crisped and browned. However, reheating the shredded pork in the microwave is an easy alternative. Microwave 6 cups meat mixture on HIGH 6 minutes, stirring once, or until thoroughly heated.

# Carnita Tacos

*Consider a Carnita Taco supper during the holidays as an alternative to chili or soup. Set up the meal, buffet-style, and let everyone prepare their own taco with favorite toppings.*

Prep: 10 min.

| | |
|---|---|
| 24 | (6-inch) corn tortillas |
| 6 | cups Carnitas meat, warmed (recipe at left) |

Toppings: queso fresco, chopped fresh cilantro, salsa verde, diced avocado, finely diced red onion, sour cream, lime wedges

Heat tortillas according to package directions. Place about ¼ cup Carnitas in center of each tortilla; top with desired toppings and a squeeze of fresh lime juice. Roll up tortillas; and serve immediately. Yield: 12 servings.

# Crabmeat Dip

*This creamy dip doubles as an appetizer and a stuffing for boneless chicken breasts. It can easily be made a day ahead and baked just before guests arrive. Reserve ½ cup of the unbaked dip for Crabmeat-Stuffed Chicken Breasts.*

Prep: 22 min.   Cook: 30 min.

| | |
|---|---|
| 1 | (8-ounce) package cream cheese, softened |
| 1 | (5.2-ounce) package buttery garlic-and-herb spreadable cheese (we tested with Boursin) |
| ½ | cup mayonnaise |
| ¼ | cup finely chopped red bell pepper |
| ¼ | cup chopped green onions |
| ¾ | cup freshly grated Parmesan cheese |
| 1 | teaspoon coarse-grained Dijon mustard |
| ½ | teaspoon Worcestershire sauce |
| 1 | teaspoon hot sauce |
| 2 | tablespoons fresh lemon juice |
| 1 | garlic clove, minced |
| 2 | tablespoons capers |
| ¼ | teaspoon freshly ground black pepper |
| 1 | pound fresh lump crabmeat, drained |

Combine first 13 ingredients, stirring well. Gently fold in crabmeat. Spoon dip into a lightly greased 8" square baking dish. Bake at 350° for 30 minutes or until bubbly. Serve with crackers or Melba toast rounds. Yield: 4½ cups.

## Crabmeat-Stuffed Chicken Breasts

**Prep: 12 min.   Cook: 33 min.**

4   skinned and boned chicken breasts
¼   teaspoon salt
½   teaspoon freshly ground pepper
½   cup uncooked Crabmeat Dip (recipe at left)
¾   cup loosely packed fresh spinach leaves
4   slices prosciutto, cut into 7" x 4" strips
2   teaspoons olive oil

Place each chicken breast between 2 sheets of heavy-duty plastic wrap; pound to ¼" thickness using a meat mallet or rolling pin. Sprinkle chicken with salt and pepper.

Spread 2 tablespoons Crabmeat Dip over each chicken breast. Divide spinach evenly over dip; roll up chicken, jelly-roll fashion. Wrap each roll with 1 slice prosciutto; secure with a wooden pick.

Heat oil in an ovenproof skillet over medium-high heat. Add chicken, and cook 3 to 4 minutes on each side or until prosciutto is lightly browned and crispy. Place skillet in oven, and bake at 350° for 25 minutes or until chicken is done. Remove wooden picks before serving. Yield: 4 servings.

**Note:** Make Crabmeat Dip no more than 1 day ahead of preparing Crabmeat-Stuffed Chicken Breasts.

## Walnut Mashed Potatoes

*Toasted nuts give fresh appeal to these spuds. Save 4 cups of the unbaked potatoes for the Shepherd's Pie recipe that follows.*

**Prep: 25 min.   Cook: 35 min.**

6   pounds baking potatoes, peeled and cut into 1" cubes (about 8 large potatoes)
¾   cup butter or margarine, cut into pieces
1½  cups half-and-half
2   teaspoons salt
½   teaspoon pepper
4   green onions, chopped
1½  tablespoons olive oil
1¼  cups chopped walnuts, toasted

Cook potatoes in boiling water to cover 30 minutes or until tender; drain well. Return potatoes to pan. Add butter, and mash with a potato masher. Add half-and-half, salt, and pepper. Mash again to desired consistency.

Sauté green onions in hot oil in a medium skillet over medium-high heat 5 minutes or until crisp-tender. Add onions and walnuts to mashed potato, stirring until blended. Yield: 14½ cups.

**Note:** Chop walnuts by hand for this recipe instead of using a processor because a processor often creates "dust" that can discolor the potatoes.

## Shepherd's Pie

*This down-home casserole has a fast prep and the comfort-food appeal of a one-dish dinner.*

**Prep: 5 min.   Cook: 44 min.**

1   pound ground beef
¾   cup chopped onion
1½  teaspoons olive oil
2   tablespoons all-purpose flour
1⅓  cups water
2   teaspoons beef bouillon granules
1   teaspoon Worcestershire sauce
¼   teaspoon salt
¼   teaspoon pepper
2   cups frozen mixed vegetables, thawed and patted dry
4   cups unbaked Walnut Mashed Potatoes (recipe at left)
¼   cup freshly grated Parmesan cheese
Paprika

Cook ground beef in a large skillet, stirring until it crumbles and is no longer pink; drain well, and set aside. Wipe skillet clean.

Sauté onion in hot oil in skillet over medium-high heat until tender. Add flour, stirring well; stir in water. Cook, stirring constantly, over medium-low heat, until thickened. Add bouillon and next 3 ingredients, stirring well. Add beef and thawed vegetables; stir well.

Spoon beef mixture into a lightly greased 2-quart casserole dish. Spread Walnut Mashed Potatoes over beef mixture; sprinkle with Parmesan cheese. Lightly sprinkle with paprika.

Bake, uncovered, at 350° for 30 minutes or until hot and bubbly. Yield: 4 servings.

# Our Best Casseroles

Here's a casserole collection that boasts a variety of big flavors. Each recipe yields enough for a crowd.

*editor's favorite*

## Gumbo Casserole with Creamed Garlic Shrimp

*A rich brown roux and the signature Cajun culinary trinity (onion, bell pepper, and celery) provide authentic flavors for this hearty dish. It's best served hot from the oven. Call ahead and ask your fishmonger to peel and devein the shrimp for you. (pictured at left)*

Prep: 40 min.   Cook: 1 hr., 22 min.

2   pounds unpeeled, medium-size fresh shrimp
1   tablespoon Creole seasoning (we tested with Tony Chachere's)
2   tablespoons bacon drippings
3   tablespoons all-purpose flour
1   tablespoon vegetable oil
⅓   cup finely chopped onion
⅓   cup finely chopped green bell pepper
⅓   cup finely chopped celery
2   garlic cloves, minced
1   teaspoon dried thyme
1   teaspoon dried oregano
¾   teaspoon salt
½   teaspoon pepper
4   green onions, chopped
½   cup chicken broth or water
2   cups whipping cream
1   pound uncooked spaghetti, broken in half and cooked according to package directions
1   cup freshly grated Parmesan cheese
Garnish: additional chopped green onions

Peel and devein shrimp, if desired. Combine shrimp and Creole seasoning in a medium bowl; set aside.

Cook bacon drippings, flour, and oil in a large skillet over medium heat, whisking constantly, 20 to 25 minutes or until roux is the dark brown color of pecan shells. Add ⅓ cup onion and next 3 ingredients; cook 5 minutes or until tender. Add thyme and next 3 ingredients; cook 1 minute, stirring constantly. Add shrimp and 4 green onions; cook over medium-high heat 3 minutes or until shrimp are almost done; transfer to a large bowl.

Add broth to skillet, scraping bottom of skillet to loosen browned bits. Add whipping cream. Bring to a boil over medium-high heat; reduce heat, and simmer 6 minutes. Add to shrimp. Stir in cooked pasta; toss well to combine. Pour into a lightly greased 13" x 9" baking dish. Sprinkle with Parmesan cheese.

Bake, uncovered, at 350° for 20 minutes or until thoroughly heated. Garnish, if desired. Yield: 8 servings.

*editor's favorite*

## Deep-Dish Spanakopita

*This Greek-flavored casserole starts out on the lowest oven rack to crisp the bottom pastry layer and finishes on the middle rack to ensure a flaky top.*

Prep: 44 min.   Cook: 56 min.

2   tablespoons olive oil
8   green onions, chopped (1 cup)
3   garlic cloves, minced
3   (6-ounce) packages fresh baby spinach or 11 cups chopped Swiss chard
¼   cup water
1   (8-ounce) package feta cheese, crumbled
½   cup freshly grated Parmesan cheese
¼   cup chopped dried tomatoes in oil
1   teaspoon dried oregano
¾   teaspoon salt, divided
¼   teaspoon pepper
½   (16-ounce) package frozen phyllo pastry, thawed (we tested with Athens)
⅓   cup butter, melted
1   tablespoon butter
1   tablespoon all-purpose flour
1   cup milk
2   ounces cream cheese, cubed and softened

Heat olive oil in a Dutch oven over medium-high heat until hot. Add green onions and garlic; sauté 3 minutes or until tender. Add spinach and water; cover and cook 8 minutes or until spinach wilts. Cool spinach completely in a colander set over a bowl. Return cooled spinach to pan. Add cheeses, tomatoes, oregano, ½ teaspoon salt, and pepper, stirring well to combine.

Trim phyllo sheets to 13" x 9", if necessary. Layer 8 sheets of phyllo in a lightly greased 13" x 9" baking dish, using half of melted butter to brush between sheets. (Keep remaining phyllo covered with a damp cloth.) Bake at 400° on lowest oven rack for 6 minutes or until lightly browned; set aside.

Melt 1 tablespoon butter in a small saucepan over medium heat. Stir in flour; cook 1 minute. Gradually whisk in milk. Cook over medium heat 2 minutes, whisking constantly. Whisk in cream cheese and remaining ¼ teaspoon salt.

Spread spinach filling over baked phyllo crust; drizzle with white sauce.

Layer remaining phyllo sheets over filling using remaining half of melted butter to brush between sheets. Using a sharp knife, score top layer of phyllo into 8 portions. Bake at 400° on middle oven rack 30 minutes or until pastry is golden. Serve hot. Yield: 8 servings.

## Roasted Vegetable Lasagna

*This white-sauced meatless lasagna will appeal to a vegetarian crowd.*

Prep: 34 min.   Cook: 1 hr., 44 min.   Other: 15 min.

| | |
|---|---|
| 1 | medium butternut squash (about 2 pounds) |
| ½ | large sweet potato, cut into ½" cubes (about 1 cup) |
| 3 | tablespoons olive oil, divided |
| 3 | cups sliced leeks (about 5 medium) |
| 1 | red bell pepper, cut into thin strips |
| 4 | cups milk |
| 4 | garlic cloves, halved |
| 3 | tablespoons butter or margarine |
| ¼ | cup all-purpose flour |
| 1 | teaspoon salt |
| ½ | teaspoon pepper |
| 9 | dried precooked lasagna noodles |
| 1 | cup grated Asiago cheese |
| 1 | cup whipping cream |
| ½ | cup grated Parmesan cheese |

Microwave butternut squash at HIGH 2 minutes. (This step softens squash for slicing.) Cut squash in half lengthwise; remove and discard seeds. Peel squash, and cut into ½" cubes. Set aside 3 cups cubed squash; reserve any remaining squash for another use.

Combine 3 cups squash, sweet potato, and 2 tablespoons olive oil on a large rimmed baking sheet. Bake at 450° for 10 minutes.

Meanwhile, combine leeks, bell pepper, and remaining 1 tablespoon oil in a large bowl. Add to partially roasted squash mixture, stirring gently. Bake at 450° for 20 minutes or until vegetables are tender, stirring after 15 minutes. Return roasted vegetables to bowl; set aside.

Combine milk and garlic in a large saucepan; bring just to a boil. Reduce heat, and simmer, uncovered, 10 minutes. Remove and discard garlic.

Melt butter in a large saucepan over medium heat; whisk in flour until smooth. Cook 1 minute, whisking constantly. Gradually whisk in warm milk; cook over medium-high heat, whisking constantly, 12 to 13 minutes or until slightly thickened. Remove from heat; stir in salt and pepper. Add to roasted vegetables, stirring gently.

Spoon 1 cup vegetable mixture into a lightly greased 13" x 9" baking dish. Top with 3 lasagna noodles; spread half of remaining vegetable mixture over noodles, and sprinkle with ½ cup Asiago cheese. Repeat procedure with 3 noodles, remaining vegetable mixture, and remaining Asiago cheese. Break remaining 3 noodles in half and lay on top of casserole. (Breaking the noodles keeps them from curling up.)

Beat cream at high speed with an electric mixer until soft peaks form. Spread whipped cream over noodles; sprinkle with Parmesan cheese. Bake, covered, at 350° for 30 minutes. Uncover and bake 13 more minutes or until golden and bubbly. Let stand 15 minutes before serving. Yield: 8 servings.

*editor's favorite • make ahead*

## Pizza Strata

*As this casserole bakes, the aroma will make you think you've ordered out for pizza.*

Prep: 21 min.   Cook: 1 hr.   Other: 16 hr., 10 min.

| | |
|---|---|
| 1 | (16-ounce) French or Italian bread loaf, cut into ½" cubes (about 20 cups) |
| 1 | cup finely chopped prosciutto (about 4 ounces) |
| ¼ | cup chopped roasted red bell pepper |
| ¼ | cup chopped green onions |
| ½ | cup freshly grated Parmesan cheese |
| 1 | (14½-ounce) can diced tomatoes, undrained |
| 1 | cup coarsely chopped pimiento-stuffed olives |
| 1 | cup (4 ounces) shredded mozzarella cheese |
| 6 | large eggs |
| 3 | cups milk |
| 1 | teaspoon dried Italian seasoning |
| ½ | teaspoon salt |
| ½ | teaspoon pepper |
| ¼ | cup chopped fresh flat-leaf parsley |

Arrange bread cubes in a single layer on large baking sheets. Let stand 8 hours to dry.

Spread half of bread cubes in a lightly greased 13" x 9" baking dish. Sprinkle prosciutto and next 3 ingredients evenly over bread cubes. Arrange remaining bread cubes evenly over Parmesan. Top with tomatoes, olives, and mozzarella cheese.

Whisk together eggs and remaining 5 ingredients. Pour egg mixture evenly over bread cubes, pressing down cubes gently to absorb liquid; cover and chill 8 hours.

Bake, uncovered, at 325° for 55 minutes or until set and top is browned. Let stand 10 minutes before serving. Yield: 8 to 10 servings.

# Chic Mac and Cheese

*Blue cheese rules in this pasta classic. Serve it alongside a grilled steak.*

**Prep: 35 min.    Cook: 1 hr., 5 min.    Other: 5 min.**

| | |
|---|---|
| 2 | tablespoons butter or margarine |
| 1 | large green bell pepper, chopped |
| 1 | large red bell pepper, chopped |
| 1 | large yellow bell pepper, chopped |
| 4 | celery ribs, finely chopped |
| ¼ | teaspoon salt |
| ½ | cup butter or margarine |
| ½ | cup all-purpose flour |
| 2 | cups whipping cream |
| 2 | cups half-and-half |
| ¼ | teaspoon celery seeds |
| ¼ | teaspoon ground white pepper |
| 1 | pound blue cheese, crumbled (we tested with Maytag) |
| 2 | large eggs |
| ½ | cup finely chopped fresh celery leaves |
| 1 | pound uncooked penne pasta |
| 1 | cup freshly grated Parmesan cheese |

Melt 2 tablespoons butter in a large skillet over medium-high heat. Add peppers and celery; sauté 8 to 10 minutes or until crisp-tender. Sprinkle with salt. Set vegetables aside.

Melt ½ cup butter in a large saucepan over low heat. Add flour, whisking until smooth; cook 1 minute. Gradually add whipping cream and half-and-half; cook over medium heat, stirring constantly, until thickened. Whisk in celery seeds and white pepper. Remove from heat; add blue cheese, whisking until cheese melts.

Whisk eggs in a medium bowl until lightly beaten. Gradually whisk about one-fourth of hot white sauce into eggs, whisking constantly; add to remaining white sauce, stirring constantly. Whisk in celery leaves.

Cook pasta according to package directions; drain and return to pan. Stir in vegetables and white sauce. Pour into a lightly greased 13" x 9" baking dish. Sprinkle with Parmesan.

Bake, uncovered, at 400° for 30 minutes or until bubbly and lightly browned. Let stand 5 minutes before serving. Yield: 12 servings.

Cheese 'n' Chile Casserole

# Cheese 'n' Chile Casserole

*Punch up the heat in this ultrarich brunch dish by using Monterey Jack cheese with peppers.*

**Prep: 18 min.    Cook: 45 min.    Other: 15 min.**

| | |
|---|---|
| 9 | large eggs |
| ¾ | teaspoon salt |
| 3 | (8-ounce) packages Monterey Jack cheese, cubed |
| 2 | (8-ounce) packages cream cheese, cubed |
| 1 | (12-ounce) container small-curd cottage cheese |
| 1 | tablespoon butter or margarine, cut into small pieces |
| ¾ | cup all-purpose flour |
| 1½ | teaspoons baking powder |
| 1 | (4.5-ounce) can chopped green chiles, drained |
| 1 | (2-ounce) jar diced pimiento, drained |

Whisk together eggs and salt in a large bowl; add cheeses and butter. Whisk flour and baking powder into cheese mixture. Add green chiles and pimiento. Pour into a lightly greased 13" x 9" baking dish.

Bake, uncovered, at 350° for 45 minutes or until set. Let stand 10 to 15 minutes before serving. Yield: 16 servings.

# Slow-Cooker Sensations

The slow cooker is ideal holiday equipment—it fills your home with inviting aromas, and it's hands-off cooking, allowing you to focus on family. Use it to make big-batch candies, party dips and dessert, and classic soups and sides.

*editor's favorite • gift idea*
## Triple Chocolate-Nut Clusters

*Candy making has never been so easy! The slow cooker is the perfect tool to keep this candy mixture warm while you're spooning it out. (pictured at left)*

**Prep: 13 min.   Cook: 2 hr.   Other: 2 hr.**

- 1  (16-ounce) jar dry-roasted peanuts
- 1  (9.75-ounce) can salted whole cashews
- 2  cups pecan pieces
- 18  (2-ounce) chocolate bark coating squares, cut in half
- 1  (12-ounce) package semisweet chocolate morsels
- 4  (1-ounce) bittersweet chocolate baking squares, broken into pieces
- 1  tablespoon shortening
- 1  teaspoon vanilla extract

Combine first 7 ingredients in a 5-quart slow cooker; cover and cook on LOW 2 hours or until chocolate is melted. Stir chocolate and nuts; add vanilla, stirring well to coat.

Drop candy by heaping teaspoonfuls onto wax paper. Let stand at least 2 hours or until firm. Store in an airtight container. Yield: 6 dozen.

*gift idea • make ahead*
## White Chocolate-Peppermint Jumbles

*Salty pretzel nuggets are coated in white chocolate and combined with peppermints for an irresistible confection. (pictured at left)*

**Prep: 42 min.   Cook: 1 hr., 30 min.   Other: 1 hr.**

- 2  (16-ounce) packages vanilla bark coating
- 1  (12-ounce) package white chocolate morsels
- 1  (6-ounce) package white chocolate baking squares
- 3  tablespoons shortening
- 1  (16-ounce) package pretzel nuggets (we tested with Snyder's of Hanover Sourdough Pretzel Nuggets)
- 1  (8-ounce) package animal-shaped crackers (3 cups)
- 1  cup coarsely crushed hard peppermint candies

Combine first 4 ingredients in a 6-quart slow cooker. Cook, covered, on LOW 1 hour and 30 minutes or until vanilla bark and chocolate look very soft. Uncover and stir until smooth. Stir in pretzels, crackers, and crushed peppermint candies.

Drop candy by heaping tablespoonfuls onto wax paper. Let stand 1 hour or until firm. Yield: about 8 dozen.

## Toffee Fondue

*Save some fondue to spoon over ice cream.*

**Prep: 5 min.   Cook: 3 hr.**

- ¾  cup butter, cut into pieces
- 2  cups firmly packed light brown sugar
- 1¼  cups light corn syrup
- 3  tablespoons water
- 2  (14-ounce) cans sweetened condensed milk
- ¾  cup almond toffee bits
- 2  teaspoons vanilla extract
- Pear slices
- Pretzel rods
- Shortbread sticks

Combine first 5 ingredients in a 4-quart slow cooker. Cover and cook on LOW 3 hours, stirring occasionally, until fondue is smooth. Stir in toffee bits and vanilla. Serve with pear slices, pretzel rods, and shortbread sticks. Yield: 6 cups.

*editor's favorite • make ahead*
## White Cheese Dip

*Look for white American cheese in the deli department. We liked the extra spice contributed by 1 can of hot tomatoes—using 2 cans of regular tomatoes yields a much milder dip.*

**Prep: 11 min.   Cook: 2 hr., 2 min.**

- 1  small onion, finely chopped
- 3  garlic cloves, minced
- 1  (10-ounce) can hot diced tomatoes and green chiles
- 1  (10-ounce) can diced tomatoes and green chiles
- 1  (4.5-ounce) can chopped green chiles
- ½  teaspoon dried oregano
- ¼  teaspoon freshly ground pepper
- 2  pounds deli white American cheese, sliced (we tested with DiLusso)
- 1  cup milk

Place onion in a medium microwave-safe bowl; cover loosely with heavy-duty plastic wrap. Microwave on HIGH 2 minutes. Stir garlic and next 5 ingredients into onion.

Roughly tear cheese slices; place in a 4-quart slow cooker. Pour milk over cheese; add onion mixture. Cover and cook on LOW 2 hours. Stir gently to blend ingredients. Yield: 8 cups.

**Make Ahead:** Spoon dip into serving-size freezer containers, and freeze up to 1 month. Thaw overnight in refrigerator. Reheat in microwave on MEDIUM (50%) power.

## The Ultimate Party Crab Dip

*It's ultimate because it's really rich and will serve a crowd for a holiday open house. Many newer slow cookers have a warm setting, which is perfect for keeping this dip hot throughout a party.*

Prep: 32 min.   Cook: 2 hr., 30 min.

2   tablespoons butter
6   green onions, chopped
2   garlic cloves, minced
1   cup heavy whipping cream
1   (14-ounce) can quartered artichoke hearts, drained and coarsely chopped
3   (8-ounce) packages cream cheese, softened
1   (8-ounce) can diced water chestnuts, drained
¾   cup chopped ham
½   cup shredded Parmesan cheese
2   tablespoons minced pickled jalapeño pepper slices or 1 fresh jalapeño, minced
¾   teaspoon salt
¼   teaspoon pepper
1   pound fresh lump crabmeat, drained
1   cup (4 ounces) shredded sharp Cheddar cheese

Melt butter in a large nonstick skillet over medium heat. Add green onions and garlic; sauté 4 minutes or until tender. Add cream and artichokes. Bring to a boil; reduce heat, and simmer 4 to 5 minutes or until reduced to 2 cups.

Beat cream cheese in a large bowl until smooth and creamy. Stir in water chestnuts and next 5 ingredients. Add artichoke cream sauce; stir until well combined. Gently fold in crabmeat.

Spoon dip into a lightly greased 3- or 4-quart slow cooker. Sprinkle with Cheddar cheese. Cook, covered, on LOW 2½ hours or until thoroughly heated and cheese melts. Serve with toasted baguette slices or crackers. Yield: about 9 cups.

*make ahead*

## Christmas Compote

*Serve this orange-kissed, sweet-tart dessert topping warm or cold over ice cream or toasted pound cake.*

Prep: 12 min.   Cook: 4 hr.

6   large Golden Delicious apples, peeled, cored, and sliced
1   cup fresh or frozen cranberries
1   cup turbinado sugar
¼   cup orange marmalade
¼   cup cranberry-apple juice drink
¼   cup port
2   tablespoons Cointreau or other orange liqueur

Combine all ingredients in a 5-quart slow cooker. Cover and cook on LOW 4 hours or until apples are tender. Cool. Serve warm or chilled. Yield: 4 cups.

*editor's favorite*

## Sweet Potato Casserole

*The slow cooker produces an undeniably good option for this favorite Southern holiday side dish.*

Prep: 24 min.   Cook: 4 hr.

2   (29-ounce) cans sweet potatoes in syrup, drained and mashed (about 4 cups)
⅓   cup butter or margarine, melted
⅔   cup firmly packed light or dark brown sugar
2   large eggs, lightly beaten
1   teaspoon vanilla extract
1   teaspoon ground cinnamon
⅓   cup whipping cream
1   cup coarsely chopped pecans
¾   cup firmly packed light or dark brown sugar
¼   cup all-purpose flour
2   tablespoons butter or margarine, melted

Combine first 6 ingredients in a large bowl; beat at medium speed with an electric mixer until smooth. Add cream; stir well. Pour into a lightly greased 3- or 4-quart oval-shaped slow cooker.

Combine pecans and remaining 3 ingredients in a small bowl. Sprinkle over sweet potatoes. Cover and cook on HIGH 3 to 4 hours or until sugar melts on top of casserole. Yield: 8 cups.

Sweet Potato Casserole

**Caribbean-Style Chicken Soup with Lime and Cilantro**

Sprinkle chicken evenly with Caribbean rub; set aside. Heat 1 teaspoon oil in a medium skillet over medium-high heat; add onion and garlic. Cook 3 minutes or until tender. Transfer mixture to a 5-quart oval slow cooker using a slotted spoon. Heat remaining 3 teaspoons oil in skillet over medium-high heat; add chicken, and cook 6 to 8 minutes, or until browned, turning occasionally. Transfer chicken to slow cooker. Add 1 cup broth to skillet, scraping skillet to loosen browned bits. Pour over chicken. Add remaining broth, adobo sauce, and next 4 ingredients to slow cooker. Cover and cook on HIGH 1 hour. Decrease temperature to LOW, and cook 3 more hours.

Remove chicken from slow cooker, and cool 10 minutes. Remove chicken from bones, returning meat to slow cooker. Stir in lime juice. Serve soup over hot cooked rice; top with cilantro, radishes, and sour cream. Serve with lime wedges. Yield: 8 cups.

* We used adobo sauce from canned chipotle chiles in adobo sauce.

*make ahead*

## Caribbean-Style Chicken Soup with Lime and Cilantro

*A squeeze of lime, crisp radishes, and fresh cilantro add zing to this earthy soup.*

Prep: 23 min.   Cook: 4 hr.   Other: 10 min.

3   bone-in chicken breasts, skinned
3   bone-in chicken thighs, skinned
1   tablespoon salt-free Caribbean rub (we tested with Spice Hunter)
4   teaspoons vegetable oil
½   cup chopped onion
1   teaspoon minced garlic
1   (32-ounce) container chicken broth
1   tablespoon adobo sauce*
1   (15-ounce) can black beans, rinsed and drained
½   cup unsweetened coconut milk
1   teaspoon salt
½   teaspoon pepper
3   tablespoons fresh lime juice
Hot cooked rice
Fresh cilantro
Thinly sliced radishes
Sour cream
Lime wedges

## Corn and Potato Chowder

*Stop by the bakery for some rustic bread to accompany this hearty chowder.*

Prep: 15 min.   Cook: 8 hr.

1   pound baking potatoes, peeled and cut into ¼" cubes (about 2 cups)
1   (14.75-ounce) can cream-style corn
1   (14.5-ounce) can diced tomatoes
1   (14-ounce) can chicken broth
½   cup chopped onion
½   cup coarsely chopped celery
¾   teaspoon dried basil
½   teaspoon salt
¼   teaspoon pepper
1   bay leaf
1   cup whipping cream
¼   cup butter or margarine
4   bacon slices, cooked and crumbled

Stir together first 10 ingredients in a 5-quart slow cooker. Cover and cook on LOW 8 hours or until potato is tender. Add whipping cream and butter, stirring until butter melts. Ladle into bowls; sprinkle each serving with bacon. Yield: 6 cups.

**Fix it Faster:** Cook bacon in the microwave or substitute packaged fully cooked bacon, prepared according to package directions.

# Great Cakes

These are our staff's favorite
layer cakes for wowing family and friends
during the holidays.

A whole lot of luscious layer cakes have come through our Test Kitchens over the past several decades. But these five are a stellar sampling of all that's good about dessert—moist layers, decadent frosting, impressive appearance, and most of all, delicious flavor.

## Butter-Pecan Cake

*The buttery goodness of white chocolate flavors this cake.*

Prep: 20 min.   Cook: 22 min.   Other: 10 min.

Butter-Pecan Frosting
6    ounces white chocolate, chopped
½    cup boiling water
1    cup butter, softened
1½   cups sugar
4    large eggs, separated
1    teaspoon vanilla extract
1    cup buttermilk
1    teaspoon baking soda
3    cups sifted cake flour
Garnish: toasted pecan halves

Prepare frosting; cover and chill. Place white chocolate in a bowl. Pour boiling water over white chocolate; stir until smooth. Set aside, and let cool.

Grease 3 (9") round cakepans; line with wax paper. Grease and flour wax paper. Set aside.

Beat butter at medium speed with an electric mixer until creamy; gradually add sugar, beating well. Add egg yolks, 1 at a time, beating after each addition until blended. Stir in white chocolate and vanilla.

Combine buttermilk and soda. Add flour to butter mixture alternately with buttermilk mixture, beginning and ending with flour. Mix at low speed after each addition until blended.

Beat egg whites at high speed until stiff peaks form. Gently fold into batter. Pour batter into prepared pans.

Bake at 350° for 20 to 22 minutes or until a wooden pick inserted in center comes out clean. Cool in pans 10 minutes; remove from pans, and cool completely on wire racks.

Spread Butter-Pecan Frosting between layers and on top and sides of cake. Garnish, if desired. Store cake in refrigerator. Yield: 1 (3-layer) cake.

*Butter-Pecan Cake*

## Butter-Pecan Frosting

Prep: 7 min.   Cook: 11 min.   Other: 1 hr.

2    tablespoons butter
1¼   cups coarsely chopped pecans
1    (8-ounce) package cream cheese, softened
1    (3-ounce) package cream cheese, softened
½    cup butter, softened
1    (16-ounce) package powdered sugar
2    teaspoons vanilla extract

Melt 2 tablespoons butter in a large skillet over medium heat. Add pecans, and cook, stirring constantly, 10 minutes or until pecans are toasted. Remove from heat. Cool completely.

Beat cream cheese and ½ cup butter at medium speed with an electric mixer until creamy. Gradually add sugar; beat until light and fluffy. Stir in buttered pecans and vanilla. Cover and chill at least 1 hour. Yield: 4 cups.

## Holiday Fig Cake

*The presence of fresh rosemary is a highlight in this moist spice cake.*

Prep: 40 min.  Cook: 45 min.  Other: 10 min.

1¾ cups fig preserves (almost 2 [11.5-ounce] jars)
3   large eggs
1   cup sugar
1   cup vegetable oil
2   cups all-purpose flour
1   teaspoon baking soda
1   teaspoon salt
1   teaspoon ground cinnamon
1   teaspoon ground allspice
½   teaspoon ground nutmeg
½   cup buttermilk
1   cup chopped pecans, toasted
1   cup finely chopped prunes
2   tablespoons chopped fresh rosemary (optional)
Honey-Cream Cheese Frosting
1¾ cups coarsely chopped pecans, toasted (optional)
Garnish: fresh rosemary sprigs

Chop large pieces of fig preserves, if necessary; set aside.

Beat eggs, sugar, and oil at medium speed with an electric mixer until blended. Combine flour and next 5 ingredients; add to sugar mixture alternately with buttermilk, beginning and ending with flour mixture. Fold in fig preserves, 1 cup chopped pecans, prunes, and, if desired, chopped rosemary.

Pour batter into 2 greased and floured 8" round cake-pans. Bake at 350° for 42 to 45 minutes or until a wooden pick inserted in center comes out clean. Run a knife around edge of pans. Cool in pans on wire racks 10 minutes; remove from pans, and cool on wire racks.

Spread Honey-Cream Cheese Frosting between layers and on top and sides of cake. Press pecan pieces onto sides of cake, if desired. Garnish, if desired. Store cake in refrigerator. Yield: 1 (2-layer) cake.

## Honey-Cream Cheese Frosting

Prep: 6 min.

1½ (8-ounce) packages cream cheese, softened
⅓   cup butter, softened
1½  tablespoons honey
4   cups powdered sugar

Beat cream cheese, butter, and honey at medium speed with an electric mixer just until smooth. Gradually add powdered sugar, beating at low speed just until blended. Yield: 3½ cups.

---

# test kitchens 10 secrets to layer cake success

### baking the layers

• Use shortening when a cake recipe calls for a "greased pan" unless otherwise specified.
• Don't sift flour before measuring, except for cake flour. Simply stir the flour, spoon it gently into a dry measuring cup, and level the top.
• Stagger cakepans on center rack of a preheated oven. If placed on separate racks, stagger pans so air can circulate.
• Keep oven door closed until minimum baking time has elapsed. Every time you open the oven door, the oven temperature drops 25 to 30 degrees. Use the oven window and light, instead, so you don't risk uneven baking.
• Keep several wire cooling racks on hand. Cakes that cool on a solid surface may become soggy.

### assembling the cake

• Be sure cake layers are completely cooled before adding filling and frosting, or frosting may slide off the cake.
• Place bottom cake layer upside-down on the serving plate. Place top layer right side up.

### frosting and freezing the cake

• Keep frosting just ahead of spatula. Do not backstroke until entire area is frosted, or spatula may drag crumbs into frosting.
• Frost sides of cake first, and top last.
• Unfrosted cake layers freeze best. Wrap cooled cake layers in aluminum foil, and then in plastic wrap. Freeze up to 5 months. Thaw cake layers in wrapping at room temperature.

*Holiday Fig Cake*

# A rosemary wreath garnish hints at the
unique use of herbs in this holiday cake.

*Double-Nut Drenched Chocolate Cake*

*editor's favorite*

# Double-Nut Drenched Chocolate Cake

*The layers of this decadent cake are drenched with*
*Frangelico liqueur and then iced with fudgy topping.*

Prep: 35 min.   Cook: 21 min.   Other: 10 min.

¾   cup butter, softened
2    cups firmly packed light brown sugar
2    large eggs
¾   cup water
¼   cup white vinegar
2    cups all-purpose flour
1    teaspoon baking soda
¼   teaspoon salt
1    cup finely chopped hazelnuts, toasted
1    tablespoon vanilla extract
¼   cup unsweetened cocoa
½   cup hazelnut liqueur (we tested with Frangelico)
Chocolate Topping
Garnish: hazelnuts

Grease 3 (8") round cakepans; line bottoms with wax paper. Grease and flour wax paper and sides of pans; set aside.

Beat butter at medium speed with an electric mixer until creamy; gradually add brown sugar, beating well. Add eggs, 1 at a time, beating until blended after each addition.

Combine water and vinegar. Combine flour, baking soda, and salt; add to butter mixture alternately with water mixture, beginning and ending with flour mixture. Beat at low speed until blended after each addition. Stir in chopped hazelnuts and vanilla. Pour one-third of batter into each of 2 prepared pans. Fold cocoa into remaining batter; pour chocolate batter into third pan.

Bake at 350° for 19 to 21 minutes or until a wooden pick inserted in center comes out clean. Cool in pans on wire racks 10 minutes; remove from pans. Peel off wax paper immediately after inverting. Cool completely on wire racks.

Brush liqueur over cake layers. Place 1 white cake layer, top side down, on serving plate; spread one-third of Chocolate Topping over top (do not frost sides). Top with chocolate cake layer; spread one-third Chocolate Topping over chocolate layer (do not frost sides). Top with remaining white layer and remaining Chocolate Topping (do not frost sides). Garnish, if desired. Allow cake to set several hours before slicing. Yield: 1 (3-layer) cake.

## Chocolate Topping

Prep: 4 min.   Cook: 9 min.   Other: 55 min.

6    (4-ounce) sweet chocolate baking bars, chopped
      (we tested with Baker's German sweet chocolate)
1    pound butter
1½   cups chopped pecans
2    teaspoons vanilla extract

Melt chocolate and butter in a heavy saucepan over medium-low heat; cool 10 minutes. Stir in pecans and vanilla; cool mixture until spreading consistency, stirring occasionally (about 45 minutes). Yield: 5 cups.

Four ingredients become sinfully good frosting.

## Hazel's Fresh Coconut Cake

*Southerner Hazel Burwell has been making this stately cake for her family for over 40 years. She brushes the layers with a coconut syrup to keep the cake moist, and adds marshmallows to the frosting to keep it soft.*

Prep: 1 hr., 15 min.   Cook: 20 min.   Other: 10 min.

1    cup butter, softened
2    cups sugar
4    large eggs
2¾  cups all-purpose flour
2    teaspoons baking powder
1    teaspoon salt
1    cup milk
1½  teaspoons vanilla extract
1½  teaspoons almond extract
2    tablespoons sugar
¼    cup fresh coconut milk
Boiled Frosting
2 to 3 cups fresh shredded coconut
       (about 2 coconuts)
Garnishes: kumquats, crab apples

Beat butter at medium speed with an electric mixer until creamy; gradually add 2 cups sugar, beating well. Add eggs, 1 at a time, beating until blended after each addition.

Combine flour, baking powder, and salt; add to butter mixture alternately with milk, beginning and ending with flour mixture. Beat at low speed until blended after each addition. Stir in flavorings. Pour batter into 3 greased and floured 9" round cakepans.

### choosing coconuts

When choosing a coconut, carefully examine the eyes at the base of the coconut. Check this area for any signs of mold or mildew. Shake several good candidates to determine which one has the most milk. Your goal is a dry, solid coconut, heavy for its size, with plenty of milk.

Bake at 350° for 18 to 20 minutes or until a wooden pick inserted in center comes out clean. Cool in pans on wire racks 10 minutes; remove from pans, and cool on wire racks.

Combine 2 tablespoons sugar and coconut milk in a small glass bowl. Microwave on HIGH 1 minute; stir until sugar dissolves. Brush 1 cake layer with half of coconut milk mixture, leaving a ½" margin around edges. Spread with 1 cup Boiled Frosting, and sprinkle with ½ cup shredded coconut. Top with second cake layer, and repeat procedure. Top with remaining cake layer. Spread remaining frosting on top and sides of cake; sprinkle with remaining coconut. Garnish, if desired. Yield: 1 (3-layer) cake.

Fresh coconut cake is the essence of Christmas.

*Hazel's Fresh Coconut Cake*

## Boiled Frosting

Prep: 9 min.   Cook: 10 min.

1½  cups sugar
½   cup water
4    egg whites
½   teaspoon cream of tartar
⅛   teaspoon salt
6    large marshmallows, cut into small pieces

Combine sugar and water in a heavy saucepan. Cook over medium heat, stirring constantly, until mixture is clear. Cook, without stirring, until syrup reaches soft ball stage or candy thermometer registers 240° (about 10 minutes).

While syrup cooks, beat egg whites at low speed with an electric mixer until foamy. Add cream of tartar and salt; beat at medium speed until soft peaks form. Increase to high speed, and add hot syrup in a heavy stream. Add marshmallows, a few pieces at a time. Beat until stiff peaks form and frosting is thick enough to spread. Yield: 7¼ cups.

New Orleans Double-Chocolate
Praline-Fudge Cake

254

# New Orleans Double-Chocolate Praline-Fudge Cake

*This cake is off-the-charts rich. If you like pralines, you'll love this candylike frosting.*

Prep: 50 min.   Cook: 29 min.   Other: 55 min.

1    cup butter or margarine
¼    cup unsweetened cocoa
1    cup water
½    cup buttermilk
2    large eggs
1    teaspoon baking soda
1    teaspoon vanilla extract
2    cups sugar
2    cups all-purpose flour
½    teaspoon salt
     Chocolate Ganache
     Praline Frosting

Grease bottoms of 3 (8") round cakepans; line with wax paper. Grease and flour wax paper and sides of pans.

Cook first 3 ingredients in a saucepan over low heat, stirring constantly, until butter melts and mixture is smooth; remove from heat. Cool.

Beat buttermilk, eggs, baking soda, and vanilla at medium speed with an electric mixer until smooth. Add butter mixture to buttermilk mixture, beating until blended. Combine sugar, flour, and salt; gradually add to buttermilk mixture, beating until blended. (Batter will be thin.) Pour batter evenly into prepared pans.

Bake at 350° for 20 to 22 minutes or until a wooden pick inserted in center comes out clean. Cool in pans on wire racks 10 minutes. Remove from pans; immediately remove wax paper. Cool completely on wire racks. (Layers will appear thin.)

Spread about ½ cup ganache between cake layers; spread remainder on sides of cake (do not frost top of cake). Chill cake 30 minutes. Pour Praline Frosting slowly over top of cake, spreading to edges and allowing some frosting to run over sides of cake. Freeze, if desired; thaw at room temperature 4 to 6 hours. Yield: 1 (3-layer) cake.

## Chocolate Ganache

Cook: 3 min.   Other: 25 min.

2    cups (12 ounces) semisweet chocolate morsels
⅓    cup whipping cream
¼    cup butter or margarine, cut into pieces

Microwave chocolate morsels and cream in a glass bowl on MEDIUM (50% power) 2 to 3 minutes or until morsels are melted, stirring after 1½ minutes; whisk until smooth. Gradually add butter, whisking until smooth. Cool, whisking often, about 25 minutes or until spreading consistency. Yield: about 2 cups.

## Praline Frosting

*Don't prepare this candylike frosting ahead because it'll harden very quickly.*

Cook: 4 min.   Other: 5 min.

¼    cup butter or margarine
1    cup firmly packed light brown sugar
⅓    cup whipping cream
1    cup powdered sugar
1    teaspoon vanilla extract
1    cup chopped pecans, toasted

Bring first 3 ingredients to a boil in a 2-quart saucepan over medium heat, stirring often; boil 1 minute. Remove from heat, and whisk in powdered sugar and vanilla until smooth. Add toasted pecans, stirring gently 3 to 5 minutes or until frosting begins to cool and thicken slightly. Pour frosting immediately over cake. Yield: about 2 cups.

# Kids *in the* Kitchen

Little ones can help stir up these playful sweets for party fun or gift giving.

Jelly beans make a fun middle for these classic vanilla cookies.

*make ahead*
## Jelly Bean Thumbprint Cookies

**Prep: 6 min.  Cook: 13 min.  Other: 8 hr.**

1    cup butter, softened
⅔   cup granulated sugar
2    egg yolks
1    teaspoon vanilla extract
2¼  cups all-purpose flour
¼   teaspoon salt
⅓   cup powdered sugar
2    tablespoons heavy whipping cream
Assorted jelly beans
Additional powdered sugar

Beat butter at medium speed with an electric mixer until creamy; gradually add ⅔ cup sugar, beating well. Add egg yolks and vanilla, beating until blended.

Combine flour and salt; add to butter mixture, beating at low speed until blended. Cover and chill dough 8 hours.

Shape dough into 1" balls, and place 2" apart on ungreased baking sheets. Press thumb into each cookie to make an indentation.

Bake at 350° for 12 to 13 minutes. Cool 1 minute on baking sheets; remove to wire racks. Make thumbprint indentations again while cookies are still warm; let cookies cool completely.

Meanwhile, combine ⅓ cup powdered sugar and heavy cream in a small bowl; stir with a fork until smooth. Spoon icing into a zip-top freezer bag; cut a tiny hole in 1 corner of bag, and squirt a small amount of icing into indentation in each cookie. Press jelly beans into center of each cookie. Let set. Dust cookies with powdered sugar. Yield: 1½ dozen.

*make ahead*
## Wreath Cookies

*With only a few ingredients, you can transform shredded wheat cereal into these whimsical holiday wreaths. Let the kids help shape and decorate them.*

**Prep: 25 min.  Cook: 3 min.  Other: 30 min.**

1    (12-ounce) package vanilla candy coating, broken up
Green paste food coloring
2½  cups coarsely crushed mini shredded whole wheat cereal biscuits (we tested with vanilla creme-flavored Frosted Mini Wheats)
Mini candy-coated chocolate pieces, red cinnamon candies, swirled holiday white morsels

Microwave vanilla candy coating in a medium bowl at MEDIUM (50% power) 3 minutes, stirring after every minute. Stir in desired amount of food coloring. Add cereal, stirring gently to coat. Drop cereal mixture by heaping tablespoonfuls onto wax paper; shape each spoonful into a wreath. Decorate with assorted candies. Let cookies stand about 30 minutes until firm. Yield: about 1½ dozen.

Wreath Cookies

# Fudge Ring

*Spooning this cookie- and candy-filled fudge into a home-made ring mold makes a fun project that the kids will want to take part in.*

**Prep: 10 min.   Cook: 12 min.   Other: 15 min.**

1   (12-ounce) package milk chocolate morsels
1   cup butterscotch morsels
1   (14-ounce) can sweetened condensed milk
1   teaspoon vanilla extract
Pinch of salt
Butter
1¼ cups candy-coated chocolate pieces, divided
½   cup coarsely crushed cream-filled chocolate sandwich
     cookies (about 5 cookies)

Combine first 3 ingredients in a saucepan, reserving condensed milk can. Cook over medium-low heat until all morsels melt, stirring often. Remove from heat; stir in vanilla and salt. Cool slightly (about 15 minutes).

Meanwhile, grease an 8" round cake pan or springform pan with butter. Line pan with 2 pieces of plastic wrap, overlapping edges and smoothing out any wrinkles. Wrap empty condensed milk can with aluminum foil, smoothing out wrinkles; place in center of cake pan.

Stir 1 cup candies and crushed cookies into fudge; spread fudge in cake pan, holding can firmly in center. (A second pair of hands is a big help here.) Sprinkle remaining ¼ cup chocolate candies over fudge, gently pressing candies into fudge. Cover and chill until firm (about 2 to 3 hours).

To unmold, carefully loosen edges with a sharp knife, and remove can from center of fudge. Carefully invert fudge onto a plate. Invert again on a serving plate or cardboard cake round for gift giving. Cut fudge into thin slices to serve. Yield: 2 pounds.

**Note:** For an easy gift giving "platter," we wrapped a cardboard cake round with wrapping paper.

Fudge Ring

▲ To unmold fudge, carefully loosen inside edges with a knife, and remove can.

▲ Lift fudge out of (springform) pan, peel away plastic wrap, and invert twice onto cardboard cake round.

# Sugar Cookie Pops

*You'll want to buy several containers of colored sugars and jimmies so you'll have plenty for coating these cookie balls.*

**Prep: 24 min.   Cook: 11 min. per batch   Other: 2 hr.**

½   cup butter, softened
½   cup shortening
1    cup granulated sugar
1    cup powdered sugar
2    large eggs
¾   cup canola or vegetable oil
2    teaspoons vanilla extract
4    cups all-purpose flour
1    teaspoon baking soda
1    teaspoon salt
1    teaspoon cream of tartar
Colored sugars, sparkling sugars, and
     multicolored jimmies
4" white craft sticks

Beat butter and shortening at medium speed with an electric mixer until fluffy; add sugars, beating well. Add eggs, oil, and vanilla, beating until blended.

Combine flour and next 3 ingredients; add to butter mixture, blending well. Cover and chill dough 2 hours or overnight.

Shape dough into 1½" balls. Roll each ball in colored sugar or jimmies in individual bowls, pressing gently, if necessary, to coat balls. Place 2" apart on ungreased baking sheets. Insert craft sticks about 1" into each cookie to resemble a lollipop.

Bake at 350° for 10 to 11 minutes or until set. Let cool 2 minutes on baking sheets; remove cookie pops to wire racks to cool completely. Yield: 4½ dozen.

Tutti Fruity Crispy Candy

## Tutti Fruity Crispy Candy

*This simple candy recipe offers several opportunities for kids to help: Let them crush the pretzels in a zip-top plastic bag, stir the cereal into the melted vanilla coating, and, best of all, break the finished candy into pieces and sample it.*

**Prep: 5 min.   Cook: 2 min.   Other: 1 hr.**

1    (24-ounce) package vanilla candy coating, broken up
2½   cups sweetened fruit-flavored multigrain cereal (we
       tested with Froot Loops)
1    cup thin pretzel sticks, coarsely broken

Line a lightly greased 15" x 10" jelly-roll pan with wax or parchment paper.

Melt candy coating in a large microwave-safe bowl according to package directions. Gently stir in cereal and pretzels. Spread candy onto wax paper. Let stand 1 hour or until firm. (Do not refrigerate.)

Break candy into pieces. Store in an airtight container. Yield: about 1¾ pounds.

## Peanut Butter 'n' Jelly Scones

**Prep: 15 min.   Cook: 20 min.**

3¼   cups all-purpose flour
⅔    cup firmly packed light brown sugar
1    tablespoon baking powder
¾    teaspoon salt
½    cup cold unsalted butter, cut into pieces
½    cup chunky peanut butter, chilled
½    cup semisweet chocolate morsels (optional)
⅔    cup whipping cream, divided
2    teaspoons vanilla extract
2    tablespoons turbinado sugar
About ¾ cup strawberry jelly

Combine first 4 ingredients in a food processor. Pulse briefly until combined. Add butter, and pulse to make a coarse meal. Add peanut butter, and pulse briefly to disperse evenly. Be careful not to overmix.

Transfer dough to a large bowl. Add chocolate morsels, if desired. Make a well in center, and add ½ cup plus 1 tablespoon whipping cream and 2 teaspoons vanilla. Stir with a fork just until dry ingredients are moistened. Knead dough in bowl 2 or 3 times to incorporate dry ingredients in bottom of bowl.

Drop mounds of dough using a ⅓-cup measure onto a baking sheet lined with parchment paper. Smooth tops, and brush scones with remaining cream. Sprinkle with turbinado sugar. Make a deep indentation in center of each scone using thumb or the back of a small spoon; fill each with a scant tablespoon jelly.

Bake at 425° for 18 to 20 minutes or until scones are lightly browned around edges. Cool completely. Yield: 1 dozen.

Peanut Butter 'n' Jelly Scones

The classic kids' sandwich flavors are reinvented here as delectable tender scones. Let your little ones help spoon jelly onto the dough.

# Our Top 10
# Cookies & Brownies

Nearly a dozen all-time best, most decadent cookies,
bars, and squares grace these pages.

# Sparkling Ginger Stars

*A heavy sugar crust and the peppery bite of fresh ginger make these gingerbread cookies scrumptious. Be sure your spices are fresh; it will make a big taste difference here.*

**Prep: 12 min.   Cook: 17 min. per batch   Other: 2 hr., 30 min.**

1½  cups all-purpose flour
½   teaspoon baking soda
½   teaspoon salt
2   teaspoons ground ginger
1   teaspoon ground cinnamon
¼   teaspoon ground cloves
¼   teaspoon freshly grated nutmeg
½   cup unsalted butter, softened
½   cup firmly packed dark brown sugar
¼   cup dark molasses
1   egg yolk
1   tablespoon grated lemon rind
1   tablespoon grated fresh ginger
½   teaspoon vanilla extract
1   large egg
2   tablespoons whipping cream
1   (3.25-ounce) jar coarse sparkling sugar (see note)

Combine first 7 ingredients in a medium bowl; stir until blended.

Beat butter at medium speed with an electric mixer until creamy; gradually add brown sugar, beating well. Beat in molasses, egg yolk, lemon rind, grated ginger, and vanilla. Stir in flour mixture; beat just until blended.

Shape dough into a ball, and divide in half. Flatten each half into a round disk; wrap each in plastic wrap, and chill 2½ hours until firm.

Line 2 large baking sheets with parchment paper. Roll out dough, 1 section at a time, to ¼" thickness on a lightly floured surface. Cut into star shapes, using a 4" cookie cutter. Place ½" apart on prepared baking sheets.

Whisk together 1 egg and whipping cream; brush egg wash lightly over cookies. Sprinkle heavily with sparkling sugar.

Bake at 325° for 17 minutes or until cookies are puffed and slightly darker around edges. Cool 2 minutes on baking sheets; remove with parchment paper to wire racks to cool completely. **Yield: 2 dozen.**

**Note:** Sparkling sugar can be purchased at gourmet grocery stores or cake decorating shops, or ordered from La Cuisine at 800-521-1176 or lacuisineus.com.

Chunky
Chocolate
Gobs

# Chunky Chocolate Gobs

*These ultrachocolate cookies are, hands down, some of the best ever to come through our test kitchen.*

**Prep: 18 min.   Cook: 12 min. per batch   Other: 30 min.**

¾   cup unsalted butter, softened
⅓   cup butter-flavored shortening
1   cup granulated sugar
⅔   cup firmly packed dark brown sugar
2   large eggs
2   teaspoons vanilla extract
2   cups all-purpose flour
⅔   cup unsweetened cocoa
1   teaspoon baking soda
¼   teaspoon salt
2   cups cream-filled chocolate sandwich cookies, coarsely chopped (16 cookies)
3   (1.75-ounce) Mounds bars, chilled and chopped
1   to 2 cups semisweet chocolate morsels

Beat butter and shortening at medium speed with an electric mixer until creamy; gradually add sugars, beating until light and fluffy. Add eggs and vanilla, beating until blended.

Combine flour and next 3 ingredients; gradually add to butter mixture, beating until blended. Stir in cookies, candy bars, and desired amount of chocolate morsels. Chill dough 30 minutes.

Drop dough by ¼ cupfuls 2" apart onto baking sheets lined with parchment paper. Bake at 350° for 10 to 12 minutes or until barely set. Cool on baking sheets 10 minutes. Transfer to wire racks to cool completely. **Yield: about 2½ dozen.**

Peppermint Bonbon Cookies

## Peppermint Bonbon Cookies

*Here's a decadent holiday combination—soft and chewy chocolate on the inside with a little peppermint candy crunch on top. These gems are great plain, or we offer a double glaze option too.*

**Prep: 25 min.   Cook: 13 min. per batch   Other: 2 hr., 35 min.**

8    ounces bittersweet or semisweet chocolate, chopped
½    cup unsalted butter
1½   ounces unsweetened chocolate, chopped
½    cup finely crushed hard peppermint candies
6    tablespoons granulated sugar
3    large eggs
1    teaspoon vanilla extract
1    teaspoon peppermint extract
1½   cups all-purpose flour
¾    teaspoon baking powder
¼    teaspoon salt
½    cup semisweet chocolate morsels
Additional coarsely crushed hard peppermint candies,
       divided
½    cup powdered sugar (optional)
2½   teaspoons milk (optional)
½    cup semisweet chocolate morsels, melted (optional)

Combine first 3 ingredients in a large saucepan; cook over low heat until chocolate melts and mixture is smooth, stirring occasionally. Remove from heat, and stir in ½ cup crushed peppermint and 6 tablespoons sugar. Let cool 30 minutes.

Add eggs to melted chocolate, 1 at a time, stirring well. Stir in extracts.

Combine flour, baking powder, and salt; add to chocolate mixture, stirring until combined. Stir in chocolate morsels. Cover and chill dough 2 hours or until firm enough to shape.

Shape dough into 1½" balls; place on parchment paper-lined baking sheets. Bake at 325° for 12 to 13 minutes or until cookies are puffed and cracked on top. Sprinkle coarsely crushed peppermints onto cookies; press candy lightly into cookies. Let cookies cool 5 minutes on baking sheets. Transfer to wire rack to cool completely.

Whisk together powdered sugar and milk; drizzle over cooled cookies, if desired. Drizzle with melted chocolate, if desired. Sprinkle cookies again with chopped peppermint, if desired. Let cookies stand until glaze and chocolate are firm. Yield: about 2½ dozen.

## Crunchy Frostbite Cookies

**Prep: 22 min.   Cook: 14 min. per batch   Other: 1 hr.**

2    cups all-purpose flour
2    teaspoons baking soda
1    teaspoon baking powder
¼    teaspoon salt
1    cup shortening
¾    cup granulated sugar
¾    cup firmly packed light brown sugar
2    large eggs
1    teaspoon vanilla extract
1½   cups uncooked regular oats
1½   cups cornflakes cereal
12   ounces white chocolate baking squares, chopped
3    tablespoons shortening
½    teaspoon peppermint extract

Combine flour, baking soda, baking powder, and salt; stir well until blended.

Beat 1 cup shortening at medium speed with an electric mixer until creamy; gradually add sugars, beating well. Add eggs and vanilla; beat well. Add flour mixture, mixing just until blended. Stir in oats and cornflakes.

Drop dough by heaping tablespoonfuls, 2" apart, onto lightly greased baking sheets; flatten slightly. Bake at 325° for 12 to 14 minutes. Cool slightly on baking sheets. Transfer cookies to wire racks to cool completely.

Microwave white chocolate and 3 tablespoons shortening in a medium-size microwave-safe bowl at HIGH 1 minute or until white chocolate melts, stirring once. Stir in peppermint extract. Dip flat bottom of each cookie into melted white chocolate, letting excess drip back into bowl. Place dipped cookies, dipped side up, on wax paper; let stand 1 hour or until white chocolate sets. Yield: about 3 dozen.

Crunchy Frostbite Cookies

White Chocolate-
Oatmeal-Raisin
Cookies

*editor's favorite • make ahead*

# White Chocolate-Oatmeal-Raisin Cookies

*Using fiori di sicilia, an Italian citrus-and-vanilla flavoring, gives these easy drop cookies a subtle taste of orange.*

**Prep: 10 min.   Cook: 15 min. per batch   Other: 5 min.**

| | |
|---|---|
| 1 | cup all-purpose flour |
| ½ | teaspoon baking soda |
| ½ | teaspoon ground cinnamon |
| ¼ | teaspoon salt |
| ½ | cup plus 2 tablespoons unsalted butter, softened |
| ½ | cup granulated sugar |
| ½ | cup firmly packed light brown sugar |
| 1 | large egg |
| 1 | teaspoon fiori di sicilia or orange extract (see note) |
| 1 | cup uncooked regular oats |
| 8 | ounces white chocolate, chopped (about 2 cups) |
| ½ | cup raisins or golden raisins |

Combine first 4 ingredients in a medium bowl.

Beat butter at medium speed with an electric mixer until creamy; gradually add sugars, beating well. Beat in egg and orange flavoring just until combined. Add flour mixture and oats; stir until blended. Stir in white chocolate and raisins. Cover and chill dough 1 hour, if desired.

Line 2 large baking sheets with parchment paper. Drop batter by heaping tablespoonfuls, 3" apart, onto prepared baking sheets.

Bake at 350° for 13 to 15 minutes or until lightly browned. Cool on baking sheets 5 minutes. Transfer cookies to wire racks to cool completely. Yield: about 2½ dozen.

**Note:** Order fiori di sicilia from bakerscatalogue.com or call 800-827-6836. It's very affordable, and a small vial will perfume your kitchen for a long time.

# Lemon-Coconut Snowballs

*Lemon and coconut add a new twist to the traditional wedding cookie. Don't be shy when rolling these in powdered sugar—the more powdered sugar, the bigger the snowball!*

**Prep: 25 min.   Cook: 20 min. per batch   Other: 35 min.**

| | |
|---|---|
| 1 | cup unsalted butter, softened |
| ½ | cup powdered sugar |
| 1 | teaspoon coconut extract |
| 1 | teaspoon vanilla extract |
| 2¼ | cups all-purpose flour |
| 1½ | tablespoons grated lemon rind |
| ½ | teaspoon salt |
| 1 | cup sweetened flaked coconut, lightly toasted |
| 1½ | cups powdered sugar |

Beat butter at medium speed with an electric mixer until creamy; gradually add ½ cup powdered sugar and extracts, beating well. Add flour, lemon rind, and salt, beating until combined. Stir in coconut. Cover and chill dough 30 minutes.

Shape dough into generous 1" balls; place 1" apart on parchment paper-lined baking sheets. Bake at 350° for 15 to 20 minutes or until golden on bottom but pale on top. Transfer cookies to wire racks to cool 5 minutes.

Place 1½ cups powdered sugar in a bowl, and roll warm cookies in powdered sugar, coating well. Cool cookies completely on wire racks. Roll cooled cookies in powdered sugar again, coating well. Yield: 2 dozen.

Dark Chocolate-Espresso Shortbread

Cover dough portions with plastic wrap; gently press or roll each portion of dough into a 5½" circle. Lightly score each round with a sharp knife into 6 or 8 wedges.

Bake rounds at 325° for 23 minutes or until shortbread feels firm to the touch. Gently score each round again with a sharp knife. Slide parchment from baking sheets onto wire racks. Let shortbread cool completely on parchment. Cut shortbread into wedges along scored lines.

Melt chocolate baking bars separately in small bowls in the microwave according to package directions. Partially dip wide end of each shortbread wedge in unsweetened chocolate. Place on a wax paper-lined jelly-roll pan, and freeze briefly to set chocolate. Then partially dip other half of wide end of each wedge in white chocolate. Freeze briefly to set white chocolate. Yield: 1½ to 2 dozen.

*gift idea*
## Pistachio-Cranberry Biscotti

**Prep: 28 min.   Cook: 49 min.   Other: 10 min.**

6     tablespoons unsalted butter, softened
¾     cup sugar
2     large eggs
1     tablespoon grated orange rind
1½   teaspoons orange extract
2¼   cups all-purpose flour
1½   teaspoons baking powder
½     teaspoon salt
1     cup orange-flavored sweetened dried cranberries
¾     cup shelled natural salted pistachio nuts, chopped

Beat butter and sugar in a large bowl at medium speed with an electric mixer until light and fluffy. Add eggs, beating well; beat in orange rind and extract.

Combine flour, baking powder, and salt; add to butter mixture, beating at low speed until blended. Stir in cranberries and pistachios.

Divide dough in half. Using lightly floured hands, shape each portion into a 14" x 2" log. Place both logs 3" apart on a large baking sheet lined with parchment paper.

Bake at 325° for 28 minutes or until firm to the touch. Cool logs on baking sheet 10 minutes.

Cut each log into ½"-thick diagonal slices with a serrated knife using a gentle sawing motion. Place slices, cut side down, on baking sheet. Bake 9 minutes; turn cookies over, and bake 12 more minutes. Transfer biscotti to wire racks to cool completely. Yield: 1½ dozen.

*editor's favorite • make ahead*
## Dark Chocolate-Espresso Shortbread

*Edges tipped with unsweetened chocolate and white chocolate enhance the coffee flavor in these cookies.*

**Prep: 33 min.   Cook: 23 min.**

1¼   cups all-purpose flour
¼     cup cornstarch
¼     cup unsweetened cocoa
1     teaspoon instant espresso powder or instant coffee powder (we tested with Café Bustello)
¼     teaspoon salt
1     cup unsalted butter, softened
1     cup powdered sugar
3     ounces unsweetened chocolate baking bars
3     ounces white chocolate baking bar (we tested with Ghirardelli)

Combine first 5 ingredients in a medium bowl; set aside.

Beat butter at medium speed with an electric mixer until fluffy; gradually add powdered sugar, beating well. Stir in dry ingredients; beat just until blended.

Line 2 baking sheets with parchment paper. Divide dough into 3 equal portions. Place 2 portions on opposite ends of 1 baking sheet. Place remaining portion on second baking sheet.

Peanut Butter
Candy Bar
Brownies

editor's favorite • make ahead

# Peanut Butter Candy Bar Brownies

*Peanut butter sandwich cookies become the crumb crust for these hunky bars loaded with chunks of candy bar.*

**Prep: 26 min.   Cook: 35 min.**

1   (16-ounce) package peanut-shaped peanut butter
     sandwich cookies, crushed
½  cup butter, melted
1   (14-ounce) can sweetened condensed milk
½  cup creamy peanut butter
1   tablespoon vanilla extract
5   (1.5-ounce) packages chocolate-covered peanut butter
     cup candies, coarsely chopped
2   (2.1-ounce) chocolate-covered crispy peanut but-
     tery candy bars, coarsely chopped (we tested with
     Butterfinger)
1   cup semisweet chocolate morsels
½  cup honey-roasted peanuts
½  cup sweetened flaked coconut

   Combine crushed cookies and butter in a medium bowl.
Press crumb mixture into bottom of a greased aluminum
foil-lined 13" x 9" pan, allowing foil to extend over ends of
pan. Bake at 350° for 6 to 8 minutes.
   Combine condensed milk, peanut butter, and vanilla in a
medium bowl, stirring until smooth.
   Sprinkle chopped candy, chocolate morsels, peanuts, and
coconut over crust. Drizzle condensed milk mixture over
coconut.
   Bake at 350° for 27 minutes or until lightly browned.
Remove to a wire rack, and let cool in pan. Use foil to
lift uncut brownies out of pan. Peel foil away from sides of
uncut brownies, and cut into bars. Yield: 28 small bars or
18 large bars.

Pistachio-Cranberry
Biscotti

Death by Caramel Bars

Add to butter mixture, stirring just until blended. Fold in chopped candy bars.

Spoon batter into a greased aluminum foil-lined 13" x 9" pan coated with cooking spray, allowing foil to extend over ends of pan. (Pan will be very full.) Spoon dollops of dulce de leche over batter; swirl slightly into batter with a knife. Bake at 325° for 1 hour and 5 minutes. Remove to a wire rack, and cool completely. (This may take several hours.) Use foil to lift uncut brownies out of pan. Peel foil away from sides of uncut brownies, and cut into bars. Yield: 2 dozen.

*Find dulce de leche with other Mexican ingredients or on the baking aisle.

*editor's favorite*
## Mudslide Brownies

*Yummy ingredients from the popular drink make a splash in these decadent bars.*

**Prep: 21 min.  Cook: 35 min.**

6    (1-ounce) unsweetened chocolate baking squares
½    cup plus 2 tablespoons unsalted butter, divided
1    cup granulated sugar
1    cup firmly packed light brown sugar
3    large eggs
4    teaspoons espresso powder, divided (we tested with Café Bustello)
2    tablespoons plus 2 teaspoons coffee liqueur, divided
1½  cups all-purpose flour
½    teaspoon salt
1    cup chopped pecans, toasted
2    tablespoons whipping cream or half-and-half
2    tablespoons vodka
2¼ to 2½ cups powdered sugar
Garnish: chocolate-covered espresso coffee beans, chopped

Melt 4 chocolate baking squares and ½ cup butter in a heavy saucepan over low heat, stirring occasionally. Remove from heat, and transfer to a large bowl. Add sugars; stir well. Stir in eggs, 2 teaspoons espresso powder, and 2 teaspoons coffee liqueur. Add flour and salt, stirring until blended. Stir in pecans.

Spread batter into a lightly greased aluminum foil-lined 13" x 9" pan (or see note on next page). Bake at 325° for 20 to 25 minutes or until brownies appear set on top. Cool completely in pan on a wire rack.

Melt remaining 2 chocolate baking squares and 2 tablespoons butter in heavy saucepan, stirring occasionally.

*editor's favorite • make ahead*
## Death by Caramel Bars

*These showy brownies are nice and tall with pockets of caramel goo. They are wicked enough on their own, but for an over-the-top dessert, add a scoop of vanilla ice cream and drizzle with caramel sauce.*

**Prep: 24 min.  Cook: 1 hr., 5 min.**

3    cups firmly packed light brown sugar
2    cups unsalted butter, melted
3    large eggs, lightly beaten
1    tablespoon vanilla extract
4    cups all-purpose flour
1    cup uncooked regular oats
1    teaspoon baking powder
½    teaspoon baking soda
¾    teaspoon salt
6    (2.07-ounce) chocolate-coated caramel-peanut nougat bars, chopped (we tested with Snickers)
1    (14-ounce) can dulce de leche*

Combine first 4 ingredients in a large bowl; stir well. Combine flour, oats, baking powder, baking soda, and salt.

Mudslide Brownies

Remove from heat; transfer to a medium bowl. Stir in remaining 2 teaspoons espresso powder, whipping cream, vodka, and remaining 2 tablespoons coffee liqueur. Add enough powdered sugar to make a good spreading consistency, beating at medium speed with an electric mixer until smooth. Spread frosting over cooled brownies; garnish, if desired. Let stand until frosting is set. Use foil to lift uncut brownies out of the pan. Cut into bars to serve. Yield: 3 dozen small or 1 dozen large.

**Note:** For really thick, showy brownies, we baked these in an 11" x 7½" pan at 325° for 26 to 28 minutes.

# Snacks & Munchies *Swap*

Move over cookie swap; this get-together encourages savory or sweet pick-up food of all kinds to sample and share with friends.

Crispy Chocolate Popcorn

*editor's favorite • gift idea*

# Crispy Chocolate Popcorn

**Prep: 30 min.   Cook: 1 hr.**

2    cups milk chocolate morsels, divided
1½ cups firmly packed light brown sugar
¾   cup butter
¾   cup light corn syrup
¾   teaspoon salt
1½ teaspoons vanilla extract
¾   teaspoon baking soda
2    (3.5-ounce) bags natural-flavored microwave popcorn,
      popped
2    cups peanuts or cashews

Combine 1 cup chocolate morsels, brown sugar, and next 3 ingredients in a heavy saucepan; cook over medium heat, stirring constantly, until mixture come to a boil. Remove from heat, and stir in vanilla and baking soda.

Distribute popcorn and nuts evenly into 2 lightly greased roasting pans. Be sure to remove all unpopped kernels of popcorn before pouring chocolate mixture over popcorn. Pour chocolate mixture evenly over popcorn and nuts, stirring well with a lightly greased spatula.

Bake at 250° for 1 hour, stirring every 15 minutes. Spread on wax paper to cool, breaking apart large clumps as mixture cools. Sprinkle remaining 1 cup chocolate morsels evenly over hot popcorn; let cool. Store in airtight containers. Yield: about 29 cups.

# Christmas Gorp

**Prep: 25 min.**

1½ cups white chocolate baking morsels
¾ cup creamy peanut butter
¼ cup plus 2 tablespoons butter
1 tablespoon honey
¼ teaspoon ground cinnamon (optional)
8 cups crispy corn and rice cereal squares (we tested with Crispix)
1 (8-ounce) package pretzel-flavored fish-shaped crackers (3 cups)
1½ cups powdered sugar
2 cups salted, roasted almonds with skins
2 cups red and green candy-coated chocolate pieces
1½ cups sweetened dried cranberries or raisins

Combine first 4 ingredients and cinnamon, if desired, in a heavy saucepan. Cook over medium heat, stirring until morsels and butter melt. Place cereal and crackers in a large bowl; add melted white chocolate mixture. Stir until well coated. Let cool slightly.

Place powdered sugar in a large zip-top plastic bag. Add coated cereal mixture in batches; seal bag, and toss well to coat. Combine sugar-coated cereal mixture, almonds, and remaining ingredients in a large bowl. Stir gently to blend. Store in an airtight container. Yield: 18 cups.

**Package these festive fortune cookies (shown at right) in those familiar to-go cartons. The cartons are available in a variety of colors online or at your local party store.**

# Holiday Fortune Cookies

*Wear gloves while shaping these fortune cookies fresh from the oven. They cool and crisp quickly, so bake and shape them two at a time. Bake more at one time if you have helpers. To make paper fortunes, type them, triple spaced, on a computer. Cut them out, fold in half, and place in middle of cookies before folding.*

**Prep: 5 min.   Cook: 12 min. per batch**

½ cup all-purpose flour
1 tablespoon cornstarch
¼ cup sugar
¼ teaspoon salt
¼ teaspoon ground cinnamon
⅛ teaspoon ground nutmeg
¼ cup canola oil
2 large egg whites
1 tablespoon water
1 teaspoon vanilla extract
2 (2-ounce) vanilla candy coating squares
Red decorator sugar
Purple decorator sugar

Whisk together first 6 ingredients in a medium bowl. Add oil and egg whites, whisking until smooth. Whisk in water and vanilla extract.

Drop a rounded teaspoonful of batter onto a well-greased baking sheet. Using back of a spoon, spread batter into a 3" circle. Repeat procedure with another rounded teaspoonful of batter. Bake at 300° for 10 to 12 minutes or until light golden brown.

Working quickly, immediately remove each cookie from pan with a spatula, and flip over into gloved hand; place prepared fortune in center of each cookie and fold each cookie in half. Grasp end of each cookie, and place over the edge of a bowl, drawing the edges down to form a crease. Place cookies, ends down, in muffin pans to maintain shape; let cookies cool completely. Repeat procedure with remaining batter, baking 2 cookies at a time.

To decorate, microwave vanilla coating in a small bowl at MEDIUM (50% power) 2 minutes, stirring after 1 minute. Dip outer edge of each cookie in vanilla coating, and then into red or purple sugar; set aside to let coating harden. Yield: about 2 dozen.

Holiday Fortune
Cookies

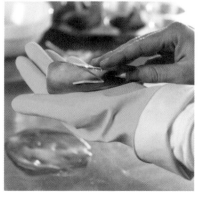

▲ Place paper fortune in center of cookie, and quickly fold cookie in half.

▲ Grasp end of each cookie, and place over the edge of a bowl, drawing the edges down to form a crease.

▲ Place cookies, ends down, in muffin pans to set the shape.

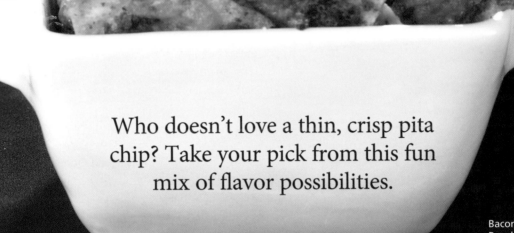

Who doesn't love a thin, crisp pita chip? Take your pick from this fun mix of flavor possibilities.

Bacon, Cheddar, and Ranch Pita Chips; Parmesan-Herb Pita Chips

*make ahead • quick & easy*

## Barbecue Pita Chips

Prep: 6 min.   Cook: 15 min.

¼  cup butter, melted
1½ tablespoons barbecue seasoning (we tested with McCormick's Grill Mates)
1½ tablespoons lemon juice
3   (6") pita rounds

Combine butter, barbecue seasoning, and lemon juice in a small bowl.

Split each pita bread into 2 rounds. Cut each round into 8 wedges. Place wedges on a lightly greased baking sheet. Brush rough side of each wedge with butter mixture. Bake at 350° for 15 minutes or until crisp. Remove from oven; transfer to wire racks to cool. Yield: 4 dozen chips.

*make ahead • quick & easy*

## Bacon, Cheddar, and Ranch Pita Chips

Prep: 6 min.   Cook: 15 min.

¼  cup olive oil
1½ tablespoons Ranch dressing mix
3   (6") pita rounds
⅓  cup real bacon bits (we tested with Hormel)
½  cup (2 ounces) shredded sharp Cheddar cheese

Combine olive oil and dressing mix in a small bowl.

Split each pita bread into 2 rounds. Cut each round into 8 wedges. Place wedges on a lightly greased baking sheet. Brush rough side of each wedge with oil mixture. Sprinkle wedges with bacon bits and then cheese. Bake at 350° for 15 minutes or until crisp. Remove from oven; transfer to wire racks to cool. Yield: 4 dozen chips.

## Taco Pita Chips

**Prep: 6 min.   Cook: 15 min.**

¼   cup olive oil
1½  tablespoons taco seasoning
3   (6") pita rounds
1   (8-ounce) package shredded Mexican four-cheese blend

Combine olive oil and taco seasoning in a small bowl.

Split each pita bread into 2 rounds. Cut each round into 8 wedges. Place wedges on a lightly greased baking sheet. Brush rough side of each wedge with oil mixture. Sprinkle wedges with cheese. Bake at 350° for 15 minutes or until crisp. Remove from oven; transfer to wire racks to cool. Yield: 4 dozen chips.

## Parmesan-Herb Pita Chips

**Prep: 6 min.   Cook: 15 min.**

⅓   cup olive oil
4   teaspoons dried Italian seasoning
1   teaspoon garlic salt
3   (6") pita rounds
½   cup freshly grated Parmesan cheese

Combine olive oil, Italian seasoning, and garlic salt.

Split each pita bread into 2 rounds. Cut each round into 8 wedges. Place wedges on a lightly greased baking sheet. Brush rough side of each wedge with oil mixture. Sprinkle wedges with cheese. Bake at 350° for 15 minutes or until crisp. Transfer to wire racks to cool. Yield: 4 dozen chips.

## Sea Salt and Cracked Pepper Pita Chips

**Prep: 6 min.   Cook: 15 min.**

3   (6") pita rounds
¼   cup olive oil
½   teaspoon sea salt
½   teaspoon freshly ground black pepper

Split each pita bread into 2 rounds. Cut each round into 8 wedges. Place wedges on a lightly greased baking sheet. Brush rough side of each wedge with oil. Sprinkle with salt and pepper. Bake at 350° for 15 minutes or until crisp. Transfer to wire racks to cool. Yield: 4 dozen chips.

## Famous Sausage Ball Muffins

*This recipe has been around for years, and every cook has definite opinions and memories related to it. We found the recipe fun to revisit as easy mini muffins and with some flavor variations.*

**Prep: 5 min.   Cook: 15 min. per batch**

2   cups all-purpose baking mix
1   pound hot or regular pork sausage (we tested with Jimmy Dean)
2   cups (8 ounces) shredded sharp Cheddar cheese (we tested with Cracker Barrel)

Combine all ingredients in a large bowl, pressing together with hands. Spoon rounded tablespoonfuls into lightly greased 1¾" miniature muffin pans. Bake at 400° for 13 to 15 minutes or until lightly browned. Remove from pans, and serve warm with desired sauce, such as Ranch dressing, honey mustard, or barbecue sauce. Yield: 4 dozen.

**Note:** To make traditional Sausage Balls, shape mixture into ¾" balls, and place on ungreased baking sheets. Bake at 400° for 15 to 18 minutes or until lightly browned. Yield: about 8 dozen. Freeze uncooked sausage balls, if desired. Bake frozen balls for 18 to 20 minutes.

**Dressed-Up Sausage Ball Muffins:** Add ⅓ cup finely chopped onion, 1 tablespoon garlic powder, and ¼ teaspoon hot sauce to sausage-cheese dough. Proceed with recipe. Yield: 4 dozen.

**Southwest Sausage Ball Muffins:** Use Pepper Jack cheese instead of Cheddar, and add 1 (4.5-ounce) can chopped green chiles, drained and patted dry with paper towels, to sausage-cheese dough. Bake 20 minutes. Yield: about 4½ dozen.

**Mediterranean Sausage Ball Muffins:** Add ⅔ cup chopped pimiento-stuffed green olives. Use 1 cup Cheddar cheese and 1 cup crumbled feta cheese. Proceed with recipe. Yield: about 4½ dozen.

**Sausage Ball Cocktail:** Skewer 2 or 3 warm Sausage Balls onto a small wooden pick or skewer. Spoon a few tablespoons Ranch dressing into a martini glass; add skewered sausage balls.

from:

# GIFTS FROM THE HEART

Share the true spirit of the season with cleverly packaged gifts from the kitchen.

# Gifts *from* the Kitchen

Homemade goodies like these taste best when delivered with love during the holiday season.

*editor's favorite • gift idea • make ahead*

# Smoked Sea Salt Chocolate-Covered Turtles

*Savor the best of both salty and sweet in each bite of these unique candies.*

Prep: 25 min.   Cook: 25 min.   Other: 45 min.

| | |
|---|---|
| 1 | (14-ounce) package caramels |
| 2 | tablespoons butter |
| 2 | tablespoons water |
| 3 | cups pecan halves, toasted |
| 8 | (2-ounce) chocolate candy coating squares |
| 1 | cup bittersweet chocolate morsels |
| 4 | (1-ounce) bittersweet chocolate baking squares |
| 2 | tablespoons shortening |

Smoked sea salt (see note)

Combine first 3 ingredients in a heavy saucepan over low heat, stirring constantly, until smooth. Stir in pecan halves. Remove from heat; cool in pan 5 minutes.

Drop candy by tablespoonfuls onto a jelly-roll pan lined with lightly greased wax paper. Freeze 30 minutes.

Melt chocolates and shortening in a heavy saucepan over low heat, stirring until smooth. Dip caramel candies into chocolate mixture, 4 or 5 at a time, allowing excess chocolate to drip off; place on lightly greased wax paper. Quickly sprinkle tops with sea salt. Chill until firm. **Yield: 2 dozen.**

**Note:** McCormick smoked flavor sea salt grinder is readily available and is what we first tested and tasted on this candy. Then we went online and found some other fine options. See Halen Môn Salt below (order at www.saltworks.us).

*gift idea • make ahead*

# Double Chocolate-Covered Toffee Grahams

*Recapture delicious memories with this nostalgic snack— crisp graham crackers dunked in chocolate.*

Prep: 20 min.   Cook: 4 min.   Other: 20 min.

| | |
|---|---|
| 2 | sleeves graham crackers (18 whole crackers) |
| 6 | (2-ounce) vanilla candy coating squares, cut in half |
| 4 | (1-ounce) white chocolate baking squares, chopped |
| 4 | tablespoons shortening, divided |
| 6 | (2-ounce) chocolate candy coating squares, cut in half |
| 4 | (1-ounce) semisweet chocolate baking squares, chopped |
| ½ | cup toffee bits |

Break each graham cracker in half.

Place vanilla squares, white chocolate squares, and 2 tablespoon shortening in a microwave-safe bowl. Microwave at HIGH 1 to 2 minutes or until white chocolate is soft; stir until smooth. Dip 18 graham cracker squares entirely in melted white chocolate. Place dipped grahams on a parchment paper-lined baking sheet. Chill 20 minutes or until white chocolate is firm. Repeat procedure with chocolate squares, remaining 2 tablespoons shortening, and remaining graham crackers. Drizzle any remaining semisweet chocolate and white chocolate over dipped grahams; sprinkle with toffee bits. Chill until firm. **Yield: 3 dozen.**

◀ Dip and sprinkle candies a few at a time so the salt will adhere before the chocolate hardens.

*gift idea • make ahead*

## Pecan-Chocolate Chip Cookie Brittle

**Prep: 17 min.   Cook: 19 min.**

1½   cups all-purpose flour
1     teaspoon baking powder
¼     teaspoon baking soda
¼     teaspoon salt
¾     cup butter, melted and cooled slightly
½     cup granulated sugar
⅓     cup firmly packed light brown sugar
1     teaspoon vanilla extract
1     cup semisweet chocolate mini-morsels
1     cup pecan pieces, toasted (see note)
½     cup sweetened flaked coconut, toasted (see note)

Combine first 4 ingredients; set aside.

Stir together butter and next 3 ingredients in a large bowl; add flour mixture, stirring until smooth. Stir in chocolate morsels, pecans, and coconut. (Dough will look crumbly.)

Press dough evenly into a lightly greased 15" x 10" jelly-roll pan, pressing almost to edges.

Bake at 350° for 19 minutes or until lightly browned and cookie "slab" seems crisp. Cool completely in pan. Break cookie into pieces. **Yield: 1 to 2 dozen cookie pieces.**

**Note:** You can toast pecan pieces and coconut in the same pan at 350° for 8 minutes.

*editor's favorite • gift idea*

## Chipotle-Chocolate Toffee

*This candy has an awesome flavor surprise—not for the fainthearted. (pictured on page 216)*

**Prep: 6 min.   Cook: 30 min.**

1¼   cups unsalted butter
1     cup granulated sugar
½     cup firmly packed light brown sugar
⅓     cup water
1     tablespoon light corn syrup
½     teaspoon salt
1     tablespoon chopped chipotle pepper plus 1 tablespoon adobo sauce from can
2     cups natural almonds with skins, coarsely chopped
1     cup dark chocolate or semisweet chocolate morsels

Melt butter in a 3-quart heavy saucepan over medium-low heat. Add granulated sugar and next 4 ingredients;

Pecan-Chocolate Chip Cookie Brittle

We like the thought of calling this "brittle" because it's a big slab of crisp chocolate chip cookie that you break into irregular pieces after it bakes.

cook until sugars dissolve, stirring constantly. Attach candy thermometer to pan. Increase heat to medium; add chopped chipotle pepper and sauce. Cook, stirring often, at a gentle boil 10 minutes. Add almonds, and continue boiling and stirring for 10 minutes or until thermometer registers 290°.

Remove from heat. Carefully pour candy onto a buttered jelly-roll pan; spread candy to ¼" thickness. Sprinkle with chocolate morsels. Let stand 2 minutes or until chocolate melts; spread chocolate using an offset spatula. Cool until chocolate hardens. Break toffee into pieces. **Yield: 1¼ pounds**

## Chocolate-Cherry Sugar-Crusted Shortbread

**Prep: 8 min.   Cook: 40 min.   Other: 30 min.**

1      cup butter, softened
½     cup powdered sugar
2½   cups all-purpose flour
⅛     teaspoon salt
¼     cup semisweet chocolate mini-morsels
¼     cup finely chopped dried cherries
1      teaspoon vanilla extract
1      tablespoon granulated sugar
½     cup granulated sugar

Beat butter at medium speed with an electric mixer until creamy; add powdered sugar, beating well.

Combine flour and salt; gradually add to butter mixture, beating until well blended. Stir in chocolate mini-morsels, cherries, and vanilla.

Line an 8" square pan with aluminum foil, allowing foil to extend over edges of pan. Lightly grease foil and sprinkle with 1 tablespoon granulated sugar. Press dough into pan.

Bake at 325° for 40 minutes or until golden. Cool 30 minutes or until slightly warm in pan. Use foil to gently lift shortbread from pan. Cut shortbread into 1" squares using a sharp knife. Roll shortbread squares in ½ cup granulated sugar. **Yield: 64 cookies.**

## Somewhat like little dessert croutons, these are great nibbles to enjoy with a cup of tea or cocoa.

Chocolate-Cherry
Sugar-Crusted Shortbread

Kitchen Sink Brownies

Coat a 13" x 9" pan with cooking spray. Line pan with aluminum foil, allowing ends to hang over short sides of pan. Tuck overlapping ends under rim on short sides. Coat foil with cooking spray; set pan aside.

Combine first 5 ingredients in a small bowl.

Beat butter and sugars at medium speed with an electric mixer until smooth; add eggs, coffee, and vanilla, beating just until blended. Add flour mixture; beat at medium speed until blended. Stir in sandwich cookie crumbs and remaining 4 ingredients.

Spoon batter into prepared pan, spreading evenly.

Bake at 325° for 55 to 58 minutes. Cool completely in pan on a wire rack. Cover and chill at least 2 hours.

Carefully invert brownies from pan using overlapping foil as handles; remove foil. Invert brownies again onto a cutting board. Cut brownies into squares. **Yield: 2 dozen.**

**Note:** We like this technique of lining a pan with foil before baking brownies. It sure makes cutting baked brownies neat and easy.

*editor's favorite • gift idea*
## Cookie Biscotti Sticks

*Liven up your next coffee break with these extravagant cookie sticks. They're impressive in size and mimic biscotti in length and crunch.*

**Prep: 11 min.   Cook: 26 min.   Other: 3 hr., 20 min.**

1      cup firmly packed light brown sugar
⅔      cup butter
¼      cup light corn syrup
¼      cup creamy peanut butter
1      teaspoon vanilla extract
3½     cups uncooked regular oats
1      (12-ounce) package semisweet chocolate morsels
1      cup butterscotch morsels
2      tablespoons shortening
½      cup creamy peanut butter
½      cup coarsely chopped peanuts

Stir together brown sugar, butter, and corn syrup in a large saucepan; cook over medium heat until sugar dissolves and butter melts. Remove from heat. Stir in ¼ cup peanut butter and vanilla. Gently stir in oats. Press into bottom of an ungreased 13" x 9" pan lined with aluminum foil. Bake at 375° for 20 to 22 minutes or until browned.

Melt together chocolate morsels, butterscotch morsels, and shortening in a saucepan over medium heat, stirring until smooth; stir in ½ cup peanut butter. Spread over

*editor's favorite • gift idea • make ahead*
## Kitchen Sink Brownies

*Decadence abounds in each bite of these chunky candy-studded brownies full of good things you've probably got in the pantry.*

**Prep: 22 min.   Cook: 58 min.   Other: 2 hr.**

1½     cups all-purpose flour
1      cup unsweetened cocoa
½      teaspoon baking powder
¼      teaspoon baking soda
¼      teaspoon salt
1½     cups butter, melted
1½     cups granulated sugar
1½     cups firmly packed light brown sugar
4      large eggs
¼      cup brewed espresso or French roast coffee
2      teaspoons vanilla extract
1      cup chopped cream-filled chocolate sandwich cookies (10 cookies)
4      (1.45-ounce) milk chocolate candy bars with almonds, chopped (we tested with Hershey's)
½      cup dark chocolate morsels (we tested with Ghirardelli)
½      cup white chocolate morsels
1      cup pecan pieces, toasted

Cookie Biscotti Sticks

baked cookie crust; sprinkle with peanuts. Let cool in pan on a wire rack 20 minutes. Cover and chill 2 to 3 hours or until firm. (Or pop them in the freezer to speed cooling. Just be sure to let them stand 5 minutes at room temperature before cutting.)

Lift uncut cookies out of pan using foil as handles. Cut crosswise into approximately 1"-thick sticks using a large chef's knife. Wrap in cellophane bags or plastic wrap for gift giving. **Yield: 1 dozen.**

◀ Use a sharp knife to cut through the crisp baked cookie crust. Work slowly so long cookie sticks don't crumble.

▲ Pair Pound Cake Minis and Fudgy Espresso Brownie Bites in holiday gift bags. Both are made using mini muffin pans.

*editor's favorite • gift idea*

## Fudgy Espresso Brownie Bites

*These petite brownies are rich and gooey, especially if you bake them the lesser time. You'd never guess they start with a mix. Pile some in a bag for gift giving.*

**Prep: 18 min.   Cook: 14 min.**

1     tablespoon espresso powder
¼     cup hot water
½     cup vegetable oil or canola oil
2     large eggs
1     (18.3-ounce) package fudge brownie mix (we tested with Betty Crocker)
1     cup semisweet chocolate morsels
1     cup coarsely chopped walnuts

Dissolve espresso powder in hot water in a 1-cup glass measuring cup, stirring with a small whisk. Cool slightly. Whisk in oil and eggs until blended.

Place brownie mix in a large bowl; break up large lumps with the back of a spoon. Stir in espresso mixture until blended. Stir in chocolate morsels and walnuts. Spoon mixture into 38 lightly greased (1¾") miniature muffin cups, filling full.

Bake at 375° for 12 to 14 minutes or until tops are shiny and crusty and centers are set. Cool completely in pans on wire racks. Remove from pans using a slight twisting motion. **Yield: 38 brownies.**

*editor's favorite • gift idea*

## Baby Pound Cakes

*Enjoy these pound cake bites for breakfast or as a late-night snack by the fire, or split and toast them with butter. Vanilla bean paste, which can be found at specialty food stores, gives these cakes a sublime goodness. And just as with classic pound cake, we loved the crusty top edges on these, too.*

**Prep: 28 min.   Cook: 25 min.   Other: 10 min.**

1½     cups butter, softened
1     (8-ounce) package cream cheese, softened
3     cups sugar
6     large eggs
3     cups all-purpose flour
¼     teaspoon salt
1     tablespoon vanilla bean paste or vanilla extract
½     teaspoon almond extract

Beat butter and cream cheese at medium speed with an electric mixer about 2 minutes or until creamy. Gradually add sugar, beating well, 5 to 7 minutes. Add eggs, 1 at a time, beating just until yellow disappears.

Combine flour and salt. Gradually add to butter mixture, beating at low speed just until blended; stir in vanilla and almond flavorings. Spoon batter into paper-lined standard-size muffin pans, filling three-fourths full.

Bake at 350° for 22 to 25 minutes or until a wooden pick inserted in center comes out clean. Cool in pans on wire racks 10 minutes; remove from pans, and let cool completely on wire racks. **Yield: 2½ dozen.**

**Pound Cake Minis:**

Spoon batter into paper-lined (1¾") miniature muffin cups, filling three-fourths full. Bake at 350° for 16 to 18 minutes or until a wooden pick inserted in center comes out clean. Cool in pans on wire racks 10 minutes; remove from pans, and let cool completely on wire racks. **Yield: about 9 dozen.**

**Fluted Baby Pound Cakes:**

Spoon batter into a greased ¼-cup capacity mini fluted tube pan, filling three-fourths full. (We tested with a 12-cavity mini fluted tube pan.) Bake at 350° for 20 minutes or until a wooden pick inserted in center comes out clean. Cool in pans on wire racks 10 minutes; remove from pans, and let cool completely on wire racks. Dust with powdered sugar or drizzle with Jelly Bean Thumbprint Cookies glaze of powdered sugar and heavy cream (see page 333), if desired. **Yield: 2½ dozen.**

Fluted Baby Pound Cakes

## Chai Tea Mix

*For optimal enjoyment of this trendy flavor-packed drink, be sure your spices are fresh.*

**Prep: 14 min.**

| | |
|---|---|
| 2½ | teaspoons ground ginger |
| 2 | teaspoons ground cinnamon |
| ¾ | teaspoon ground cloves |
| ¾ | teaspoon ground cardamom (optional) |
| 1 | teaspoon ground allspice |
| 1 | teaspoon ground nutmeg |
| ½ | teaspoon freshly ground black pepper |
| 1½ | cups unsweetened instant tea or decaffeinated instant tea |
| 1½ | to 2 cups sugar |
| 1 | cup nonfat dry milk powder |
| 1 | cup powdered nondairy creamer |
| 1 | cup French vanilla-flavored powdered nondairy creamer |

Combine spices and tea in a food processor or blender. Blend 1 to 2 minutes or until mixture becomes a fine powder. Pour into a large bowl. Add sugar to food processor or blender (without cleaning it), and process until superfine, about 30 seconds. Add sugar to bowl of spices. Stir in milk powder and creamers; blend well. Spoon mix into gift jars, if desired.

To serve, stir 2 heaping tablespoons Chai Tea Mix into a mug of hot milk or boiling water. **Yield: 5½ cups mix.**

**Chocolate Chai Mix:** Add ½ cup unsweetened cocoa along with dry milk powder to the blend above. Follow serving directions above. (We recommend milk here.)

**Chai Shake:** Blend ¼ cup Chai Tea Mix, 1 cup milk, and 3½ cups vanilla ice cream in a blender.

**White Chocolate Chai:** Add ¼ cup finely chopped premium white chocolate (such as Lindt or Ghirardelli) to 1 cup Chai Tea Mix. Stir well. Follow serving directions above with 2 heaping tablespoons per cup of hot milk or boiling water.

Chai Shake

Chunky Tapenade

*gift idea • make ahead • quick & easy*

# Chunky Tapenade

*Serve this chunky French favorite as an hors d'oeuvre accompanied with baguette slices, enjoy it with pan-seared tuna or salmon, or on a sandwich of crusty bread and goat cheese. The recipe is easily doubled or tripled if you have multiple gifts to give.*

**Prep: 10 min.**

½   cup pitted chopped kalamata olives
½   cup chopped pimiento-stuffed green olives
½   cup drained and chopped roasted red bell pepper
¼   cup olive oil
2   tablespoons finely chopped fresh flat-leaf parsley
2   tablespoons drained capers
1½  teaspoons chopped fresh thyme
1¼  teaspoons grated lemon rind
¼   teaspoon freshly ground black pepper
2   oil-packed anchovy fillets, rinsed, patted dry, and minced
1   garlic clove, minced

Combine all ingredients in a bowl, and toss gently until blended. Store in an airtight container in the refrigerator up to 1 week. Serve at room temperature. **Yield: 1¾ cups.**

Use a computer to generate gift tags with serving suggestions included. ▶

# Wrapped in Style

When you give gifts from your kitchen, you'll want
them to look as good as they taste. Here are some simple ideas.

Instant Spiced Tea Mix, page 187
Citrus Curd, page 186

Thoughtfulness takes on a special meaning during the holidays. In the hustle and bustle of such busy times, taking a moment to deliver homemade treats brightens the season and spreads the joy. Here are a few tips and gift-giving ideas.

- Purchase a wide selection of jars, buckets, and decorative tins at grocery and variety stores. Also check out tag sales for bargain-priced containers.
- Decorate jar lids with festive fabric scraps, colored or textured tissue papers, or napkins. Cut with decorative-edge scissors to fit, if desired.
- Shop crafts stores for small kitchen utensils and decorations to tie on packages.
- Generate recipe cards on the computer using colored paper stock and kitchen-themed designs.
- Wash a potato chip, drink mix, or mixed nuts container. Glue fabric around the container, or spray-paint the container. Glue ribbon or fabric trim around the bottom of the container. Spray-paint the plastic lid, if desired. Fill the container with cookies, and cover with the plastic lid.

Triple Chocolate-Nut Clusters, White Chocolate-Peppermint Jumbles, page 319

Gingerbread Biscotti, page 310

Homemade Caramel Sauce, page 311

## Goodies for Giving

*Select any of the following for scrumptious food gifts this holiday season.*

- Triple Chocolate-Nut Clusters (page 319)
- White Chocolate-Peppermint Jumbles (page 319)
- Old-Fashioned Peanut Brittle (page 307)
- Homemade Caramel Sauce (page 311)
- Chocolate-Almond-Coconut Macaroons (page 301)
- Coconut-Chocolate Pastries (page 302)
- White Chocolate-Dipped Oatmeal-Cranberry Cookies (page 303)

# CHRISTMAS EXPRESS

Be party-ready in minutes with recipes that are
fast and fabulous. Every recipe features a
make-ahead or time-saving twist.

# Christmas *Express*

Check out this easy and fast holiday fare—each recipe is ready in 30 minutes or less, and many can be made ahead.

# Spicy Crawfish Spread

*Serve this sassy Cajun spread with corn chips, vegetable crudites, or crackers.*

Prep: 4 min.   Cook: 6 min.

| | |
|---|---|
| 3 | tablespoons butter |
| ¾ | cup finely diced onion |
| ¾ | cup finely diced celery |
| 4 | garlic cloves, minced |
| 2 | tablespoons all-purpose salt-free seasoning blend (we tested with Paul Prudhomme's Magic Seasoning) |
| ½ | teaspoon cayenne pepper |
| 8 | ounces peeled, cooked crawfish tails, finely chopped |
| 1 | (8-ounce) package cream cheese, softened |

Garnish: celery leaf

Melt butter in a small skillet over medium-high heat. Add onion, celery, and garlic; sauté 5 minutes or until onion and celery are tender. Add seasoning blend and pepper; sauté 30 seconds. Combine sautéed vegetables and crawfish tails in a bowl. Add softened cream cheese, and stir gently to combine. Garnish, if desired. **Yield: 2¼ cups.**

Spicy Crawfish Spread

# Orecchiette with Broccoli in Garlic Oil

*This simple pasta dish offers a nice way to get kids to eat broccoli.*

Prep: 4 min.   Cook: 22 min.

| | |
|---|---|
| 1 | tablespoon salt |
| 1 | (12-ounce) package orecchiette pasta (about 4 cups) or other small shaped pasta |
| 1 | (12-ounce) package fresh broccoli florets |
| ½ | cup olive oil |
| 8 | garlic cloves, thinly sliced |
| ¾ | teaspoon salt |
| ¼ | teaspoon dried crushed red pepper |
| 3 | tablespoons minced fresh flat-leaf parsley |

Stir 1 tablespoon salt and pasta into 3 quarts boiling water in a Dutch oven. Cook 3 minutes less than package directions state. Stir in broccoli florets; cook 3 minutes or until pasta is al dente, and broccoli is crisp-tender. Drain and return pasta and broccoli to Dutch oven.

While pasta cooks, combine olive oil and next 3 ingredients in a small saucepan. Cook over medium-low heat 6 minutes or until garlic is golden, stirring often. Remove from heat. Add garlic oil and parsley to pasta, and toss well. Serve hot. **Yield: 4 servings.**

# Raspberry-Glazed Beets with Chèvre

*Goat cheese makes a wonderful finishing touch for these slightly sweet, quick-to-heat beets.*

Prep: 2 min.   Cook: 15 min.

| | |
|---|---|
| ¾ | cup chicken broth |
| ½ | cup red raspberry preserves (we tested with Smucker's Simply Fruit) |
| ¼ | teaspoon salt |
| 3 | (14½-ounce) cans sliced beets, drained |
| ¼ | cup butter or margarine |
| ¼ | cup crumbled chèvre |

Bring first 3 ingredients to a boil in a large saucepan over high heat. Add beets, and boil 8 to 10 minutes or until liquid is reduced to a syrup, stirring often. Remove from heat. Stir in butter. Top each serving with crumbled chèvre. Serve immediately. **Yield: 8 servings.**

## Stovetop Sweet Potatoes with Maple and Crème Fraîche

*These sweet potatoes are beaten with a mixer and heated on the stove, keeping your oven free for other holiday baking. Crème fraîche is a surprise ingredient blended in along with maple syrup for an indulgent twist to traditional sweet potato casserole. And instead of marshmallow topping, try these cinnamon-glazed pecans. You won't be able to stop nibbling on them.*

**Prep: 8 min.   Cook: 15 min.**

2    cinnamon sticks, broken
¼    cup sugar
3    tablespoons butter
1    cup pecan halves
¼    teaspoon salt
3    (15-ounce) cans candied yams or sweet potatoes in syrup, drained
¼    cup butter, softened
2    tablespoons finely chopped crystallized ginger
1    teaspoon salt
¼    teaspoon freshly grated nutmeg
1    cup crème fraîche*
¼    cup pure maple syrup
1    teaspoon maple extract or vanilla extract
1    teaspoon balsamic vinegar

Grind cinnamon sticks to a fine powder in a coffee grinder; set aside.

Cook sugar and 3 tablespoons butter in a small saucepan over medium-high heat 3 minutes or until melted and golden. Add pecans, and cook 2 minutes until pecans are toasted and glazed, stirring frequently.

Stir in cinnamon and ¼ teaspoon salt. Spread pecans on wax paper, and set aside to cool.

Combine sweet potatoes, ¼ cup butter, ginger, 1 teaspoon salt, and nutmeg in a large bowl. Beat at low speed with a hand mixer 1 minute; beat at high speed 2 minutes.

Gently fold crème fraîche, maple syrup, extract, and balsamic vinegar into sweet potatoes. Transfer to a saucepan. Bring to a simmer over medium-low heat. Simmer, covered, 10 minutes, stirring occasionally. Spoon potatoes into a serving dish, and sprinkle with glazed pecans. **Yield: 8 to 10 servings.**

*Find crème fraîche with other specialty cheeses in the deli section of many upscale markets.

## Roasted Broccoli with Orange-Chipotle Butter

*Here's a high-flavored side dish worthy of the finest dinner menu. Fresh orange flavor and smoky chipotle pepper hit hot roasted broccoli and sizzle with goodness. Chicken, beef, or pork make fine partners.*

**Prep: 2 min.   Cook: 17 min.**

2    (12-ounce) packages fresh broccoli florets
2    tablespoons olive oil
¼    cup butter, softened
2    teaspoons freshly grated orange rind
1    teaspoon minced canned chipotle peppers in adobo sauce
½    teaspoon salt

Combine broccoli and oil in a large bowl; toss to coat. Place broccoli in a single layer on an ungreased jelly-roll pan. Roast at 450° for 15 to 17 minutes or until broccoli is crisp-tender.

While broccoli roasts, combine butter and next 3 ingredients in a large bowl. Add roasted broccoli to bowl, and toss to coat. Serve hot. **Yield: 6 to 8 servings.**

Roasted Broccoli with Orange-Chipotle Butter

Crisp Chicken with
Hearts of Palm Salad

*quick & easy*

# Crisp Chicken with Hearts of Palm Salad

Prep: 17 min.  Cook: 9 min.

4    skinned and boned chicken breasts (about 1½ pounds)
1    cup Japanese breadcrumbs (panko)
1    large egg
½    teaspoon salt
½    teaspoon freshly ground black pepper, divided
5    tablespoons olive oil, divided
1    (14-ounce) can hearts of palm, drained and sliced
½    cup diced red onion
1    small green bell pepper, diced
1    tablespoon red wine vinegar
2    tablespoons chopped fresh flat-leaf parsley or cilantro
Garnish: flat-leaf parsley or cilantro

Place chicken between 2 sheets of heavy-duty plastic wrap; flatten to ¼" thickness using a meat mallet or rolling pin. Spread breadcrumbs in a shallow plate. Beat egg in a shallow bowl.

Sprinkle chicken with salt and ¼ teaspoon pepper. Dip 1 chicken breast in beaten egg; coat with breadcrumbs. Repeat with remaining chicken. Cook chicken in ¼ cup hot oil in a large skillet over medium-high heat 4 minutes on each side or until done.

While chicken cooks, make salad. Gently toss together remaining 1 tablespoon oil, remaining ¼ teaspoon pepper, hearts of palm, and next 4 ingredients. Serve chicken topped with salad. Garnish, if desired. **Yield: 4 servings.**

Turkey and Black Bean Chili

Heat oil in a Dutch oven over medium-high heat. Add turkey and salt; cook, stirring until turkey crumbles and is no longer pink. Push meat to outer edges of pan, and add onion and garlic to center of pan. Sauté 3 minutes.

Add chili seasoning, and cook 1 minute. Add tomatoes, broth, chipotle pepper, and 1 tablespoon adobo sauce. Bring to a boil. Cover, reduce heat, and simmer 5 minutes. Add beans; cook 5 minutes or until thoroughly heated. Serve with desired toppings. **Yield: 6 cups.**

*quick & easy*

## Broiled Sirloin with Smoky Bacon Mushrooms

*Using precooked bacon and presliced mushrooms gets this gourmet fare to the table fast.*

Prep: 8 min.   Cook: 16 min.   Other: 5 min.

4    fully cooked hickory smoked bacon slices
1    medium onion, cut vertically into thin slices
1    tablespoon butter, melted
2    garlic cloves, minced
2    (8-ounce) packages sliced fresh mushrooms
1¾   teaspoons salt, divided
3    tablespoons chopped fresh flat-leaf parsley
⅛    teaspoon freshly ground black pepper
2    (1-pound) sirloin steaks (1¼" thick)
½    teaspoon freshly ground black pepper

Reheat bacon according to package directions until crisp; coarsely crumble. Sauté onion in butter in a large skillet over medium heat 5 minutes until beginning to brown. Stir in garlic, mushrooms, and ¾ teaspoon salt. Sauté 10 minutes or until mushrooms are tender and liquid evaporates. Stir in bacon, parsley, and ⅛ teaspoon pepper.

While mushrooms cook, sprinkle both sides of steaks with remaining 1 teaspoon salt and ½ teaspoon pepper.

Broil 5½" from heat 7 minutes on each side or until desired degree of doneness. Let stand 5 minutes before slicing. Cut steaks into thin slices; arrange on a serving platter, and top with mushrooms. **Yield: 4 to 6 servings.**

*make ahead • quick & easy*

## Turkey and Black Bean Chili

*Take advantage of packaged seasoning mixes, such as the chili mix called for below. Seasoning mixes are great because they include a number of spices in one package so they cut down on the time it takes to measure individual spices. We used canned black beans here, but pinto or kidney beans are equally good.*

Prep: 5 min.   Cook: 19 min.

2    tablespoons olive oil
1¼   pounds ground turkey
½    teaspoon salt
1    large onion, chopped
2    tablespoons chopped garlic
1    (1.25-ounce) package chili seasoning mix
1    (15-ounce) can diced tomatoes in sauce or crushed
     tomatoes in puree
1    cup chicken broth
1    chipotle pepper in adobo sauce, chopped
1    tablespoon adobo sauce
1    (15-ounce) can black beans, rinsed and drained
Toppings: sour cream, shredded Monterey Jack cheese,
     fresh cilantro sprigs, diced avocado

# Pepper Steak with Roasted Red Pepper Pesto

*Using a grill pan allows you to grill year-round. A cast-iron skillet works well as a grill pan substitute.*

**Prep: 4 min.   Cook: 15 min.**

| | |
|---|---|
| 1½ | pounds sirloin steak (1½" thick) |
| ½ | teaspoon salt |
| 1 | tablespoon coarsely ground black pepper |
| 2 | tablespoons olive oil |
| 1 | (7-ounce) jar refrigerated pesto |
| 1 | (7-ounce) jar roasted red bell peppers, drained and chopped |
| 1 | tablespoon lemon juice |

Sprinkle both sides of steak with salt and 1 tablespoon pepper; brush with olive oil. Place grill pan over medium-high heat until hot. Cook steak in hot grill pan 5 to 7 minutes on each side or until desired degree of doneness. Transfer steak to a carving board, and let stand 5 minutes.

Meanwhile, combine pesto, chopped roasted red pepper, and lemon juice in a small bowl.

Cut steak into thin slices, and transfer to a serving platter. Serve with red pepper pesto. **Yield: 4 to 6 servings.**

Sausage Italian Bread Pizza

# Sausage Italian Bread Pizza

*Choose your favorite sauce for this quick pizza. Most supermarkets have a good selection of jarred pasta and pizza sauces ranging in flavor from simple marinara to roasted pepper.*

**Prep: 12 min.   Cook: 19 min.**

| | |
|---|---|
| 1 | pound mild or hot Italian sausage |
| 2 | tablespoons olive oil, divided |
| 1 | onion, halved and thinly sliced |
| 2 | garlic cloves, minced |
| 1 | cup pizza or pasta sauce |
| 1½ | teaspoons dried oregano |
| ¼ | teaspoon dried crushed red pepper |
| ¼ | teaspoon salt |
| 1 | (1-pound) loaf semolina bread (about 14" long) |
| ⅔ | cup ricotta cheese, divided |
| 2 | cups (8 ounces) shredded mozzarella cheese, divided |
| ¼ | cup grated Parmesan cheese, divided |

Remove and discard casings from sausage. Cook sausage in a large skillet over medium-high heat 8 minutes, stirring until meat crumbles and is no longer pink. Push meat to outer edges of pan; add 1 tablespoon oil. Add onion and garlic; cook 5 minutes or until onion is softened. Remove from heat; stir in pizza sauce and next 3 ingredients.

Cut bread in half lengthwise using a serrated knife, and scoop out center of each bread half, leaving a ½" border; discard scooped-out bread or reserve for making breadcrumbs.

Spread ⅓ cup ricotta down center of each bread half. Top each evenly with sausage mixture, mozzarella, and Parmesan cheese. Drizzle pizzas evenly with remaining 1 tablespoon oil. Place pizzas on a lightly greased baking sheet.

Bake at 425° for 6 minutes or until cheese is melted and pizzas are thoroughly heated. **Yield: 4 servings.**

# Monterey Jack Omelets with Bacon, Avocado, and Salsa

*Omelets make wonderful quick suppers. This southwestern-flavored omelet makes two hefty or four regular servings.*

**Prep: 9 min.   Cook: 7 min.**

6    fully cooked bacon slices
1    cup (4 ounces) shredded Monterey Jack cheese, divided
1    avocado, diced
¼    cup bottled salsa
¼    cup minced fresh cilantro
6    large eggs
2    tablespoons water
½    teaspoon salt
¼    teaspoon freshly ground black pepper
¼    cup butter, divided

Reheat bacon according to package directions until crisp; coarsely crumble. Stir together bacon, ½ cup cheese, avocado, and salsa; set aside to use as filling. Combine remaining ½ cup cheese and cilantro in a bowl.

Whisk together eggs, water, salt, and pepper. Melt 2 tablespoon butter in a 9" nonstick skillet over medium-high heat. Pour half of egg mixture into skillet, and sprinkle with half of cilantro-cheese mixture. As egg starts to cook, gently lift edges of omelet with a spatula, and tilt pan so uncooked portion flows underneath. Sprinkle 1 side of omelet with half of bacon filling. Fold in half. Cook over medium-low heat 45 seconds. Remove from pan, and keep warm. Repeat procedure with remaining butter, egg mixture, cilantro-cheese mixture, and bacon filling. Serve hot. **Yield: 2 servings.**

# Chicken with Cranberry Mojo

**Prep: 9 min.   Cook: 6 min.**

1    teaspoon salt
1    teaspoon ground cumin
½    teaspoon ground coriander
¼    teaspoon freshly ground black pepper
6    skinned and boned chicken breasts
2    tablespoons olive oil
Cranberry Mojo

Combine first 4 ingredients in a small bowl; set aside. Place chicken breasts between 2 sheets of heavy-duty plastic wrap, and flatten to ¼" thickness using a meat mallet or rolling pin.

Sprinkle chicken with spice mixture. Cook chicken in hot oil in a large nonstick skillet over medium heat 2 to 3 minutes on each side or until done. Serve with Cranberry Mojo. **Yield: 4 servings.**

## Cranberry Mojo

2    cups fresh cranberries
½    cup frozen cranberry juice concentrate, thawed
¼    cup fresh cilantro leaves
2    tablespoons olive oil
1    tablespoon fresh lime juice
1    tablespoon honey
1    garlic clove, sliced
¼    teaspoon ground cumin
¼    teaspoon salt

Combine all ingredients in a food processor; pulse 3 times or until mixture is coarsely chopped. Serve over chicken. **Yield: 1½ cups.**

# Cranberry Chicken Salad Empanadas

*Look for a premium, freshly made deli chicken salad, or use leftover holiday turkey. One empanada makes the perfect appetizer; two with a small salad fit the entrée bill.*

**Prep: 10 min.   Cook: 16 min.**

1    (15-ounce) package refrigerated piecrusts
1    cup deli chicken salad
⅓    cup sweetened dried cranberries
⅓    cup pecan pieces, toasted
1    large egg, lightly beaten

Working with 1 crust at a time, unroll piecrust according to package directions onto a lightly floured surface. Cut each piecrust into 4 (4½") circles.

Combine chicken salad, cranberries, and pecans in a bowl. Spoon about 2 tablespoons chicken salad mixture in center of each circle. Brush edges of circles with beaten egg. Fold dough over filling for each empanada, pressing edges with a fork to seal. Place empanadas onto a lightly greased baking sheet, and brush with beaten egg. Repeat procedure with remaining piecrust circles, chicken salad mixture, and beaten egg.

Bake at 400° for 16 minutes or until lightly browned. Serve warm or at room temperature. **Yield: 8 empanadas.**

Cranberry Parfaits

# Cranberry Parfaits

**Prep: 22 min.**

1¼ cups fresh or frozen cranberries
½ cup light corn syrup
1 teaspoon grated orange rind
1 cup whipping cream
1 cup sifted powdered sugar
1½ cups sour cream
½ teaspoon vanilla extract
Garnish: cranberries cut in half

Process 1¼ cups cranberries and corn syrup in a food processor until finely chopped. Transfer to a small bowl, and stir in orange rind.

Beat whipping cream until foamy; gradually add powdered sugar, beating until stiff peaks form.

Stir together sour cream and vanilla extract in a medium bowl. Fold in half of whipped cream. Fold in remaining whipped cream.

Spoon about 1 tablespoon cranberry syrup into each of 6 parfait glasses; top with about ⅓ cup sour cream mixture. Repeat layers once. Garnish, if desired. **Yield: 6 servings.**

# Ginger Streusel-Topped Cheesecake

*This easy dressed-up cheesecake is topped with big chunks of crunchy gingersnap streusel. Serve it warm from the oven, and scoop it into dessert bowls.*

**Prep: 5 min.   Cook: 19 min.**

1   cup coarsely crushed gingersnaps (we tested with
     Nabisco)
½   cup butter, softened
½   cup sugar
½   cup all-purpose flour
1   tablespoon finely chopped crystallized ginger
1   (30-ounce) frozen New York style cheesecake (we
     tested with Sara Lee)

Combine first 5 ingredients, mixing well with a spoon. Sprinkle streusel over top of frozen cheesecake. Bake at 425° for 16 to 19 minutes or until streusel is browned. Scoop warm cheesecake into serving bowls. **Yield: 8 servings.**

Ginger Streusel-Topped Pumpkin Pie

**Ginger Streusel-Topped Pumpkin Pie:** Prepare topping as directed for cheesecake. Sprinkle topping over a small deli-baked pumpkin pie. Bake again at 425° for 18 to 20 minutes to brown the streusel. Let stand 15 minutes. Slice to serve. **Yield: 8 servings.**

▲ This frozen cheesecake comes wrapped in a collar. Just top the cheesecake with homemade streusel and pop it in the oven to bake the streusel.

Ginger Streusel-Topped Cheesecake

*editor's favorite • make ahead*

## Cheesecake-Stuffed Dark Chocolate Cake

*Though it isn't ready in 30 minutes, there's a lot that is express about this grand cake. It's even better once you've chilled it. (also pictured on page 374)*

**Prep: 26 min.   Cook: 32 min.   Other: 1 hr., 10 min.**

Unsweetened cocoa
1     (18.25-ounce) package devil's food cake mix
1     (3.4-ounce) package chocolate instant pudding mix
3     large eggs
1¼   cups milk
1     cup canola oil
1     tablespoon vanilla extract
1½   teaspoons chocolate extract (optional)
1     teaspoon almond extract
3     (1.55-ounce) milk chocolate bars, chopped (we tested with Hershey's)
3     (16-ounce) cans homestyle cream cheese frosting
3     (7.75-ounce) boxes frozen cheesecake bites, coarsely chopped (we tested with Sara Lee)
1     (12-ounce) jar dulce de leche caramel sauce (we tested with Smucker's)
Double chocolate rolled wafer cookies, coarsely broken (we tested with Pirouline)
Chocolate fudge rolled wafer cookies, coarsely broken (we tested with Pepperidge Farm)

Grease 2 (9") round cake pans, and dust with cocoa.

Beat cake mix and next 7 ingredients at low speed with an electric mixer 1 minute; then beat at medium speed 2 minutes. Fold in chopped milk chocolate bars. Pour batter into prepared pans.

Bake at 350° for 32 minutes or until cake springs back when lightly touched. Cool cake in pans on wire racks 10 minutes; remove from pans, and cool completely on wire racks. Wrap and chill cake layers at least 1 hour or up to 24 hours. (This step enables you to split cake layers with ease.)

Using a serrated knife, slice cake layers in half horizontally to make 4 layers. Place 1 layer, cut side up, on a cake plate. Spread with ½ cup cream cheese frosting; sprinkle with one-fourth of chopped cheesecake bites. Repeat procedure with remaining 3 layers, frosting, and cheesecake bites, omitting cheesecake bites on top of last layer. Frost sides and top of cake with remaining frosting. Drizzle desired amount of caramel sauce over cake, letting it drip down sides. Chill until ready to serve. Decorate cake with rolled wafer cookies and remaining chopped cheesecake bites. Store in refrigerator. **Yield: 12 servings.**

This impressive dessert makes the most of cake mix, canned frosting, frozen cheesecake bites, and a jar of caramel sauce.

Cheesecake-Stuffed Dark Chocolate Cake

◀ Sprinkle chopped cheesecake bites over each frosted cake layer.

# Make-Ahead Party Food

These scrumptious do-ahead dishes have broad
appeal, hefty yields, and big flavor.

## Deviled Eggs with Smoked Salmon and Cream Cheese

*Hard-cooked eggs get dolled up with the classic combination of smoked salmon and cream cheese. If you're buying smoked salmon for a special occasion, set aside some for this hors d'oeuvre.*

**Prep: 18 min.   Cook: 8 min.   Other: 15 min.**

6      large eggs
3      tablespoons minced smoked salmon (about 1 ounce)
3      tablespoons minced green onions
3      tablespoons softened cream cheese
1      tablespoon sour cream
1      teaspoon Dijon mustard
2      teaspoons lemon juice
¼      teaspoon salt
⅛      teaspoon ground red pepper
Garnishes: fresh dill, smoked salmon slivers, sweet paprika

Place eggs and enough water to cover in a saucepan over medium heat; bring to a boil. Cover, remove from heat, and let stand 15 minutes. Drain; return eggs to saucepan, and add enough cold water and ice to cover. Let cool. Remove shells from eggs, halve each egg lengthwise, and scrape yolks into a bowl. Reserve egg whites.

Combine yolks, salmon, and next 7 ingredients, mashing with a fork until well blended. Spoon filling into reserved whites, cover loosely with plastic wrap, and refrigerate up to 2 days. Garnish, if desired. **Yield: 12 servings.**

## Southwestern Spinach Dip

**Prep: 10 min.**

⅔      cup mayonnaise
½      (8-ounce) package cream cheese, softened
½      cup fresh cilantro leaves
2      tablespoons sliced green onions
1      teaspoon grated lime rind
2      tablespoons fresh lime juice
½      teaspoon ground cumin
½      teaspoon salt
1      jalapeño pepper, seeded and chopped
1      (10-ounce) package frozen chopped spinach, thawed
        and squeezed dry

Combine first 9 ingredients in a food processor; process until smooth. Add spinach, and pulse 3 times or until blended. Transfer dip to a bowl; cover and refrigerate up to 1 day. Serve with fresh cut vegetables, multigrain tortilla chips, or crackers. **Yield: 1½ cups.**

## Honey-Peppered Goat Cheese with Fig Balsamic Drizzle

**Prep: 8 min.**

1      (11-ounce) package or 4 (3-ounce) logs fresh goat cheese
⅓      cup olive oil
¼      cup honey
½      teaspoon freshly ground black pepper
1      teaspoon fresh thyme leaves
Fig balsamic vinegar* or balsamic vinegar
Garnish: fresh thyme
Lahvosh or other cracker bread

Using a sharp knife, carefully slice goat cheese in ½"-thick slices. Place cheese in an 11" x 7" dish or other serving platter. Drizzle with oil. Combine honey and pepper; drizzle over cheese. Sprinkle with 1 teaspoon thyme leaves. Cover and chill up to 2 days.

Remove cheese from refrigerator 1 hour before serving. Just before serving, drizzle a little vinegar over cheese. Garnish, if desired. Serve with lahvosh or other specialty cracker bread. **Yield: 6 to 8 appetizer servings.**

*Find fig balsamic vinegar at Williams-Sonoma or other cook stores.

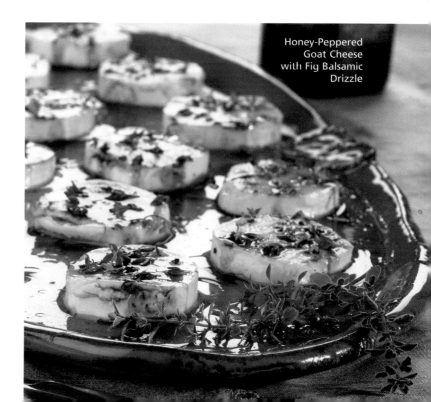

Honey-Peppered
Goat Cheese
with Fig Balsamic
Drizzle

◆◇◆◇◆◇◆◇◆◇◆◇◆◇◆◇◆◇◆◇◆◇◆◇◆◇◆◇

## Mediterranean Mezze

Mezze are small plates of food served midday in Greece and other Mediterranean countries. Although traditionally meant to be eaten as a nosh with drinks, these little plates make wonderful hors d'oeuvres. Variety is the key word here and, in addition to the 3 recipes that follow, the Mezze table can be augmented with store-bought items such as black and green olives, cheese, roasted red peppers, nuts (pistachios and almonds), pepperoncini (pickled Tuscan peppers), and, of course, pita bread.

◆◇◆◇◆◇◆◇◆◇◆◇◆◇◆◇◆◇◆◇◆◇◆◇◆◇◆◇

# Hummus

*This version of hummus was such a hit that we gave it our highest rating.*

**Prep: 7 min.**

1      (19-ounce) can chickpeas (garbanzo beans)
2      garlic cloves, chopped
⅓     cup extra-virgin olive oil
⅓     cup water
⅓     cup fresh lemon juice
⅓     cup tahini*
½     teaspoon salt
1      tablespoon extra-virgin olive oil
2      tablespoons minced fresh flat-leaf parsley
2      tablespoons pine nuts, toasted
Pita bread, cut into wedges

Combine first 7 ingredients in a food processor; process until smooth. Transfer hummus to a serving bowl; cover and refrigerate up to 5 days before serving.

To serve, drizzle hummus with 1 tablespoon olive oil, and sprinkle with parsley and toasted pine nuts. Serve with pita wedges. **Yield: 2 cups.**

*Tahini is a popular ingredient used in Middle Eastern cooking. It's a thick paste made from ground sesame seeds. Tahini can be found with the peanut butter or with organic foods at your grocer.

*editor's favorite • make ahead*

# Babaghanouj

*This dip (pronounced* bah-bah-gah-NOOSH*) gets wonderful smoky flavor from two sources—grilled eggplant and smoked paprika. Look for smoked paprika at specialty food stores or spice stores. It's one of those secret ingredients that turns an ordinary dish into an extraordinary one. Of course, you can make it with regular paprika, but you won't have the same smoky essence. This dip is best made ahead, as the flavors tend to mellow.*

**Prep: 15 min.    Cook: 14 min.    Other: 40 min.**

Olive oil-flavored cooking spray
1      medium eggplant, cut in half lengthwise (about 1 pound)
2      tablespoons extra-virgin olive oil
2      large garlic cloves, chopped
2      tablespoons tahini
2      tablespoons fresh lemon juice
1      tablespoon sour cream
½     teaspoon salt
⅛     teaspoon ground red pepper
Extra-virgin olive oil
Smoked paprika
Pitted kalamata olives, halved
Pita chips

Spray cut sides of eggplant with cooking spray. Grill eggplant, skin side down, covered with grill lid, over medium-high heat (350° to 400°) 10 minutes. Turn eggplant halves over, and grill 4 minutes or until flesh is nicely browned and tender. Remove from grill, and let stand 20 minutes or until cool to the touch.

Scoop pulp from eggplant halves into a large wire-mesh strainer; let drain 20 minutes. Combine drained pulp, 2 tablespoons olive oil, and next 6 ingredients in a food processor. Process until smooth. Transfer to a bowl; cover and refrigerate up to 1 week.

To serve, transfer dip to a serving bowl; drizzle with a small amount of olive oil, and sprinkle with smoked paprika and olives. Serve with pita chips. **Yield: 1⅔ cups.**

# Tzatziki

*This refreshing cucumber yogurt dip can be served as part of the traditional Mezze (see note at far left), but it's also perfect as a sauce for poached salmon or other cold seafood. Be sure to look for Greek yogurt. It's thick, rich, and pre-drained. Plain yogurt can be substituted; see note below.*

Prep: 16 min.

2    large cucumbers, peeled, seeded, and grated (about 1¼ pounds unpeeled)

2    cups Greek yogurt or 4 cups plain yogurt, drained (see note)

2    garlic cloves, minced

3    tablespoons fresh lemon juice

1½  tablespoons chopped fresh dill

1½  tablespoons chopped fresh mint

½   teaspoon salt

Press grated cucumber between layers of paper towels to remove excess moisture. Stir together cucumber, yogurt, and remaining ingredients. Cover and refrigerate up to 5 days. **Yield: 2¾ cups.**

**Note:** To drain plain yogurt, line a sieve with a double thickness of cheesecloth; set sieve over a bowl. Spoon yogurt into sieve, and let drain in refrigerator at least 3 hours.

# Peach and Pecan Tapenade with Goat Cheese

*We gave this traditional French condiment a Southern twist with pecans and dried peaches. The result is a beautiful spread that's sure to impress.*

Prep: 8 min.   Cook: 9 min.   Other: 30 min.

1    cup orange juice

2    cups dried peaches, chopped (we tested with Sun-Maid)

1    cup pitted kalamata olives, chopped

2    tablespoons olive oil

2    tablespoons honey

1    tablespoon capers, drained

½   teaspoon dried thyme

¼   teaspoon freshly ground pepper

1    cup chopped pecans, toasted

12  ounces goat cheese

Specialty crackers

Peach and Pecan Tapenade with Goat Cheese

Bring orange juice to a boil in a small saucepan over medium heat. Remove from heat, and add chopped dried peaches. Cover and let stand 30 minutes. Drain, if necessary.

Combine olives and next 5 ingredients in a serving bowl. Stir in peaches and pecans. Place tapenade on a serving platter with goat cheese and crackers. Spread cheese on crackers, and smear with tapenade. **Yield: 3¾ cups.**

**Make Ahead:** Prepare tapenade, omitting nuts. Cover and store in refrigerator up to 2 days. Stir in nuts just before serving.

## Bourbon BBQ Baby Back Ribs

*Prebaking these ribs gives them a rich browned exterior. The subsequent long, slow stint in the slow cooker produces fall-off-the-bone, fork-tender ribs.*

**Prep: 10 min.   Cook: 10 hr., 9 min.   Other: 30 min.**

| | |
|---|---|
| 5 | pounds pork baby back ribs, racks cut in half |
| 1½ | teaspoons salt |
| 1 | teaspoon pepper |
| 1 | cup ketchup |
| 1 | cup firmly packed light brown sugar |
| ½ | cup bourbon |
| ¼ | cup prepared horseradish |
| ½ | teaspoon hot sauce |

Place ribs, meaty-side up, in a large roasting pan. Sprinkle ribs with salt and pepper.

Bake at 475° for 30 minutes. Meanwhile, combine ketchup and next 4 ingredients in a small bowl.

Arrange ribs in a 6-quart slow cooker, adding sauce on each layer of ribs. Depending on the shape of your slow cooker—oval or round—you may have to cut each rib rack into thirds instead of in half. Cover and cook ribs on LOW 9 hours. Remove ribs from slow cooker; cover to keep warm.

Pour drippings and sauce from slow cooker into a saucepan. (Skim a few ice cubes across the surface of sauce to remove fat, if desired, and discard.) Bring sauce to a boil; reduce heat, and simmer over medium heat 20 minutes or until sauce thickens. (Sauce will reduce by about half.) Brush sauce over ribs before serving. **Yield: 5 servings.**

**Make Ahead:** These ribs can hold for several hours after finishing in the slow cooker. Place sauced-up ribs on a rimmed baking sheet; cover tightly with foil. Place in a preheated 190° oven to keep warm.

Bourbon BBQ
Baby Back Ribs

You might not consider ribs as holiday food for entertaining, but this lip-smacking recipe will make you think twice.

▲ Arrange ribs in a single layer in a large roasting pan.

# Boeuf Bourguignon

*We almost insist you make this beef stew a day ahead and just reheat when ready to serve. The rich flavors meld together and only get better with time. One key to success: Be sure to brown the beef well. Do this in batches in a very hot pan—this creates an intense layer of flavor that will permeate the dish.*

**Prep: 12 min.   Cook: 4 hr.   Other: 8 hr.**

2½    cups Cabernet Sauvignon or other dry red wine
2      cups beef broth
2      tablespoons fresh rosemary leaves
3      tablespoons minced garlic
4      pounds boneless beef chuck roast, cut into 2" pieces and well trimmed
6      ounces thick-sliced bacon, cut into ½" pieces
2      cups beef broth
¼     cup olive oil
1      (8-ounce) package small button mushrooms, halved
1½    teaspoons salt, divided
1      (1-pound) package frozen pearl onions, thawed and drained
5      carrots, peeled and cut into 2" pieces
3      tablespoons cornstarch
¼     cup water
Salt and pepper to taste
Minced fresh flat-leaf parsley

Combine first 4 ingredients in a large zip-top freezer bag. Add beef, and seal bag; refrigerate overnight. Drain meat and aromatics, reserving liquid. Pat meat dry with paper towels.

Cook bacon in a large Dutch oven over medium heat 8 minutes or until crisp. Drain bacon on paper towels, and set aside; reserve drippings in pan.

Add meat to Dutch oven in 3 batches, and cook without crowding meat 10 to 15 minutes per batch or until well browned; set aside. Pour off any remaining bacon drippings; return browned meat and reserved marinade to Dutch oven, and add 2 cups broth. Bring mixture to a boil; reduce heat, and simmer, partially covered, 2 hours and 45 minutes or until meat is tender.

Meanwhile, heat 2 tablespoons oil in a large nonstick skillet over medium-high heat until hot. Add mushrooms and ¼ teaspoon salt; cook 12 to 15 minutes or until browned, stirring after 10 minutes. Set mushrooms aside. Heat remaining 2 tablespoons oil in same skillet; add onions, carrots, and ¼ teaspoon salt, and cook 10 minutes or until golden brown, stirring often. Add mushrooms,

onions, and carrots to meat in Dutch oven. Stir in 1 teaspoon salt. Continue simmering stew 15 minutes or until vegetables are tender.

Combine cornstarch and water; stir into stew, and cook 3 to 5 minutes or until thickened. Add salt and pepper to taste. Sprinkle with bacon and parsley before serving. **Yield: 8 servings.**

**Note:** You can prepare the beef stew, cool it completely, and keep it refrigerated up to 3 days.

# Meat Lover's Chili

*This chili is better the second and even third day, but feel free to enjoy it freshly made with minced red onion, shredded Monterey Jack cheese, chopped fresh cilantro, sour cream, and a basket of warm flour tortillas.*

**Prep: 17 min.   Cook: 1 hr., 21 min.**

3      pounds ground chuck
3      medium onions, chopped
1      large green bell pepper, chopped
3      tablespoons minced garlic
½     cup chili powder
1      tablespoon ground cumin
1      (14-ounce) can beef broth
1      tablespoon dried oregano
1½    teaspoons salt
2      (28-ounce) cans diced tomatoes, undrained
3      (15-ounce) cans pinto beans, rinsed and drained

Brown beef in a large Dutch oven over medium heat. Drain beef, reserving ¼ cup drippings in pan.

Add onion, bell pepper, and garlic to drippings; sauté over medium-high heat 6 to 8 minutes or until vegetables are tender. Return beef to Dutch oven.

Stir in chili powder and cumin; cook over medium heat 3 minutes, stirring occasionally. Stir in beef broth and next 3 ingredients. Reduce heat, and simmer, covered, 50 minutes, stirring occasionally. Add pinto beans, and cook 20 more minutes. **Yield: 16 cups.**

# Tortilla Chicken Casserole

*Get a jump start on dinner with this southwestern comfort-food casserole that can be made up to 2 days ahead. Serve with an array of toppings: diced avocado, sour cream, lime wedges, sliced pickled jalapeño, fresh cilantro, and salsa.*

**Prep: 17 min.   Cook: 1 hr.**

| | |
|---|---|
| 3 | tablespoons vegetable oil |
| 1½ | cups minced red bell pepper |
| 1½ | cups minced onion |
| 2 | tablespoons minced garlic |
| ½ | teaspoon salt |
| 2½ | teaspoons ground cumin |
| ¼ | cup all-purpose flour |
| 1½ | cups chicken broth |
| 1 | cup sour cream |
| 5 | cups chopped cooked chicken or turkey |
| 12 | corn tortillas |
| 3 | cups (12 ounces) shredded Monterey Jack cheese |

Heat oil in a large nonstick skillet over medium heat until hot. Add bell pepper and next 3 ingredients; sauté 5 minutes or until vegetables are soft. Stir in cumin, and cook 1 minute. Stir in flour; cook 3 minutes. Add chicken broth and sour cream; simmer 5 minutes, stirring frequently. Add chicken, and stir to blend.

Soften tortillas by layering them between damp paper towels and heating in microwave, in several batches, at HIGH for 30 seconds.

Arrange 4 tortillas in a lightly greased 3-quart baking dish. Top with one-third of chicken mixture (about 2 cups), sprinkle with 1 cup cheese, and cover with 4 more tortillas. Repeat layers with another one-third of chicken mixture, 1 cup cheese, 4 tortillas, and ending with remaining chicken and 1 cup cheese. Cover with aluminum foil, and refrigerate up to 2 days.

Bake, uncovered, at 350° for 35 to 45 minutes or until bubbling and browned. **Yield: 8 servings.**

**Note:** You can also freeze this casserole. Follow the make-ahead directions above but freeze after preparing. When ready to cook it, bake foil-covered frozen casserole at 350° for 1 hour and 15 minutes or until thoroughly heated.

# Chicken à la King

*A classic American dish evoking childhood memories for some of us, Chicken à la King is elegant enough for a party buffet, and yet comfort food at its best. Serve the creamy chicken over our Crisp Cheddar-Cornmeal Waffles, and it'll be a hit. The dish can be prepared 2 days ahead, stored covered, and chilled.*

**Prep: 25 min.   Cook: 1 hr.**

| | |
|---|---|
| 4 | cups chicken broth |
| 2 | pounds skinned and boned chicken breasts |
| 6 | tablespoons butter, divided |
| 4 | red bell peppers, diced ½" |
| 1 | medium onion, diced ½" |
| 1 | (8-ounce) package fresh mushrooms, quartered |
| 1 | teaspoon salt |
| ⅛ | teaspoon ground red pepper |
| 6 | tablespoons all-purpose flour |
| 2 | cups whipping cream |
| 3 | tablespoons dry sherry |
| 2 | tablespoons lemon juice |

Salt and pepper to taste
Crisp Cheddar-Cornmeal Waffles
Garnishes: toasted sliced almonds, flat-leaf parsley

Pour broth in a Dutch oven or stockpot; bring to a boil. Add chicken; reduce heat to medium-low, and cook, uncovered, 10 minutes. Remove chicken from broth; coarsely chop, and set aside. Strain broth through a sieve into a saucepan; simmer, uncovered, over medium heat until reduced to 2½ cups (10 to 20 minutes).

Melt 3 tablespoons butter in a large skillet over medium heat. Sauté red bell pepper and onion 4 minutes or until tender. Add mushrooms, salt, and ground red pepper; sauté 4 minutes. Remove from heat, and set aside.

While broth continues to simmer, preheat waffle iron, and cook waffles.

Melt remaining 3 tablespoons butter in Dutch oven over low heat; whisk in flour until smooth. Cook 3 minutes, whisking constantly. Gradually whisk in reserved 2½ cups broth and 2 cups whipping cream; cook over medium heat, whisking constantly, until sauce is thickened and bubbly.

Add chicken and reserved vegetables to sauce. Stir in sherry and lemon juice; cook over medium heat, just until thoroughly heated. Add salt and pepper to taste. Serve over waffles. Garnish, if desired. **Yield: 12 cups.**

Chicken à la King with Crisp
Cheddar-Cornmeal Waffles

## Crisp Cheddar-Cornmeal Waffles

Prep: 12 min.   Cook: 10 min. per batch

*These waffles are crisp and interesting on their own or with syrup, but crown them with some Chicken à la King and they become fancy brunch fare.*

1    cup all-purpose flour
1    cup yellow cornmeal
2    teaspoons baking powder
1    teaspoon baking soda
½    teaspoon salt
1½   cups (6 ounces) shredded sharp Cheddar cheese
½    cup chopped toasted pecans
3    large eggs
1    cup buttermilk
1    cup club soda
⅓    cup canola or vegetable oil

Sift together first 5 ingredients in a large bowl. Stir in cheese and pecans. Combine eggs and next 3 ingredients; gently stir into dry ingredients just until blended.

Spoon a heaping 1 cup batter evenly onto a preheated, lightly greased waffle iron. Cook 5 to 10 minutes or until crisp and done. Repeat with remaining batter.

Transfer waffles to a baking sheet, and keep warm, uncovered, in the oven at 200° until ready to serve. Waffles can be frozen in zip-top freezer bags and reheated in oven or toaster oven. **Yield: 16 (4") waffles.**

**Note:** To make Belgian waffles, spoon 2 cups batter into a preheated, greased Belgian waffle iron with 4 square grids. Cook until crisp and done.

## Twice-Baked Smoky Sweet Potatoes

*Like a twice-baked potato, this sweet potato version mashes yummy ingredients together and then gets a crusty cheese topping with a surprise ingredient. The results pair well with pork tenderloin, turkey, or ham.*

**Prep: 21 min.  Cook: 1 hr., 12 min.**

| | |
|---|---|
| 6 | medium sweet potatoes (3½ pounds) |
| ⅓ | cup butter or margarine |
| ½ | cup whipping cream, half-and-half, or milk |
| ¼ | teaspoon salt |
| ¼ | teaspoon smoked paprika |
| ⅛ | teaspoon ground red pepper |
| ½ | cup crushed amaretti cookies (about 4 cookies) |
| ¼ | teaspoon smoked paprika |
| ¾ | cup grated Parmigiano-Reggiano cheese |

Scrub potatoes, and prick each potato once. Place on a baking sheet. Bake at 450° for 1 hour or until tender.

When potatoes are cool enough to handle, cut a strip from top of each potato; carefully scoop out potato pulp, leaving ⅛"-thick shells. Set shells aside. Place pulp, butter, and next 4 ingredients in a medium bowl. Mash with a potato masher, or beat at medium speed with an electric mixer until smooth; spoon into potato shells. Cover and chill up to 2 days.

When ready to bake, place stuffed potatoes on a large, round microwave-safe, ovenproof platter, and cover with a paper towel. Microwave potatoes at HIGH 6 minutes or until thoroughly heated.

Combine crushed cookies, ¼ teaspoon paprika, and cheese. Sprinkle over potatoes. Bake at 400° for 6 minutes or until browned. **Yield: 6 servings.**

**Note:** You can find smoked paprika at specialty grocery stores or spice stores.

## Citrus Cheesecake

*The beauty of pomegranate seeds nestled against sectioned oranges and candied orange peel gives this creamy cheesecake grande dame status. Baking it in a water bath makes it extra creamy.*

**Prep: 8 min.  Cook: 55 min.  Other: 8 hr.**

| | |
|---|---|
| 4 | navel oranges |
| ¾ | cup sugar |
| ¾ | cup water |
| ¼ | cup sugar |
| 2 | cups graham cracker crumbs |
| ½ | cup butter, melted |
| ⅓ | cup sugar |
| ½ | teaspoon ground ginger |
| 3 | (8-ounce) packages cream cheese, softened |
| 1¼ | cups sugar |
| 1 | (8-ounce) container sour cream |
| 4 | large eggs |
| 1 | tablespoon grated lemon rind |
| 2 | teaspoons vanilla extract |
| 1 | teaspoon orange extract |
| 1 | large pomegranate, seeds removed |

Using a zester and working from top of orange to bottom, remove peel from oranges in long strips. Combine ¾ cup sugar and ¾ cup water in a small saucepan over medium-low heat, stirring until sugar dissolves. Bring to a boil; reduce heat, and simmer 2 minutes. Add orange peel; simmer 15 minutes.

Meanwhile, peel and section zested oranges. Seal orange sections in a zip-top plastic bag, and refrigerate until ready to garnish cheesecake.

Drain orange peel well. Toss with ¼ cup sugar in a small bowl. Place candied peel in a thin layer on wax paper to dry. Store in an airtight container up to 2 days.

Combine graham cracker crumbs and next 3 ingredients; stir well. Press mixture firmly on bottom and 2" up sides of a lightly greased 9" springform pan.

Bake at 350° for 14 to 16 minutes; let cool. Wrap bottom and sides of pan in aluminum foil and place in a large roasting pan; set aside. (Wrapping the pan is insurance against leaks in case your pan is older and not 100% airtight.)

Beat cream cheese at medium-high speed with an electric mixer until creamy. Gradually add 1¼ cups sugar, beating just until blended. Add sour cream, beating just until blended. Add eggs, 1 at a time, beating well after each addition. Stir in lemon rind and extracts.

Citrus Cheesecake

Pour batter into baked crust. Add hot water to roasting pan to a depth of 2". Bake at 350° for 55 minutes or until edges are set and center is almost set. Carefully remove pan from water bath, and immediately run a knife around edge of pan. Cool completely on a wire rack; cover and chill 8 hours.

To serve cheesecake, remove sides of springform pan. Place cheesecake on a serving platter. Arrange orange sections in concentric circles on top of cake. Pile pomegranate seeds in center of cheesecake. Decorate with candied orange peel. **Yield: 12 servings.**

▲ To make candied citrus peel, use a zester and work from top to bottom of fruit.

▲ Place candied peel in a thin layer to dry after it's been cooked and sugared.

# 5 Ingredient 15 Minute Holiday Recipes

*Get the festivities started with these simple and stylish recipes.*

*Warm Brie with Pear Preserves*

What could be more enticing during the holidays than recipes with only five ingredients and 15 minutes of work time? We think you'll like this variety that includes sweet and savory, drink and dessert. We don't include salt, pepper, water, cooking spray, or garnish in the ingredient count. For speedy results with pasta and baked goods respectively, put your water on to boil and preheat the oven as your first step.

*quick & easy*

## Warm Brie with Pear Preserves

*Leaving the edible white rind on the Brie and cutting the cheese into wedges are two steps toward a quick finish. Serve Brie with thin gingersnaps, fruit, or crackers.*

Prep: 10 min.   Cook: 4 min.

½   cup pear preserves
2    tablespoons sweet white wine (we tested with Riesling)
1½  teaspoons chopped fresh thyme or ½ teaspoon dried thyme
2    (8-ounce) rounds Brie
¼   cup chopped walnuts
Garnishes: fresh thyme sprigs, walnut halves

Combine first 3 ingredients in a small glass bowl; set bowl aside.

Cut each round of Brie into 6 wedges. Place wedges close together on a lightly greased baking sheet; sprinkle each round with 2 tablespoons chopped walnuts.

Bake at 450° for 4 minutes or just until cheese begins to soften in the center. Meanwhile, microwave preserves mixture on HIGH 20 seconds or just until thoroughly heated. Using 2 spatulas, carefully remove each Brie intact from baking sheet, and immediately place on a serving platter. Spoon melted preserves over Brie. Garnish, if desired. Serve hot. Yield: 12 servings.

**Fix it Faster:** Heat Brie with toppings, 1 round at a time, in the microwave on HIGH 1½ minutes on a microwave-safe plate. You don't even have to cut Brie into wedges.

*quick & easy*

## Peppermint Patty Hot Chocolate

*Garnishes make this drink fun to serve. For children, omit the peppermint schnapps.*

Prep: 1 min.   Cook: 13 min.

4    cups milk
4    cups whipping cream
½   cup sugar
3    (4-ounce) semisweet chocolate baking bars, broken into pieces (we tested with Ghirardelli)
¼   teaspoon salt
¾   cup peppermint schnapps
Garnishes: canned whipped topping, crushed hard peppermint candies

Heat first 3 ingredients in a large saucepan over medium-high heat until sugar dissolves and mixture is thoroughly heated. Remove from heat; add chocolate and salt, whisking until chocolate melts. Stir in peppermint schnapps. Garnish, if desired. Serve immediately. Yield: 11 cups.

**Note:** For added indulgence, dip a peppermint patty lollipop into hot chocolate. It will partially melt and add an extra peppermint punch. We tested with peppermint patty candies and 4″ and 6″ white lollipop sticks.

*Peppermint Patty Hot Chocolate*

*quick & easy*

# Banana Bread French Toast

*Serve warm with your favorite syrup.*

Prep: 2 min.   Cook: 13 min.

4   large eggs, lightly beaten
1   cup milk
3   tablespoons butter or margarine, divided
1   (16-ounce) loaf banana crunch swirl bread (we tested
    with Cobblestone Mill Breakfast Swirl)
Toppings: chopped pecans, sliced banana

Whisk together eggs and milk.

Melt 1½ tablespoons butter in a large nonstick skillet over medium-high heat. Lightly dip bread slices, 1 at a time, in egg mixture. Cook bread slices, in batches, 2 to 3 minutes on each side or until golden. Add remaining butter to skillet as needed.

Top each serving with pecans and sliced banana, if desired. Serve hot. Yield: 4 to 5 servings.

## Spicy Queso Dip

*This is no ordinary cheese dip. It's chock-full of spinach, sausage, black beans, and green chiles.*

Prep: 3 min.    Cook: 9 min.

1    (16-ounce) package mild ground pork sausage
2    (16-ounce) cartons refrigerated hot queso dip (we tested with Gordo's Cheese Dip)
1    (10-ounce) package frozen chopped spinach, thawed and well drained
1    (15-ounce) can black beans, drained
1    (10-ounce) can diced tomatoes and green chiles, undrained

Cook sausage in a large skillet over medium-high heat, stirring until sausage crumbles and is no longer pink. Drain.

Meanwhile, heat queso dip according to package microwave directions in a 2-quart microwave-safe bowl. Stir in sausage, spinach, and beans. Drain tomatoes and green chiles, reserving juice. Add tomatoes and green chiles to dip. Stir in enough reserved juice to get a good consistency (about 2 to 3 tablespoons). Serve hot with tortilla chips. Yield: 7½ cups.

## Chicken and Prosciutto Pasta with Sage Butter

*Fresh sage and portobello mushrooms give this simple dish robust flavor. For quick results, put the water on to boil right as you begin.*

Prep: 7 min.    Cook: 15 min.

2    (9-ounce) packages refrigerated chicken and prosciutto tortellini (we tested with Buitoni)
½    cup butter, divided
2    (8-ounce) packages baby portobello or cremini mushrooms, sliced (about 6 cups)
1½  tablespoons chopped fresh sage
1    cup freshly grated Asiago or Parmesan cheese

Cook tortellini according to package directions; drain. Return pasta to warm pot.

While pasta cooks, melt ¼ cup butter in a large skillet over medium-high heat. Add mushrooms, and sauté 3 minutes or until tender. Remove from heat; add to pasta.

Heat remaining ¼ cup butter in a small microwave-safe bowl on HIGH 30 seconds or until butter melts. Stir in sage. Add to pasta. Sprinkle with grated cheese; toss and serve immediately. Yield: 4 servings.

## Peppered Beef Fillets with Pomegranate Jus

*The 1-inch thickness of the fillets is important for uniform cooking. Press fillets with the palm of your hand to make fillet thickness match.*

Prep: 4 min.    Cook: 12 min.

6    beef tenderloin fillets (about 1″ thick)
¼    teaspoon salt
¼    cup au poivre marinade, divided (see Note)
⅔    cup minced onion or shallot
⅔    cup refrigerated pomegranate juice or red wine
3    ounces Gorgonzola or blue cheese

Sprinkle fillets evenly with salt. Rub fillets with 3 tablespoons au poivre marinade. Place a large nonstick skillet over medium-high heat until hot. Add fillets, and cook 5 minutes on each side or until desired degree of doneness. Remove fillets from skillet, and keep warm.

Add remaining 1 tablespoon au poivre marinade to skillet. Add onion, and sauté 30 seconds, scraping browned bits from bottom of skillet. Add pomegranate juice. Bring to a boil, and cook 1 minute.

To serve, pour pomegranate jus over fillets, and top each serving with cheese. Yield: 6 servings.

**Note:** We tested with LuLu Au Poivre marinade from Williams-Sonoma. You can otherwise use our similar homemade marinade. Combine ¼ cup extra-virgin olive oil, 1½ teaspoons cracked black pepper, 1 teaspoon each dried parsley flakes and dried oregano, ¼ teaspoon fine-grained sea salt, and 1 large garlic clove, pressed.

*Pork Chops with
Shallot-Cranberry
Sauce*

## Sweet Potato Soup

*Ground red pepper puts a spicy kick in this soup. The
soup is good without the pepper, too.*

Prep: 10 min.   Cook: 5 min.

1    (40-ounce) can yams in heavy syrup
1    (14-ounce) can vegetable or chicken broth
½    cup fresh orange juice
1 to 2 tablespoons minced fresh ginger
1½ cups coconut milk (we tested with Taste of Thai)
1    teaspoon salt
¼    teaspoon ground red pepper

Drain yams, reserving ½ cup syrup. Discard remaining
syrup. Place yams in a blender or food processor. Add
½ cup syrup, broth, orange juice, and ginger. Process 2 to
3 minutes or until smooth, stopping to scrape down sides.
Pour pureed mixture into a medium saucepan. Stir
in coconut milk and remaining ingredients. Cook over
medium heat, stirring often, until soup is thoroughly
heated. Ladle soup into bowls. If desired, drizzle additional
coconut milk into soup. Run a knife through each bowl to
make a decorative design. Yield: 6 cups.

*quick & easy*
## Pork Chops with Shallot-Cranberry Sauce

*For an easy and impressive presentation, perch these skillet
chops on a mound of mashed potatoes.*

Prep: 7 min.   Cook: 13 min.

4    boneless pork loin chops (¾" thick)
¾    teaspoon salt, divided
½    teaspoon freshly ground black pepper
2    tablespoons butter, divided
2    shallots, finely chopped (¼ cup)
1    (12-ounce) container cranberry-orange crushed fruit
1½ teaspoons chopped fresh thyme
Garnish: fresh thyme

Sprinkle both sides of pork with ½ teaspoon salt and
pepper. Melt 1 tablespoon butter in a large skillet over
medium-high heat. Add pork, and cook 4 to 5 minutes on
each side or to desired degree of doneness. Remove pork
from skillet; cover and keep warm.
Add remaining 1 tablespoon butter to skillet, stirring just
until butter melts. Add shallots, and sauté 1 to 2 minutes.
Add crushed fruit and remaining ¼ teaspoon salt to
skillet; bring to a boil. Return pork and any juices to skillet; cook 1 minute or until heated. Sprinkle with chopped
thyme, and serve hot. Garnish, if desired. Yield: 4 servings.

*quick & easy • editor's favorite*
## Rosemary Roasted Grape Tomatoes

*These tiny tomatoes take on a sweetness when roasted.
Serve them as a simple side dish, or toss with hot
cooked pasta.*

Prep: 5 min.   Cook: 8 min.

2    pints grape tomatoes
1    tablespoon chopped fresh or dried rosemary
1    tablespoon olive oil
½    teaspoon salt
½    teaspoon freshly ground pepper
Garnish: fresh rosemary sprigs

Rinse tomatoes, and pat dry with paper towels.
Combine tomatoes and next 4 ingredients; toss gently
to coat. Place tomatoes in a single layer in a shallow
roasting pan.
Bake at 475° for 7 to 8 minutes or until tomato skins are
blistered and start to pop, stirring once. Garnish, if desired.
Yield: 4 servings.

## Caramel-Chocolate Tartlets

*Dulce de leche is a fancy name for caramel. It makes these bite-size sweets really rich.*

Prep: 14 min.  Other: 1 min.

1   (13.4-ounce) can dulce de leche (we tested with Nestlé)*
2   (2.1-ounce) packages frozen mini phyllo pastry shells, thawed (we tested with Athens)
1   cup double chocolate morsels (we tested with Ghirardelli) or regular semisweet morsels
⅓   cup roasted salted peanuts, chopped, or coarsely chopped pecans, or both

Spoon 1 heaping teaspoon dulce de leche into each pastry shell. Microwave chocolate morsels in a small glass bowl on HIGH 1 to 1½ minutes or until melted, stirring twice. Spoon 1 teaspoon chocolate over dulce de leche. Sprinkle tartlets with peanuts or pecans. Freeze 1 minute to set chocolate. Yield: 30 tartlets.

**Tip:** Make the tartlets ahead, and freeze them in the plastic pastry trays sealed in zip-top freezer bags.

*Find dulce de leche on the baking aisle or the Mexican food aisle, or make your own. Pour 1 (14-ounce) can sweetened condensed milk into an 8″ dish or pieplate; cover with foil. Pour ½″ hot water into a larger pan. Place covered pieplate in pan. Bake at 425° for 1 hour and 25 minutes or until thick and caramel colored (add hot water to pan as needed). Remove foil when done; cool.

*preparing Caramel-Chocolate Tartlets*

▲ Spoon 1 heaping teaspoon dulce de leche into each pastry shell.

▲ Keep tartlets in pastry trays, and freeze in zip-top bags.

*make ahead*

# Banana Cream Cake

*We liked this cake served partially frozen. We found bakery pound cake easiest to slice when it's partially frozen, too.*

Prep: 15 min.   Other: 2 hr.

1   round bakery pound cake (about 3 pounds)
1   (15.6-ounce) jar banana jam*
3   large bananas, sliced and divided
1   (12-ounce) container frozen whipped topping, thawed
1   cup chopped pecans
Garnish: 3 (1.4-ounce) chocolate-covered toffee candy bars, chopped

Turn cake on its side, and slice evenly into 3 layers.

Place bottom layer on a serving platter. Spread with 3 tablespoons banana jam. Top with half of banana slices. Spread ½ cup whipped topping over banana slices; sprinkle with ¼ cup pecans. Top with second cake layer. Repeat layering ingredients; top with remaining cake layer.

Frost assembled cake with remaining whipped topping. Sprinkle remaining pecans over cake. Garnish, if desired. Serve right away or cover and chill until ready to serve. Freeze cake 2 hours if you want to serve it partially frozen. Yield: 1 (3-layer) cake.

*We used banana jam from Williams-Sonoma. Serve leftover jam on toast or biscuits. If you can't find banana jam, use mashed ripe banana sweetened with a touch of honey.

Banana Cream Cake

*Ambrosia Trifle*

*quick & easy ▪ make ahead*

## Ambrosia Trifle

*Layer these ingredients in one big bowl or several small hurricane glasses that each hold two servings.*

Prep: 7 min.   Cook: 8 min.

1   cup sweetened flaked coconut
1   (24-ounce) package prepared vanilla pudding (we tested with Jello Pudding Snacks)*
1   (8-ounce) container frozen creamy whipped topping, thawed
2   (24-ounce) jars refrigerated mandarin oranges (we tested with Del Monte Sun Fresh)
½   round bakery pound cake, cut into 1" cubes

Place coconut on a baking sheet. Bake at 350° for 8 minutes or until lightly browned; set aside.

Meanwhile, stir together pudding and 1½ cups whipped topping. Drain oranges, reserving liquid.

Layer half of cake cubes in 6 (2-cup) stemmed glasses or a 3-quart glass bowl or trifle dish. Brush cake cubes with reserved liquid; spoon half of pudding evenly over cubes. Top with half of oranges. Repeat layers, ending with oranges. Dollop with desired amount of whipped topping; sprinkle with toasted coconut. Chill until ready to serve. Yield: 10 to 12 servings.

*As an option, you can use a (5.1-ounce) package vanilla instant pudding that yields about 3 cups.

321

# Quick-Fix *Food Gifts*

*Each of these recipes has a time-saving twist—we've added a homemade touch to purchased or packaged foods.*

Marinated Cheese and Olives

*make ahead*

## Marinated Cheese and Olives

*The shortcut here: dressing up cubed cheese and olives.*

Prep: 5 min.   Other: 8 hr.

4   (8-ounce) packages cubed colby-Jack cheese
1   (10-ounce) jar or 2 (7-ounce) jars kalamata olives, drained
1   (16-ounce) bottle olive oil and vinegar dressing
1   tablespoon dried Italian seasoning
½   teaspoon dried crushed red pepper
6   garlic cloves, crushed
6   fresh rosemary sprigs

Combine all ingredients except rosemary in a large bowl; stir gently. Cover and chill at least 8 hours or up to 24 hours.

Divide cheese and olives into 6 glass containers. Place 1 rosemary sprig in each container. Pour remaining dressing evenly into containers. Cover and refrigerate up to 2 weeks. Yield: 8 cups.

*quick & easy • make ahead*

## Roasted Chili-Cheese Dip

*We liked this dip served on tacos and burritos.*

Prep: 17 min.   Cook: 8 min.

2   tablespoons butter or margarine
½   cup finely chopped sweet onion
2   large garlic cloves, minced
4   (8-ounce) containers refrigerated Mexican cheese dip (we tested with Olé)
1   (16-ounce) jar fire-roasted red and green chiles, drained and finely chopped (we tested with Melissa's)
1   teaspoon ground cumin

Melt butter in a large skillet over medium-high heat. Add onion; sauté 3 minutes or until tender. Add garlic; sauté 1 minute. Reduce heat to medium; stir in cheese dip, chiles, and cumin, stirring constantly until cheese melts. Serve warm with tortilla chips, or spoon dip into small jars or containers. Cover and chill. Give jars of dip as gifts along with reheating instructions. Yield: 5 cups.

**Note:** To reheat 1 cup dip, place in a microwave-safe bowl. Microwave dip on HIGH for 3 minutes, stirring after 1½ minutes.

## Cheddar Cookies

*This simplified cheese straw recipe uses self-rising flour, a food processor, and a cookie scoop to cut down on time. Look for a lever-release cookie scoop in specialty kitchen shops or large home-goods stores.*

Prep: 24 min.   Cook: 12 min. per batch

2   cups self-rising flour
¾   cup cold butter, cut into pieces
1   (8-ounce) package shredded sharp Cheddar cheese
¾   teaspoon ground red pepper
3   tablespoons ice water
Toasted, salted pecan halves (optional; see Note)

Process flour and butter in a food processor until mixture resembles coarse meal. Add cheese and pepper; pulse 6 to 8 times or until combined. With processor running, gradually add water through food chute, and process just until dough forms a ball.

Drop dough by level tablespoonfuls 2" apart onto ungreased baking sheets. Flatten each cookie with the bottom of a glass; gently press 1 pecan half into center of each cookie, if desired.

Bake in batches at 400° for 12 minutes. Let cool on baking sheets 2 minutes. Remove cookies to wire racks to cool. Store in an airtight container. Yield: 4½ dozen.

**Note:** To toast pecan halves, coat them with cooking spray, and place in a large skillet. Cook over medium heat 6 to 7 minutes or until lightly toasted. Remove pecans to a paper towel, and sprinkle lightly with salt. Let cool.

*Cheddar Cookies*

*Chocolate-Covered Cherry Cookies*

Bake at 375° for 8 to 10 minutes. Cool 2 minutes. Gently press 1 cherry candy in center of each cookie. Cool completely on baking sheets; transfer to wire racks.

Combine powdered sugar and liqueur in a small bowl, stirring until smooth. (Glaze should be thick, yet easy to drizzle.) Place glaze in a small zip-top plastic bag. Snip a tiny hole in 1 corner of bag. Drizzle glaze over cookies. Let stand until set. Yield: 3½ dozen.

**Note:** Depending on the size candy box you buy, you may need two boxes for these cookies.

## Chocolate-Almond Croissants

*Bakery-style croissants or frozen croissants work fine in this recipe. If using frozen croissants, slice them while frozen.*

Prep: 28 min.   Cook: 7 min.   Other: 3 hr.

1   (12½-ounce) can almond filling
1   dozen small croissants, split in half horizontally*
1   cup double chocolate morsels (we tested with Ghirardelli) or regular semisweet chocolate morsels
1   cup sliced almonds, toasted

Stir almond filling. Spread each croissant bottom with about 2 tablespoons almond filling. Cover with tops; place on a large foil-lined baking sheet, and bake at 325° for 7 minutes or until lightly toasted.

Place chocolate morsels in a small microwave-safe bowl; microwave on HIGH 1 to 2 minutes or until melted, stirring once. Spread melted chocolate over croissants. Sprinkle almonds over chocolate. Let stand at room temperature 2 to 3 hours or until chocolate is firm. Yield: 1 dozen.

*If you use frozen Sara Lee Petit French Style Croissants, you'll need 2 (6-ounce) packages.

## Chocolate-Covered Cherry Cookies

*Place these cookies in candy cups, and give them in a gift box.*

Prep: 12 min.   Cook: 10 min. per batch

⅓   cup butter, softened
⅓   cup shortening
1   large egg
1   (17.5-ounce) package chocolate chip cookie mix (we tested with Betty Crocker)
½   cup unsweetened cocoa
42   assorted chocolate-covered cherries (we tested with Russell Stover hand-dipped Cherry Cordials)
½   cup powdered sugar
4   to 5 teaspoons cherry liqueur or maraschino cherry juice

Beat butter and shortening in a large bowl at medium speed with an electric mixer until fluffy; add egg, beating until blended.

Combine cookie mix and cocoa; gradually add to butter mixture, beating well. Shape dough into 1″ balls. Place balls 2″ apart on ungreased baking sheets.

# Bittersweet Sugar Cookie Macaroons

*Sandwich these coconut-covered sugar cookies together with chocolate. The shortcut: portioned cookie dough (see photo below).*

Prep: 28 min.   Bake: 13 min. per batch   Other: 5 min.

1   (18-ounce) package refrigerated ready-to-bake sugar cookie bar dough (we tested with Nestlé)
3   cups sweetened flaked coconut
1   (4-ounce) bittersweet chocolate baking bar, chopped (we tested with Ghirardelli)
2   tablespoons whipping cream

Cut each cookie dough portion into 4 equal pieces. Roll dough pieces in coconut; shape into balls. Place balls 2″ apart on lightly greased baking sheets.

Bake at 350° for 12 to 13 minutes or until edges are golden. Cool on baking sheets 5 minutes; transfer to wire racks to cool completely.

Combine chocolate and whipping cream in a small glass bowl. Microwave on HIGH 30 seconds; stir. Spoon melted chocolate into a small zip-top plastic bag. Snip a small hole in 1 corner of bag. Pipe ½ to 1 teaspoon chocolate mixture onto center of 40 cookie bottoms. Top with remaining half of cookies, pressing gently to adhere. Let sandwich cookies stand on wire racks for chocolate to harden. Yield: 40 sandwich cookies.

## *making macaroon sandwich cookies*

▲ Cut each portion of cookie dough into four pieces.

▲ Pipe chocolate onto flat sides of half the baked cookies.

▲ Sandwich the chocolate with remaining cookies.

*Chocolate-Raspberry Petits Fours*

If additional frosting is needed, scrape off excess frosting from baking sheet, and reheat.

Microwave white chocolate morsels in a glass measuring cup on HIGH 1 minute or until melted, stirring after 30 seconds. Place white chocolate in a zip-top freezer bag. Snip a tiny hole in 1 corner of bag; drizzle melted white chocolate over brownies. Chill brownies 30 minutes or until chocolate is firm. Yield: 30 petits fours.

**Note:** Look for plastic flavor injectors in the kitchen gadget section at Wal-Mart.

## Pistachio Pastry Twists

*Wrap these flaky pastries in cellophane, and tie with ribbon, or deliver them in a vase. Add a monogram sticker to the vase to personalize the gift.*

Prep: 28 min.   Cook: 19 min. per batch

2    egg yolks
1    tablespoon water
⅓    cup sugar
½    teaspoon ground cinnamon
½    teaspoon ground cardamom
1    (17.3-ounce) package frozen puff pastry sheets, thawed
½    cup finely chopped roasted pistachios
2    tablespoons butter or margarine, melted

Whisk together egg yolks and water in a small bowl. Combine sugar, cinnamon, and cardamom.

Carefully roll each sheet of puff pastry into a 9½" square on a lightly floured work surface. Brush each sheet with egg wash, and sprinkle with 2 tablespoons sugar mixture. Sprinkle chopped pistachios evenly over 1 sheet, leaving a ¼" border; top with remaining sheet, sugared side down. Firmly press edges to seal. Brush top of pastry with melted butter; sprinkle with remaining sugar mixture. Cut pastry into ¾"-thick strips, using a pizza cutter. Twist each strip 3 times, and place 2" apart on lightly greased baking sheets.

Bake at 400° for 19 minutes or until golden. Remove from pans immediately, and cool on wire racks. Yield: 10 twists.

**Note:** To reheat pastry twists, bake at 450° for 5 minutes or just until heated. Cool. (As they cool, they crisp up.)

*make ahead*
## Chocolate-Raspberry Petits Fours

*Place these moist little brownie bites in candy cups for gift giving.*

Prep: 50 min.   Other: 30 min.

2    (11-ounce) boxes prebaked mini brownies (we tested with Entenmann's Little Bites Brownies)
⅓    cup seedless raspberry jam
1    tablespoon raspberry liqueur (optional)
1    (15-ounce) container pourable milk chocolate frosting (we tested with Betty Crocker)
½    cup white chocolate morsels

Place brownies on a wire rack set over a baking sheet.

Microwave jam in a glass measuring cup on HIGH 10 to 15 seconds or just until slightly melted; stir until smooth. Stir in liqueur, if desired. Pour a small amount of jam into a flavor injector; inject each brownie through the side with a small amount of jam. Refill injector as needed until all brownies are filled.

Microwave pourable frosting in original container on HIGH 20 seconds. Pour or spoon frosting over brownies.

*Pistachio Pastry Twists*

327

*Saffron and Golden Raisin Breakfast Bread*

Combine remaining egg yolk with 1 tablespoon water. Brush tops of loaves with egg wash, and sprinkle with turbinado sugar.

Bake at 350° for 32 minutes or until golden. Remove from pan, and cool completely on a wire rack. Yield: 1 loaf.

**Mini Breakfast Breads:** Divide dough into 3 portions. Form into 3 small loaves, and place in 3 greased 5¾" x 3¼" loafpans. Continue with recipe, letting dough rise 40 minutes and baking mini loaves at 350° for 20 minutes or until golden. Yield: 3 loaves.

**Note:** We recommend cooling this loaf on its side on a wire rack. This helps the loaf maintain its shape.

## Saffron and Golden Raisin Breakfast Bread

*Put your bread machine to work mixing this dough. We liked the bread best sliced and toasted.*

Prep: 7 min.   Cook: 32 min.   Other: 2 hr., 35 min.

¼   teaspoon saffron threads
2   teaspoons warm water
3   egg yolks, divided
¾   cup warm water (75° to 85°)
2   tablespoons butter, softened
2   tablespoons granulated sugar
1   (12-ounce) package bread machine country
     white bread mix (we tested with Fleischmann's)
½   cup golden raisins
½   cup chopped walnuts
1   tablespoon water
Turbinado sugar

Combine saffron and 2 teaspoons water in a small bowl; let stand 5 minutes. Place saffron mixture, 2 egg yolks, ¾ cup warm water, and next 5 ingredients, including yeast packet from bread mix) in a bread machine. Set bread machine to "dough" setting according to manufacturer's instructions; start machine.

When dough cycle is complete, turn dough out onto a lightly floured surface, and knead several times. Form dough into a loaf, and place in a greased 9" x 5" loafpan. Let dough rise in a warm place (85°), free from drafts, for 1 hour or until doubled in size.

## Dried Tomato and Rosemary Flatbread

*The key to crispy results here is rolling the dough out really thin.*

Prep: 10 min.   Cook: 10 min.   Other: 5 min.

1   (6½-ounce) package pizza crust mix (we tested
     with Jiffy)
½   cup warm water (100° to 110°)
¼   cup minced dried tomatoes packed in oil, drained
2   tablespoons finely chopped fresh rosemary
Olive oil
2   tablespoons olive oil
½   cup (2 ounces) shredded Italian five-cheese blend

Combine first 4 ingredients in a medium bowl; stir well. Cover and let stand at room temperature 5 minutes. Turn dough out onto a heavily floured surface, and knead 1 minute or until dough forms a smooth ball, adding more flour, if necessary. Divide dough in half.

Roll each portion of dough into a 12" x 10" rectangle; transfer dough to 2 baking sheets brushed with olive oil. (To transfer dough easily, roll dough onto rolling pin, and unroll onto baking sheets.) Roll or press each portion of dough into a 14" x 12" rectangle. (Dough should be very thin.) Brush each portion with 1 tablespoon olive oil; sprinkle evenly with cheese.

Bake at 425° for 10 minutes or until crispy and cheese is browned. Remove flatbread to wire racks, and let cool completely. To serve, break flatbread into large pieces. Store in an airtight container. Yield: 6 to 8 servings.

# Gingerbread Fruitcake

*No one will guess that this brandy-soaked loaf starts with a cookie mix.*

Prep: 12 min.   Cook: 1 hr.   Other: 40 min.

1   (7-ounce) package dried fruit bits (we tested with Sun-Maid)
¾   cup sweetened dried cranberries
6   tablespoons apricot brandy, divided
1   (14.5-ounce) package gingerbread cake and cookie mix (we tested with Betty Crocker)
1¼ cups water
1   large egg, lightly beaten
¾   cup chopped pecans, toasted

Combine dried fruit bits, cranberries, and ¼ cup brandy in a medium bowl. Let stand 30 minutes.

Place cake mix in a large bowl; make a well in center. Add water and egg, stirring just until blended. Stir in soaked dried fruit and chopped pecans. (Batter is not as thick as typical fruitcake batter.) Pour batter into a greased 9" x 5" loafpan.

Bake at 350° for 55 to 60 minutes or until a long wooden pick inserted in center comes out clean. Cool in pan on a wire rack 10 minutes; remove from pan. Poke holes in loaf at 1" intervals, using a long wooden pick. Brush remaining 2 tablespoons brandy over loaf. Cool completely on a wire rack. For best results, store in an airtight container 2 to 3 days before serving. Yield: 1 loaf.

*make ahead*

# Creamy Chicken and Polenta Casserole

*This recipe makes two casseroles. Keep one, and give the other to a friend, along with baking instructions.*

Prep: 20 min.   Cook: 36 min.   Other: 10 min.

1   (32-ounce) container chicken broth
2   tablespoons butter or margarine
½   teaspoon freshly ground black pepper
1   cup yellow cornmeal
¾   cup shredded Parmesan cheese
1   (12-ounce) jar marinated quartered artichoke hearts, drained and coarsely chopped
1   (12-ounce) jar roasted red bell peppers, drained and chopped
4   cups shredded cooked chicken (about 1 large rotisserie chicken)
1   (16-ounce) jar roasted garlic Alfredo sauce (we tested with Classico)
⅓   cup chopped fresh basil
1½ cups (6 ounces) shredded Italian five-cheese blend

Bring first 3 ingredients to a boil in a large saucepan; gradually whisk in cornmeal. Cook 4 minutes or until thickened and bubbly, stirring constantly. Remove from heat; stir in Parmesan cheese. Spoon polenta evenly into 2 (8") square disposable ovenproof pans (see Note below). Cool 10 minutes.

Sprinkle artichoke hearts, peppers, and chicken evenly over polenta. Pour Alfredo sauce over chicken in both pans. Sprinkle with basil; top with Italian cheese blend. Cover and chill until ready to bake.

Before baking, place pan on center of a baking sheet. Bake, uncovered, at 350° for 25 minutes or until casserole is thoroughly heated. Yield: 2 casseroles (4 servings each).

**Note:** We tested with Glad OvenWare disposable pans. Clip and save instructions from back or bottom panel, and share these instructions when gift giving.

These festive ingredients make an easy holiday fruitcake.

# General Index

# Recipe Index